STRUCTURED COBOL
FOR DATA PROCESSING

CW01067000

Glencoe Series in Computer Science and Data Processing

George Ledin Jr., Series Editor

Norman R. Lyons, *Structured COBOL for Data Processing*
Richard E. Mayer, *Ten-Statement Spiral BASIC: From Calculator to Computer*

Forthcoming:

Jack A. Fuller, *Business BASIC: Programming and Applications*
Curtis Gerald, *Introduction to Data Processing*
George Ledin Jr., *Fundamentals of Computer Science*
Mel Maron, *Numerical Methods for Calculators and Computers*
Joseph Paul, *Methods of Simulation for Dynamic Systems Engineering*
James Pick, *Business Data Processing*
Harvey L. Shapiro, *Introduction to Assembly Language Programming
on the PDP 10 and the PDP 11*

STRUCTURED COBOL FOR DATA PROCESSING

NORMAN R. LYONS
Naval Postgraduate School
Monterey, California

Glencoe Publishing Co., Inc.
Encino, California
Collier Macmillan Publishers
London

Glencoe Publishing Co., Inc.
17337 Ventura Boulevard
Encino, California 91316
Collier Macmillan Canada, Ltd.

Library of Congress Catalog Card Number: 79-84623
1 2 3 4 5 6 7 8 9 10   83 82 81 80 79

ISBN 0-02-470770-8

CONTENTS

PREFACE

Structured COBOL for Data Processing is the result of many years of teaching in data processing and computer science. The COBOL language itself poses something of a paradox for instructors. COBOL is probably the most widely used computer language in the world, yet its wordiness and cumbersome structure continue to cause concern. COBOL's widespread use and utility, however, demand that all who are serious about a computer career should master it. The same is true of students whose future careers may require them to manage a data processing operation or to work with programmers.

FEATURES OF THE TEXT

Pedagogy

Much of my experience in data processing has been with special data base management languages designed to be taught in the following simple sequence: at the beginning, the students are told that there is a data file containing certain information. They are first taught how to retrieve this information, then how to update it, and finally, how to create their own files. This is also the approach taken in *Structured COBOL for Data Processing*. By presenting the structure and underlying concepts, the learning process is enhanced by providing the student with immediate, successful feedback from the computer; even totally inexperienced students are able to submit successful computer jobs on their first try.

This approach avoids the tedious and, often, demoralizing task of learning every COBOL convention before actually programming. At each step, in this text, the student learns only what is needed for immediate use, and learning usually progresses quickly and without undue frustration.

In this book, I have approached ANSI COBOL as a data base management language—which it is—and taught it in a pedagogically natural sequence. Students begin by practicing information retrieval from a predefined file. All definitions pertaining to that file have been provided, and only the commands for processing the data need to be supplied by the students. Later, after a few successes in programming, students are introduced to more complex processes of data structure and file definition.

The structured programming approach is used throughout the text. This allows students to produce better code faster than is possible with nonstructured approaches. *Structured COBOL for Data Processing* also places COBOL in its proper social context: all of the examples in this book are parallel to real-world data processing situations, so that students can see how COBOL will fit into their larger career goals. Good programming practices and the reasons for following these practices are emphasized. This leads students to an early understanding of the need for following certain standards of structure and program documentation.

The predefined data base to be used in conjunction with this text contains simulated student records for 200 students at a hypothetical university. This number is enough to give students a feel for data processing problems without drowning them in data or exhausting the computer budget for the course. The examples in the text are drawn from this data base as well, so that what the students see in the book can be reinforced by actual practice. Many of the problems in the extensive sets of Study Exercises are also drawn from this data base.

Organization of the Text. Each chapter of the text has specific goals: by the end of the chapter, the student should be able to use specific new COBOL features to solve specific problems. The basic philosophy behind the book is that a student of computing learns by doing, so every chapter, except the first and sixth, involves specific programming assignments. In a computing course, students feel frustrated if they are not able to use the computer successfully early in the course; therefore, one of the aims of this book is the early and successful use of COBOL to solve realistic computing problems. Then, as more difficult COBOL concepts are introduced, the students already have a base of positive experience to build on.

Chapter 1 introduces the student to the basic computing vocabulary, data processing equipment, and the general file and record terminology used in COBOL. This chapter has no specific computing goals. Chapter 2 introduces a basic set of COBOL commands so that the student can write simple COBOL programs using only PROCEDURE DIVISION statements. It also introduces the variable names and scratch variables used in the student data base. It ends with a programming example that is a complete program similar to those required of the student in the Study Exercises.

Chapter 3 introduces the SORT statement. In most COBOL books, the SORT statement is either ignored or left until much later in the book. I feel that this is unwise, because sorting is the heart of all real-world data processing. It is impossible to do meaningful information retrieval problems (for example, phone directories or grade lists) or update problems without sorting. In this book, sorting is an integral part of the examples used from the third chapter on.

Chapter 4 introduces the basic arithmetic statements in COBOL, and Chapter 5 introduces conditional statements (IF statements) in both simple and complex forms. Chapter 6 departs from the usual sequence and presents a discussion of number systems and the coding systems used in computing. The discussion focuses on IBM 360/370 equipment, but the basics are the same for most machines.

In Chapter 7 the IDENTIFICATION and ENVIRONMENT divisions are introduced. Before this, students use a standard IDENTIFICATION and ENVIRONMENT DIVISION with all the code they write; now they learn how to write their own code for these divisions. In Chapter 8 the DATA DIVISION is introduced. Here students can see how the material they have learned in Chapter 6 applies to defining COBOL data structures.

Chapter 9 introduces the I/O commands students need to define their own COBOL files independent of the instructor-supplied master files. Chapter 10 introduces all the options of the PERFORM statement. Before this, students use only a few restricted forms of the PERFORM statement. Chapter 11 introduces some advanced features of COBOL.

Chapter 12 covers the REPORT feature. This feature is one area of COBOL that is frequently neglected in beginning texts. Some instructors (along with portions of the data processing community) feel that the RE-PORT feature takes up too much time or space on the machine. This may indeed be true on smaller machines; however, on the larger machines available today, the REPORT feature takes up little extra machine time or space, and it can result in substantial savings in programmer time, which is often a more expensive resource. In the past, the popularity of the REPORT feature has also suffered because most descriptions of it—principally those in reference manuals—have made it appear obscure and difficult. Thus, I have taken extra pains to make the presentation of this feature in Chapter 12 easy for the beginner to follow.

Supplementary Materials. An Instructor's Manual which gives solutions to the Study Exercises, suggestions for using the text, goals for each chapter, and directions for using the data base is available to instructors. The data base itself, in the form of punched computer cards, will be supplied gratis to adopters of the text.

INTRODUCTION TO COBOL AND COMPUTING

1.0 INTRODUCTION

In the years since the end of World War II, the electronic computer has revolutionized business. Many routine clerical jobs have been taken over by machines, and all jobs have been changed to some degree by computers. In some industries, notably in the banking industry, it would not be possible to keep track of all the paperwork without using computers.

Most people are aware of this revolution, but they often think only of computers' more spectacular uses. They are familiar with the machines used to control the space shots or with those used in nuclear physics. The popular conception of computers is that they are electronic brains used mostly for sophisticated mathematical problems. Indeed, computers have been indispensable in these endeavors, but most computers today are used for applications much more ordinary than headline-grabbing scientific or engineering calculations. It has been estimated that 90 percent of the computers in the world are used for conventional daily business data processing.

We are all familiar with the use of computers for producing paychecks and bills. These are typical computer applications. The first business use of computers occurred in 1954 for payroll processing, and this type of application grew rapidly through the 1950s. Computers were used to handle clerical duties that were the most troublesome to process by hand. In addition to payroll processing, accounts receivable and accounts payable used computers extensively. By 1959, such applications were widespread in large businesses.

In 1959 the U.S. government decided that data processing applications had to be standardized. The government was and is the largest user of computers in the world. Within the government, the Department of Defense (DOD) is the largest single user. In 1959 DOD called a meeting of manufacturers and some of the larger users to discuss the problem of proliferation of data processing languages. At this time, the major computer manufacturers were hard at work on their own data processing languages, and it seemed that many different languages would be competing for data processing applications. The people at this meeting eventually became the nucleus of what is called **CODASYL** (Committee on Data Systems Languages). CODASYL established a definition of a data processing language called **COBOL** (Common Business Oriented Language) and has been responsible for maintaining the standards and defining the future updates to this language.

CODASYL

Naturally, the manufacturers resisted. They had all invested substantial amounts of money and time in their own data processing languages, and a few of them thought, with some justification, that they had a better language than COBOL. For a while, it seemed that the data processing language situation might become as confused as ever and that COBOL would be merely another language among many. Then in 1961 the federal government stepped in and announced that it would not acquire any general-purpose computer that was not equipped with a COBOL compiler. Because the government was the largest user of computers, this made any further discussion about the "best" data processing language an academic one.

Since then, the use of COBOL has grown so that it is probably the most widely used computer language. This is not necessarily because it is the best or the only language for a particular application. There is a large number of computer languages, even for data processing applications. However, today COBOL is the most commonly used programming language for data processing on medium- to large-size computers. This range covers most of the important data processing applications.

On small or "mini" computers, **RPG** (Report Program Generator) or **BASIC** (Beginners All-purpose Symbolic Instruction Code) are probably the most common languages. There are other languages. IBM's **PL/I** (Programming Language One) is supposed to combine the best features of a scientific language such as **FORTRAN** (FORmula TRANslator) and COBOL. It is a promising development, but it has yet to gain acceptance with large numbers of users. **Mark IV**, marketed by the Informatics Corporation, combines the power of COBOL with a very simple instruction format. But it is rather expensive and not as widespread as COBOL. Because COBOL is both widespread and standardized, it is likely to be used for many years to come. The type of application for which it is used—namely, data processing—is the most common use of computers, and this should ensure its popularity in the future. Nobody who is serious about the data processing industry can afford to ignore COBOL and the developments connected with this language.

BASIC

PL/I
FORTRAN

Mark IV

1.1 COMPUTER CONCEPTS

In the beginning, as you learn about computers, you may feel that all computer users speak a strange language. They do, but do not let this put you off. The language they use is meaningful and not too hard to learn. After a few weeks of studying COBOL, you will be using the same terminology yourself. The purpose of this section is to provide you with some of the essential computer terms that you will use initially.

Hardware and Software

The first two terms you will encounter are **hardware** and **software.** Hardware refers to the physical devices that make up a computer system. Software refers to the *programs* that instruct the computer system in the jobs it is to do. A computer program is a set of instructions for the machine to follow, and it is written in a highly structured language that the computer can understand. COBOL is one such language, but most computers can use a variety of languages. These languages usually have specialized purposes. COBOL's purpose is data processing work. Other languages, such as FORTRAN, may be intended for scientific work, whereas others may be even more specialized.

hardware
software

Types of Software

There are basically two types of software in a computer system: **manufacturer-supplied software** and **applications software.** The manufacturer-supplied software is usually purchased with the machine and performs such tasks as controlling jobs in the machine, translating computer languages, and so on. The applications software is usually written by the user or purchased by the user from an organization other than the computer manufacturer. Applications software is the set of computer programs that do the work on the machine. Examples include payroll programs, accounts receivable programs, billing programs, and so forth.

manufacturer-supplied
software
applications software

Types of Hardware

Let us return to the discussion of the hardware or the physical devices that make up the computer system. There are essentially two types of hardware, the **mainframe** and the **peripheral devices.** The mainframe consists of the components that we identify as the computer. The two basic components of the mainframe are the **CPU (Central Processing Unit)** and the **memory.** The CPU is the machine's "brains." It performs all the mathematical functions and executes the instructions given to it by the users of the machine. You can think of it as a kind of gigantic or very powerful calculator. The memory is where the programs and data are stored while the computer is running (executing) them. A computer's memory is strictly short-term. It is not like a human being's memory in

mainframe
peripheral devices
CPU (Central
Processing Unit)
memory

IBM

a

b

IBM

FIGURE 1.1
(a) The IBM 370 System, Model 138, with Several Typical Input-Output Devices. *The units in the background are magnetic tape units. The unit to the right is a CRT terminal, and a line printer is in the center.*
(b) A Point of Sale Terminal

which everything that ever happened may be stored. Your program will reside in the computer's memory only while the computer is working on your job. After completing your job, the computer will remove your program from its memory.

The mainframe is connected to the peripheral devices or Input–Output (I/O) devices through special data channels. The data channels transfer information from the I/O devices to the mainframe of the machine. Figure 1.1 shows some typical I/O devices. When you run your COBOL program, you may have it punched on cards, and the cards are read by a card reader like the one in Figure 1.2. These cards may be read directly into the memory of the machine and the computer will begin to run the COBOL program you have written, or they may be read into another peripheral device (such as a tape or disk) where they will be stored until the computer is ready to work on them.

Input–Output Devices

Let us discuss some of the I/O devices you will be using. It is important that you understand something of the equipment the computer

FIGURE 1.2
A Card Reader and Punch
Unit

IBM

uses to process your program because this equipment will influence the way your jobs are designed and run. First, you must get your COBOL program into the machine. One way is to punch the COBOL commands on a set of data cards using a keypunch. A keypunch is much like a typewriter, and your program would be written one line to a card. Your instructor will show you how to use a keypunch if this is the technique you will use to run your jobs. After the deck has been punched, you will turn it in to be read into a card reader like the one in Figure 1.2. The card reader will read in your deck of COBOL cards very fast, but one card at a time.

Another way to enter your COBOL program into the machine is without cards. You may type your program into a **terminal** or **CRT** (**Cathode Ray Tube**) like the one shown in Figure 1.3. This particular terminal looks like a cross between a television set and a typewriter. The typed lines are displayed on a screen in front of the keyboard. The computer will let you store your program on a disk file and then recall it for running later. This type of system, in which access to the machine is through remote terminals, is becoming much more common in businesses, and it should not be long before punched cards are eliminated entirely.

terminal
CRT (Cathode Ray Tube)

Magnetic tape The COBOL statements you use must have data on which to operate. COBOL is well suited for processing large data files, and the data on these files may be stored on magnetic tape. You can think of a magnetic tape unit as similar to home sound recording units. The computer tapes are much larger, however, and the tape drives move much faster. A home recording unit may move the tape at 1⅞ inches per

FIGURE 1.3
A CRT Data Entry Terminal

NCR CORPORATION

second during playback. A computer tape drive may move at 120 inches per second. The data can be packed very densely on a computer tape. Modern computer tape can store 1,600 BPI (characters or bytes of data per inch of tape). A magnetic tape may be as much as 2,400 feet long, so this means that a magnetic tape can store 46,080,000 characters or about the average equivalent of 25,000 double-spaced typewritten pages.

A diagram of a computer tape unit is given in Figure 1.4. The data on the tape will not be stored in one continuous string. Instead, it will be broken up into blocks called **records.** When it is using magnetic tape, your COBOL program will read in the data for processing one record at a time. The data on a magnetic tape must be read **sequentially**, which means that we read the data one record at a time as we encounter the records. If we want a record that is near the end of the tape, we must read all the records that come before it. This can be a tedious process as it may take 2 or 3 minutes to get all the way to the end of a tape. Therefore, magnetic tapes are usually used for data processing applications where access to most of the records in the file will be necessary. Fortunately, this is true of a large number of data processing applications (such as payroll or checking account data processing). For this type of application, magnetic tape is a cheap and cost-effective form of data storage.

records

sequentially

Magnetic disk Another common type of I/O device is the magnetic disk. You can think of a magnetic disk as a series of phonograph records mounted on a common spindle. The surface of the disk is covered with a plastic material that can be magnetized to record data. The surface is magnetized by a set of read–write heads attached to an access arm that allows them to move back and forth over the surface of the disk. The whole operation is very rapid and demands a high degree of precision. On one of the disk surfaces, the data is stored in bands of concentric circles called **tracks.** There may be as many as 200 tracks on a single disk and as many as 20 surfaces on the whole disk pack. Figure 1.5 shows a typical disk file (containing a number of disk packs) and a diagram of an individual disk pack.

tracks

The tracks on a surface will be numbered. The group of all tracks with the same number on all surfaces is called a **cylinder.** Because all the read–write heads on the access arm move when the access arm moves, cylinder organization allows for faster I/O activity. The access arm can stay in position and read the data on successive surfaces as it comes under the read--write heads. All disk movement takes place very quickly and demands a high degree of mechanical precision from the disk drive. It takes about $1/10$ second for the access arm to move from the first track to the last track. The disk revolves about once every 20 milliseconds (a millisecond is $1/1000$ second), so it is possible to get to any data stored on the disk in about $1/10$ second. To achieve these speeds, the equipment must be precisely adjusted and be kept perfectly clean. To give you an

cylinder

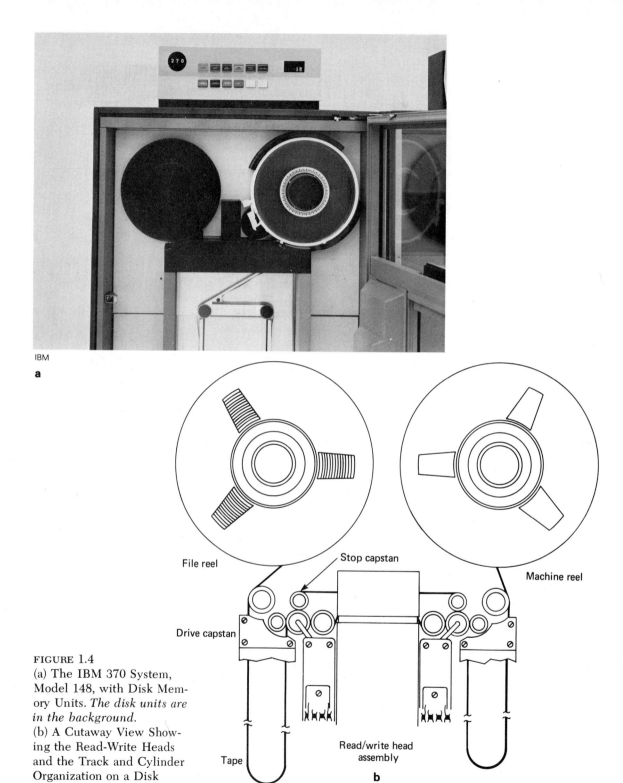

a

File reel

Stop capstan

Machine reel

Drive capstan

Read/write head
assembly

Tape

b

FIGURE 1.4
(a) The IBM 370 System,
Model 148, with Disk Memory Units. *The disk units are
in the background.*
(b) A Cutaway View Showing the Read-Write Heads
and the Track and Cylinder
Organization on a Disk

IBM

a

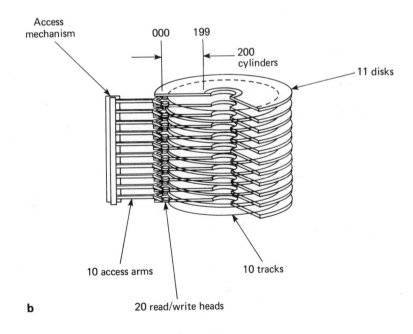

b

FIGURE 1.5
Disk Unit

idea of how tight the tolerances in a disk file are, suppose that we enlarge the scale and assume that our read–write heads are the size of a Boeing 747 jumbo jet and that the disk surface is the surface over which our jet is flying. The interesting question is At what altitude is our jet flying? On the scale we have chosen, our jet is flying at an altitude of about 1 foot, and we have to be very careful about obstacles in our path (such as overinflated basketballs). Back on our disk file scale, it means that we have to be very careful about keeping the surface of the disk clean. A particle of cigarette smoke on the surface can cause a "head crash," which may result in loss of data.

Disks are quite a bit more expensive than tapes, but because it is possible to reach data so quickly on them, they are very widely used. In many systems—for example, airline reservation systems—it is necessary to have very fast access to stored data, and a disk file can provide such speed.

There are other types of computer hardware, but they are beyond the scope of this discussion. We now return to the topic of manufacturer-supplied software. There are basically three types of manufacturer supplied software: (1) operating systems, (2) compilers, and (3) utility packages.

The **operating system** is the control program for the machine. It resides in memory and controls the execution of all other programs in the machine. It is the program that causes your program to be read into the memory and run, and it is the program that decides when you have had enough time on the machine. It is really the "brains" of the computer system and controls everything that goes on.

operating system

A **compiler** is a translator program that allows you to use your COBOL programs. No machine actually "speaks" COBOL. Each computer has its own individual machine language, and these machine languages vary widely from machine to machine and from manufacturer to manufacturer. To allow COBOL to be run on a variety of different machines, the manufacturers have provided compilers that will translate your COBOL program into your particular machine's machine language. A typical computer system will have available a number of different compilers. (COBOL, FORTRAN, BASIC, and RPG compilers are the most popular in business environments.)

compiler

A **utility package** is a special program that is used by other programs or by itself to perform special chores on the machine. Examples of utility packages are programs that copy files, sort data records, merge files, and perform library and housekeeping tasks on your data. These programs vary from machine to machine, but they are a necessary part of any computer system.

utility package

In this brief discussion, we have touched on only a few of the major points about computer systems. This should be enough to get you started and give you an overall view of computers. Much of what you learn about computers, you will learn by doing. Programming is a skill that is a little like swimming. It is not possible to learn it from books. You must learn it through practice. You can read many books and attend many lectures on swimming, but you will probably not know how to swim. It takes actual practice, and the same is true of programming. In your classes, you should ask lots of questions. Never be put off because you think a question is "dumb." Chances are, the person sitting beside you has the same question and is afraid to ask it, too. Challenge your instructor and try to get the most out of your experience with programming.

1.2   DESIGNING COMPUTER PROGRAMS

You should get used to the idea that computer programming is a process of designing a system to meet a specific goal. For the initial problems you have in this book, the goals will be quite simple. You will be asked to do things like produce a telephone directory from a file of student names. But the approaches and habits you learn now will be useful when you are solving much more complicated programming problems. There are structured, methodical approaches to computer problem solving that should be used. Computer programming should always be a conscious effort at good design rather than a trial-and-error process.

Before any programming of a computer data processing system can begin, a process known as **systems analysis** must take place. In programming "real-world" systems, this may be a formal process involving many people. For your jobs, it will mean that you should devote some time to analyze your problem at your desk before you attempt to produce any computer code. In systems analysis, an individual known as a systems analyst looks at the work flows in the system, where the computer program would be used, and how the program will interface with the people who run the system. After studying the problem, the systems analyst begins the systems design phase of the process. In this phase of the project, the documentation for the proposed system is laid out, and plans for implementation and coding are begun.

systems analysis

The whole process is known as the **system life cycle.** The phases in the system life cycle are:

system life cycle

1. PROBLEM IDENTIFICATION PHASE. In this phase, a problem is identified in the way the data processing system is working, and steps are initiated to solve it.

2. SYSTEMS ANALYSIS PHASE. The decision has been made to change the current data processing system, and a study is made of how the process to be changed works. The analyst studies the flow of work and makes recommendations about how it can be changed.

3. SYSTEMS DESIGN PHASE. The study produced by the systems analyst is used as the basis for the design of a new system. In the new system, certain manual procedures are likely to be automated, old procedures eliminated, and a study made of how to implement the new system.

4. IMPLEMENTATION PHASE. The design as proposed by the analyst has been reviewed, revised, and accepted, and work begins on the new system. Coding begins on the computer programs; equipment needed for the new system is ordered; and the operating manuals for the people who must run the system are produced.

5. TESTING PHASE. A preliminary version of the new system is ready for use, and it is installed to run in parallel with the old system. During this time, bugs (errors) are eliminated and procedures are changed, if necessary. At the end of the time, a go or no-go decision is made about the new system.

6. INSTALLATION PHASE. The new system has been found to be satisfactory and is installed. The employees who run the system are trained in its use, and the new procedures are put into effect.

7. THE POSTAUDIT PHASE. After the system has been running for a period of time (say, a year), its performance is reviewed and the results are used to initiate any necessary changes in the systems design process in the organization.

This systems design process may or may not include a computer program. The whole process applies equally well to purely manual systems. However, in modern data processing, purely manual systems are becoming rare. In this book we will be examining mostly the computer programming part of the process, but you should keep in mind that this is only part of the whole system life cycle.

Documentation

In the system life cycle, several pieces of standard documentation are usually produced to accompany the system. Many programmers, especially beginners, do not stop to consider this phase of the process. But good documentation is extremely important. The first piece of documentation is the proposal that initiates the project. It outlines the type of project desired, who wants the project, how much it will cost, and what the benefits will be. The next document is usually some set of external specifications for the system. These specifications describe how the system will work, and how it will look to the user. Both of these documents are reviewed by the appropriate groups, revised if necessary, and approved. In addition to the external specifications, a set of internal specifications for the computer programs is prepared. These internal specifications, which describe the technical details of the computer programs used in the system, should be reviewed and approved by competent computer analysts. They will form the necessary basis for any changes to the system.

After these working documents have been put in order, the systems implementation begins. After the system has been completed, a reference manual and an operator's manual are produced. These should be written as plainly as possible for the nontechnical user of the system. Finally, a **change log** and a **run log** should also be kept on the working system. The change log documents any changes made to the computer program and shows that these changes were approved by the appropriate individual in charge of the system. The organization's internal auditors will frequently insist on such controls to ensure that unauthorized changes are not made to the system. The run log contains the dates and times that the programs in the system were run as well as notes by the operator on anything unusual that occurred during these runs.

change log
run log

Although this may seem like quite a bit of paperwork to a beginner, it is all necessary. Many systems have failed not because they were not technically feasible but because there was not enough documentation on what they did to enable anyone to pick them up and run them.

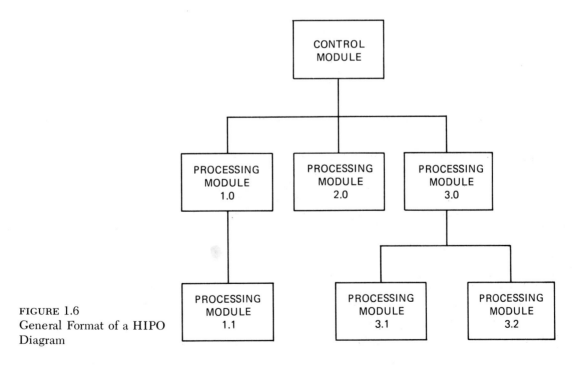

FIGURE 1.6
General Format of a HIPO
Diagram

Top-Down Approach and HIPO Structure

In designing the programs that make up the system, a very good technique to use is the **top-down** approach. Design your program as a set of pieces that will be called for use by a special control module. Figure 1.6 shows a diagram of how the structure of a program should look. The control module calls in the processing modules as they are needed to perform the different parts of the job.

top-down

This type of hierarchical diagram is used in the systems design technique called **HIPO (Hierarchy plus Input, Process, and Output).** The diagram shows the hierarchy of the modules that make up the program. Input means that the documentation should include a description of the input that the program or system will need. Process stands for a description of the processes that the computer program or system will perform on the input. Output means that there should also be a complete description of the output produced by the program. None of this is particularly new in systems design, but the idea of formalizing the process forces us to pay more attention to the components of good design.

HIPO (Hierarchy plus Input, Process, and Output)

FIGURE 1.7
HIPO Chart of a Payroll System

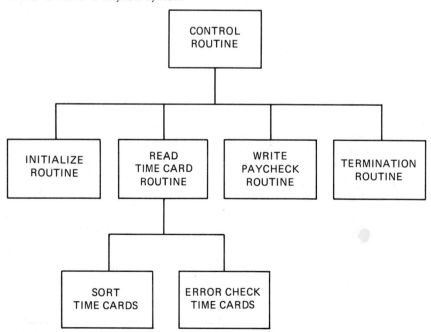

Flowcharts

A HIPO diagram might look like the one in Figure 1.7, which shows a hypothetical program for processing a payroll. An important part of the HIPO approach for describing the different processing modules is the **flowchart.** A flowchart is a diagram that uses a set of standard symbols to show the way the control flows in a computer program. Opinions differ on the usefulness of flowcharts. Most analysts regard flowcharts as useful tools, but they can be overused or used unnecessarily. Some people try to produce flowcharts that go into too much detail, which adds nothing to one's understanding of the program since that level of detail is already present in the program listing itself. A flowchart should be used as a diagram to give an overview of what the program is doing. Try to keep your flowcharts simple and limit them to one page if possible.

flowchart

The symbols used in flowcharts have been standardized by the International Standards Organization (ISO), but you will find that many organizations use their own variations. A very handy tool for producing flowcharts is a flowchart template or tracing diagram. IBM produces a very inexpensive template that conforms to the standard symbols. Some of the flowchart symbols and their meanings are given in the following list:

1. Any processing function causing a change in the value, form, or location of information.

2. Comment on some piece of the flowchart. The dotted line extends to the appropriate piece of the flowchart.

3. INPUT–OUTPUT ACTIVITY. This would apply to any type of reading or writing done by a computer program. The statement inside the box will tell which type of activity is taking place.

4. CONNECTOR. When a flowchart must extend over more than one page, a connector with a letter or number in it will be used to show where the flow of control exits from one page and enters on another.

5. DECISION. This indicates a branching of the flow of control in a program based on a decision made by the program. For example, it could show a question like "If no claimed deductions then go forward, otherwise branch to another symbol".

6. TERMINAL. This shape is used to indicate the beginning or end of a program.

7. PREDEFINED PROCESS. Refers to another block of computer code or another flowchart giving program steps.

You can do most of your flowcharting with this set of seven symbols. As you become more involved in COBOL programming, you will find that there are a few other symbols that are useful, too. These are:

8. DOCUMENT. This symbol refers to any paper document, such as line printer output.

9. PUNCHED CARD. Indicates that input or output activity will take place on punched cards.

10. MAGNETIC TAPE. Indicates that input or output activity will take place on magnetic tape.

11. ON-LINE STORAGE. Indicates that the data used is stored on some type of on-line device.

12. ON-LINE DISPLAY. Indicates that the interaction is with an on-line terminal.

13. DISK STORAGE. Indicates input or output activity to an on-line disk.

Structured Programming

It is possible to write very complicated flowcharts to describe a programming process. You are better off, however, if you try to learn a few basic structures for your flowcharts and programs and then construct your programs as variations of these structures, combining the basic forms when more complex structures are needed. This idea has come to be called **structured programming,** and you will hear a great deal about it as you go on in programming. To some writers, it is a cure for all the ills in programming. Some suggest that these techniques can be used to prove correctness in programs in the same way you would prove a theorem in mathematics. Other authors would say that structured programming is simply a fancy name for what good programmers have been doing for years.

structured programming

This author feels that structured programming is a good development because it encourages programmers to pay attention to the design of their programs rather than simply to try to write the computer code out any old way. The basic building blocks of structured program design are shown in Figure 1.8.

There are three basic structures. The first is the **simple sequence.** In this structure, you simply execute the commands to the computer in a sequence, one after another. The second type, the **decision structure,** can be thought of as the IF A THEN B ELSE C structure. If the condition represented by A is true, then you do the block of code represented by B. If the condition A is not true, you skip the block of code called B and do the block of code represented by C. The third type, the **repetition structure,** is the DO B WHILE A type of loop. The computer will keep performing the block of code called B as long as the condition in A holds true. As soon as the condition in A becomes false, it falls through the decision block and goes on to the next program segment.

simple sequence

decision

repetition

To a beginner, it may seem very difficult to restrict the types of code that you write in a COBOL program to these simple structures. Actually, this is not the case. First, each of the process blocks can themselves be complicated structures. By combining the three basic forms, you can produce complex programs. But complexity should never be your goal in producing computer code. You should always try to produce computer programs that can be understood by anyone competent in the language. Structured programming aids in this understanding because reliance on structures allows another programmer to determine what your code is doing.

Structured programming by itself is not enough, however. You should also be careful to put meaningful comments into your programs to give future readers a good idea of the purpose of each of your program's segments, and you should provide adequate documentation on the code you write.

Simple sequence structure

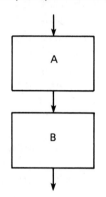

IF A THEN B ELSE C decision structure

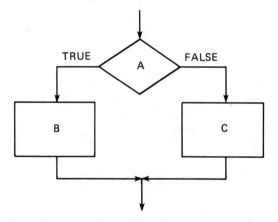

DO A WHILE B repetition structure

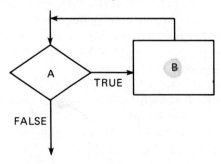

FIGURE 1.8
Basic Structures in Computer Programming

Advantages of Using a Structured Program

There are three major advantages to using a disciplined, structured approach in designing your computer programs. They are:

1. You will find it possible to write programs faster using a structured approach.

2. The code produced using a disciplined approach requires less debugging time. (It's easier to write correct code when a structured approach is used from the beginning.)

3. The code produced is easier to maintain (update and change) than conventionally produced computer code.

Let us discuss some of the aspects of these advantages. First, productivity is increased. The average productivity for programmers writing in higher level languages (like COBOL) is about eight lines of tested code per work day. This may sound unbelievably small, but the key word here is *tested*. Writing the computer code takes little time, but debugging the resulting code can be very time-consuming. A structured approach to the production of code usually requires much less debugging to make the code operational, and programmer productivity rises. So, the first and second advantages cited above are intimately related.

The third advantage is one that may be difficult for beginners to grasp. You may say, "A computer program is only a set of instructions. It is not like an automobile engine that wears out with time and use, so what is this business about maintenance?" You are correct. Computer programs do not wear out like machines, but they must still be maintained. Computer programs are used to run real-world clerical systems, and clerical procedures change frequently because of changes in government regulations, growth in organizations, and different managerial styles. Once a computer program has been written, it must be frequently updated to reflect such changes. These updates are often done by somebody other than the original programmer. If the original programmer used a well-documented, structured approach in writing the code, the work of the maintenance programmer will be much easier.

As we learn COBOL, we will also be trying to learn the steps we should take in producing good structured programs. COBOL has its own type of structure, which does not conform exactly to the ideas currently used in structured programming. However, COBOL was intended to be self-documenting and designed in such a way that programs in COBOL could be easily maintained. As you go on in COBOL, you will have to judge for yourself how well the original designers succeeded in their goal. In any computer language, however, your work will be much easier if you think about your systems design *before* you begin producing code. Never be afraid to throw out code if the design is too complicated. It is often simpler to completely redesign a bad program (or system) than it is to patch it up so that it works somehow.

1.3   FLOWCHARTING EXAMPLE

Suppose you were given a stack of graded examinations, and you were asked to compute the average grade using a calculator and a paper and pencil. Could you do it? This seems like a silly question; of course, you would have no trouble with this job.

But now, let us try a little harder question. Could you tell somebody else how to do this job? Think about this one before you answer. You cannot just say "Average the grades on those exams and give me the answer." Does the person you are talking to know what an average is? What a calculator is and how to use it? How to write and count? These may seem like silly objections, but they are not. We have assumed that the person assigned this task knows quite a bit.

Suppose you had a very fast, efficient slave who could do this arithmetic for you. But also suppose the slave is rather stupid and must be told *exactly* what to do. It interprets things literally and will do exactly what you tell it to, no matter how silly your orders may be. This is the situation in which we find ourselves with computer programming. The computer is a very fast, efficient slave; it will do whatever you tell it to—exactly. But this responsiveness will get you into trouble. You have to tell the computer *exactly* what you mean. If what you say is not what you mean, you are in trouble. There is no computer yet invented that has a DO WHAT I MEAN statement available.

Let us go back to our grade-averaging problem. Eventually, we would like to produce a flowchart of this task that we could use to build a computer program. But for now, let us concentrate on setting this task up so that it could be done by a human being. This approach is a reasonable one for many computer problems. Try to figure out how you would do it manually, and then write the corresponding steps that you would need for the computer. The steps we would need are:

1. Turn on the calculator and zero it out. (Flip the on–off switch to on, and press the "clear" button.)

2. If there are no exams left in the stack, go to step 6, otherwise go on to the next step.

3. Add the grade on the test to the total in the calculator, and discard the test.

4. Make a mark on the paper.

5. Go back to step 2.

6. Count up the number of marks on the paper and divide the total in the calculator by this number.

7. The number in the calculator display is the answer (the arithmetic mean or average).

8. Stop.

These eight steps are what you could call an **algorithm.** An algorithm is a set of steps that define a process. A recipe in a cookbook is a type of algorithm, so is a set of steps for solving a mathematical problem,

algorithm

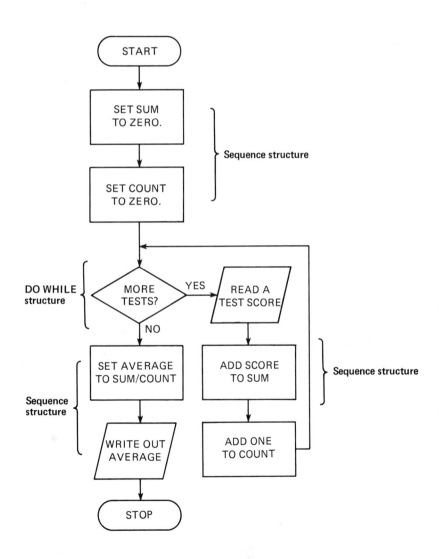

FIGURE 1.9
Process to Average Test
Grades

such as this problem of averaging grades. To set up a flowchart for it, we will have to set up some variables to store the values we are using. These variables will take the place of the calculator and the scratch paper that we used in the eight steps. The variables are:

SUM   *contains the running sum of the grades*
COUNT   *contains the count of the number of students*

The flowchart in Figure 1.9 gives the diagram of the solution to this problem. Let us look at this flowchart in terms of the structured programming concepts we discussed in the last section. You will see that it is made up of three sequence structures and a DO WHILE structure. The DO WHILE structure has one of the sequence structures imbedded in it. So, you can see that the structures we presented in Section 1.2 allow us quite a bit of flexibility after all.

This section has only introduced you to the ideas of flowcharting and structure. We will be using them throughout the book, and it is by using them that you will become fully familiar with the concepts involved. Flowcharts can be a very useful part of the documentation associated with a program or a system (although they are no substitute for readable English), and you should know how to use them well.

STUDY EXERCISES

1. What is CODASYL?

2. What does COBOL stand for?

3. What do RPG, BASIC, FORTRAN, and PL/I stand for? What are they?

4. Explain the difference between hardware and software.

5. What is a computer program?

6. What is the CPU in a computer?

7. How long is your job kept in the main memory of a computer? Would you be able to go back next week and expect to find your job there?

8. What does CRT stand for and what is it?

9. What is a magnetic tape?

10. Suppose that you have a magnetic tape 1,200 feet long packed at a density of 800 BPI. What is the maximum number of characters that you could get on this tape?

11. What is a magnetic disk?

12. Explain what a track and cylinder are.

13. What does a COBOL compiler do? Is it hardware or software?

14. What is a system life cycle?

15. What is a HIPO diagram?

16. Match each flowchart symbol below with its definition.

   1. Magnetic tape
   2. Magnetic disk
   3. Termination symbol
   4. Connector
   5. On-line display
   6. Document
   7. Input–output activity
   8. Punched card
   9. Process
   10. Decision block

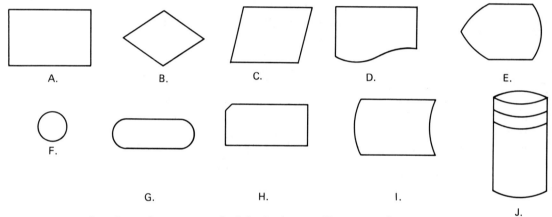

A.   B.   C.   D.   E.

F.

G.   H.   I.

J.

17. Write a flowchart of a process to find the highest and lowest grades in a set of graded tests.

18. Write a flowchart of the process of starting a car. This process should work for as many different types of cars as possible. Will your process work for all cars? If not, why not? What are the exceptions? Is it feasible to write a set of instructions for starting a car that will work for all cars?

COBOL FOR SIMPLE PROBLEM SOLVING

2.0 INTRODUCTION

COBOL is a language intended for processing data files. From what you have seen of clerical operations in your everyday life, you should be familiar with the types of things that one would like to be able to do with files. We want to be able to create them, destroy them, update them, and retrieve them when we need the information contained in them. This holds true whether we are dealing with a manual operation or a computer operation. Only the methods we use to do these operations differ from one type of system to another.

As an example of a manual filing system, look at the sample student record card pictured in Figure 2.1. This card might be used at a small college to contain the basic information about a student's activities in a particular semester. This piece of paper represents the student's record. The records of all students would be grouped together in a large student file. If you wanted to read a particular student's record in this manual filing system, all you would have to do is walk over to the filing cabinet where the record was kept and retrieve the correct record.

If the student records are kept in computer readable storage, you have a problem. You cannot read the data directly, but you can write a COBOL program that will read it for you and print out the results. Figure 2.2 shows an example of such a COBOL program. This program is a very simple one; it only reads out the data on the first student record on a file called MASTER-FILE. It prints out a few values of fields from that file and then it quits.

Let us examine this program in detail. First of all, we should point out that it is only a part of a COBOL program. A COBOL program is divided up into four major divisions:

1. IDENTIFICATION DIVISION

2. ENVIRONMENT DIVISION

3. DATA DIVISION

4. PROCEDURE DIVISION

Every COBOL program must have all four of these divisions, and they must always be present in the above order. The IDENTIFICATION DIVISION contains information that names the program and identifies its purpose and its programmer. The ENVIRONMENT DIVISION contains information about the computer environment in which the job will be run. The DATA DIVISION contains the names of the files and variables that will be used and describes their structure. The PROCEDURE DIVISION contains the descriptions of the processes that COBOL is to perform on the files. Each of the divisions is introduced by the names above.

In Figure 2.2, however, we have given only one of the four divisions— the PROCEDURE DIVISION. This is the approach we will be using through the beginning chapters of this book. We have defined a standard

FIGURE 2.1
Sample Student Record

Student Number:_____ Name:_____
                                              Last   First   Initial

Address:_____
              Street   City   State   Zip

Phone:_____ Age:_____ Sex:_____ Birthday:_____
                                                             Month   Day   Year

College:_____ Major:_____

Advisor:_____ Credits:_____GPA:_____

Courses

Course Number	Course Name	Credit Hours	Pass–Fail	Grade
1.				
2.				
3.				
4.				
5.				

Room Fees: _____
Tuition Fees: _____
College Fees: _____
Miscellaneous: _____
Total Charges:_____

code for the IDENTIFICATION, ENVIRONMENT, and DATA divisions, and you will write all of your first COBOL programs using these definitions.

We will return to the standard set of definitions in a minute, but first, let us examine the program in Figure 2.2 and explain what it is doing.

Notice that each line in the program is numbered. These numbers are for the convenience of the programmer. The computer does not use them other than to check to see if they are in the proper sequence (if they are not, it issues a warning message). COBOL text begins in column 8 of the card. The first card, PROCEDURE DIVISION introduces this block of code as the PROCEDURE DIVISION of our COBOL program. The word READ-A-RECORD is a user-defined name and is the paragraph name of the code we are using here. The cards with line numbers 10020 through 10040 are the exceptions to our assertion that COBOL text begins in column 8. These cards are not COBOL text but simply comment cards. The asterisk in column 7 introduces them as comments, and the COBOL compiler ignores them except for printing them out.

The actual work of our program begins with line 10050. This is an OPEN statement, which performs housekeeping chores to prepare the MASTER-FILE for input. The computer would instruct the operator to have the file ready for work when this statement was executed. The next line is a READ statement, which causes the first record to be read in from the MASTER-FILE. If there is no data on the MASTER-FILE, the computer is instructed to stop the run by the AT END STOP RUN phrase in the READ statement. If the data is on the MASTER-FILE, a single record is read into a predefined record area (not shown in Figure 2.2 but one that will be defined for you). The student record has the same general format as the manual record shown in Figure 2.1.

FIGURE 2.2
Sample COBOL Program to
Read a Single Record

```
COLUMNS 1      6 7 8
        |      | |
        |      | |
        010000 PROCEDURE DIVISION.
        010010 READ-A-RECORD.
        010020*   THIS COBOL PROGRAM READS A SINGLE          ⎫ These lines are
        010030*   RECORD FROM THE MASTER-FILE AND            ⎬ comments—note
        010040*   PRINTS OUT THE NAME AND ADDRESS VALUES.    ⎭ the asterisks in
        010050    OPEN INPUT MASTER-FILE.                      column 7
        010060    READ MASTER-FILE AT END STOP RUN.
        010070    DISPLAY FIRST-NAME OF MASTER-RECORD,
        010080       LAST-NAME OF MASTER-RECORD.
        010090    DISPLAY STREET OF MASTER-RECORD,
        010100       CITY OF MASTER-RECORD,
        010110       STATE OF MASTER-RECORD,
        010120       ZIP OF MASTER-RECORD.
        010130    STOP RUN.
```

The next two statements (beginning in line 10070 and 10090) are DISPLAY statements. They use more than one card and end at the period. The first DISPLAY statement prints out the first name and the last name of the student whose name is on the MASTER-FILE. This generates a single line of printout. The second DISPLAY generates a second line of printout and prints the student's address. After this has been done, the run is stopped. The words PROCEDURE, DIVISION, OPEN, INPUT, READ, AT END, STOP, RUN, and DISPLAY are all special COBOL words. The other words used in this program are user-defined words that represent variables used by the program or the names of files.

COBOL is a language designed primarily for manipulating data files. Therefore, to learn how to use it effectively, it is necessary to have a data file on which you can practice. For this purpose, a special data file called the MASTER-FILE has been created. It is similar in structure to the student record shown in Figure 2.1. You will use it for most of your initial work in COBOL. Later, you will learn how to define your own data files and design your own applications in COBOL.

To use this file, you must know two things about it. First, you will have to know the names of the fields in the file. In some computer languages, it is possible to make up any name you want for a variable, and the computer will automatically define that variable for you. This is not true in COBOL. All data names must be defined before they can be used. This has already been done for you in the MASTER-FILE. The second thing that you will have to know is how long the data fields are and how the data is coded. The field lengths tell you what to expect when the data is printed. The coding will tell you how to interpret what is printed. Most data processing systems will have a **code book** for the system. This code book gives the meanings of the data stored in the data fields. For example, in the field giving the student's sex, is the correct code "M" for male and "F" for female, or is it 0 for male and 1 for female? This is the type of question that would be answered by the system code book. Such a document is essential to anyone using the system. Figure 2.3 gives the layout of the records in the MASTER-FILE.

The field names in Figure 2.3 are the ones you will have to use when you are writing COBOL programs later on. The names must be spelled exactly as they are given in Figure 2.3. The second column in the figure gives the length of the field in characters. The third column gives the type of the field. An **alphanumeric** field can contain either letters or digits. You cannot compute with an alphanumeric field. You may only print it out or move its contents around. A **numeric** field contains only numbers and a sign code (in Chapter 6, we will have more details on how numbers are represented internally). You can compute with the values in a numeric field, but you should probably not try to print them out. Because of the way in which the sign is coded in the data, printing a numeric field gives strange-looking results. If you want to print the contents of a numeric field, you will have to edit the field appropriately.

code book

alphanumeric

numeric

FIGURE 2.3
Layout of the MASTER-
FILE

FIELD NAME	LENGTH	TYPE	CONTENTS
STUDENT-NO	10	Alphanumeric	This is ten digits for the student number. It contains no imbedded spaces or other nonnumeric characters. It is right justified with leading zeros.
LAST-NAME	20	Alphanumeric	The last name, left-justified.
FIRST-NAME	20	Alphanumeric	The first name, left-justified.
INIT	1	Alphanumeric	The middle initial.
STREET	20	Alphanumeric	The street address, left-justified.
CITY	20	Alphanumeric	The name of the student's home city, left-justified.
STATE	2	Alphanumeric	The name of the student's home state using the U.S. Post Office's two character codes for states.
ZIP	5	Alphanumeric	The zip code.
PHONE	7	Alphanumeric	The student's home phone with no imbedded blanks or dashes.
SEX	1	Alphanumeric	M stands for male, F for female.

FIGURE 2.3
(Continued)

FIELD NAME	LENGTH	TYPE	CONTENTS
AGE	2	Numeric	The student's age.
BIRTHDAY	6	Numeric	The student's birthdate in mmddyy (month-day-year) format.
MM	2	Numeric	The first two digits of the BIRTHDAY field, representing the month of the student's birth, right-justified.
DD	2	Numeric	The third and fourth digits of the BIRTHDAY field representing the day of the student's birth, left-justified.
YY	2	Numeric	The last two digits of the BIRTHDAY field representing the year of the student's birth, left-justified.
COLLEGE	20	Alphanumeric	The student's college at the university, left-justified.
MAJOR	20	Alphanumeric	The student's major, left-justified.
ADVISOR	20	Alphanumeric	The name of the student's faculty advisor, last name first, followed by a comma, followed by the first initial.

FIGURE 2.3
(Continued)

FIELD NAME	LENGTH	TYPE	CONTENTS
CREDITS	3	Numeric	The number of credits earned toward graduation.
AVERAGE	5	Numeric	The student's GPA. There are three places after the decimal.

Course Table
This block of entries is repeated 5 times.

NUMBR	6	Alphanumeric	The course's catalog number, left-justified.
NAME	20	Alphanumeric	The course's catalog name, left-justified.
HOURS	2	Numeric	The number of credit hours earned by passing the course, right-justified.
P-F	1	Alphanumeric	A flag telling whether the student has selected the Pass-Fail grading option in this course. If so, this field is zero. Otherwise, it is one.
GRADE	3	Numeric	The student's grade with A = 4.0, B = 3.0, and so on. There are two places after the implied decimal point.

End of Course Table

FIGURE 2.3
(Continued)

FIELD NAME	LENGTH	TYPE	CONTENTS
ROOM-BAL	7	Numeric	The balance owed on the student's room and board bill. There are two places after the implied decimal point.
TUITION-BAL	7	Numeric	The balance owed on the student's tuition bill. There are two places after the implied decimal point.
OTHER-BAL	7	Numeric	The total balance of other fees owed by the student. There are two places after the implied decimal point.
TOTAL-BAL	7	Numeric	The sum of the previous three fields. There are two places after the implied decimal point.

In addition to these specific data fields, there are also some scratch fields that you may use for computing intermediate results. The names of these fields and their uses are given below.

Name	Description
X1 through X5	These fields are used for computations. They are 7 places long with two places after the implied decimal. You should not try to print the values in these fields.

FIGURE 2.3
(Continued)

FIELD NAME	LENGTH	TYPE	CONTENTS

XP1 through XP5   These fields are used for printing the results of computations.
They may not be used for computation. The results of a computation
are moved into one of these fields,
and they will be printed with a
decimal point. There are two places
after the decimal.

XD1 through XD5   These are the same as the XP
fields, except that they will be
printed with a dollar sign ($)
in front.

D1 through D5   These fields are used for holding
alphanumberic variables.

MORE-DATA   This is a three-place alphabetic
field. It is used as a flag for
your program to tell when it is
out of data on its input file.

You may do this editing by using the MOVE statement (to be discussed in the next section of this chapter) and the scratch fields given at
the end of Figure 2.3. You could move the field you wished to print to a
scratch field especially used for printing and then print the scratch field.
Say, for example, that you wished to print out the GPA (grade–point
average) given in the field AVERAGE. If a student had a 3.0 average, the
printout would be 300. To avoid this, move the contents of the AVERAGE
field to one of the XP fields. The following example shows how this
would work:

```
MOVE AVERAGE OF MASTER-RECORD TO XP1.
DISPLAY XP1.
     Resulting Printout:  3.00

MOVE AVERAGE OF MASTER-RECORD TO XD1.
DISPLAY XD1.
     Resulting Printout:  $3.00
```

The example assumes that the field AVERAGE contained a 3. The decimal point in the AVERAGE field does not actually appear. The computer keeps track internally of the location of the decimal point.

In Chapters 6 and 7, you will learn more about the requirements of COBOL for editing data items. The brief introduction given here plus a little practice should be enough for now.

2.1   BASIC COBOL CONVENTIONS

Before we can begin writing any COBOL programs, you will have to learn some of the basic rules for the COBOL language and the words that make it up. You will quickly discover that computers are very particular about the instructions that are given them. A computer is a very powerful slave, and it will do exactly what you say. You will also discover that what you actually say (in the computer's language) may not always be what you meant to say. Read this section carefully and refer to it later on when confronted by problems arising from some of these points.

COBOL has a basic set of fifty-one characters used in forming instructions (statements). This does not mean that a COBOL program can work with only fifty-one symbols. It can manipulate any characters as data that are legal in the particular computer's character set. But the COBOL language itself requires only fifty-one characters. These characters and their uses are given in Figure 2.4.

COBOL has a number of rules for the use of the characters in its character set. These rules are:

1. When the definition of any statement in this book uses a punctuation symbol, that symbol is always required.

2. When a period, semicolon, or comma is used in a statement, there should never be a space before it, and there should always be a space after it.

3. A left parenthesis must not be immediately followed by a space. A right parenthesis must not be preceded immediately by a space.

4. At least one space must separate any two COBOL words.

5. An arithmetic operator must always have spaces on both sides of it. The only exception to this is a unary operator—that is, a single minus or plus sign in front of a number.

FIGURE 2.4
Basic COBOL Character Set

The complete COBOL character set consists of the
following 51 characters.

Digits 0 through 9 (10 characters)
Letters A through Z (26 characters)
Special Characters (15 characters)
+   plus sign
-    minus sign
     blank or space
*   asterisk
/   slash
=   equal sign
>   greater than inequality
<   less than inequality
$ dollar sign
,   comma
.   period or decimal point
'   quotation mark (Check this. Some machines
     may use the " [double quotation] instead)
(left parenthesis
)   right parenthesis
;   semicolon

Of the previous 51 characters, the following groups
have special purposes.

1. The digits 0 through 9, the letters A
through Z, and the hyphen or minus sign are
used to form words.

2. The quotation mark, left and right parentheses, comma, period, and semicolon are
used for punctuation.

3. The asterisk, slash, plus, and minus
signs are used in arithmetic expressions.

4. The greater than, less than, and the
equals sign are used in relational tests.

Some examples of the use of these rules are given here:

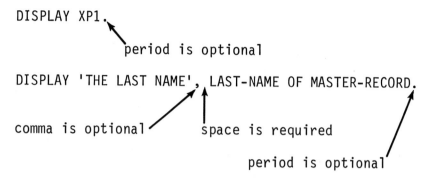

```
DISPLAY XP1.
```

period is optional

```
DISPLAY 'THE LAST NAME', LAST-NAME OF MASTER-RECORD.
```

comma is optional   space is required

period is optional

You should refer to these rules when you start writing COBOL statements. For students used to other computer languages, COBOL sometimes seems particularly fussy in its demands for punctuation and spacing.

Once you get used to these rules while actually writing COBOL code, however, you will seldom refer to them later.

Words

The characters in the character set are used to build **words.** A word is a group of thirty or fewer characters, beginning with a letter and made up of either letters, numbers, or the hyphen (-). Some examples of COBOL words are:

words

```
READ
COMPUTE-THE-AVERAGE
DISPLAY
PROCEDURE
```

A word may be a **reserved word,** which means that it has its own special meaning in the COBOL language. Appendix A contains a list of reserved words. Some examples are:

reserved word

```
READ
MOVE
PROCEDURE
DISPLAY
```

It is a common mistake to use reserved words as data names in your own program. If you begin getting strange error messages from the computer, refer to Appendix A to see if you have used a reserved word incorrectly.

The other type of word in COBOL is a programmer-supplied **name.**   name
Some examples are:

```
MASTER-FILE
READ-A-RECORD
AVERAGE
FIRST-NAME
MASTER-RECORD
```

These programmer-supplied names are used for such things as variables or data files. All the names for the fields in the MASTER-FILE are programmer-supplied names. They are not part of the COBOL language, but you will use them in your programs as if they were.

The reserved words that make up the COBOL language are divided into two types, **key words** and **optional words.** A key word is a word   key words
required in a particular COBOL statement for the computer to interpret   optional words
the statement. An optional word is one that may be included in a COBOL statement to improve readability for users. The computer does not need the word to figure out what the statement means. Some examples are:

```
READ MASTER-FILE END STOP RUN.
READ MASTER-FILE RECORD AT END STOP RUN.
```

These two READ statements mean exactly the same thing. The words RECORD and AT in the second statement are examples of optional words. They make the statement look more familiar, but the computer does not need them. We will discuss optional words and key words later in the section when we talk about how to define a COBOL statement.

Constants and Literals

In addition to words, it is also possible to use constants in COBOL. There are two types of constants, or literals as they are sometimes called: **numeric constants** and **nonnumeric literals.** A numeric constant is simply   numeric constants
a number; it does not change its value during the running of a program.   nonnumeric literals
The rules for writing numbers in COBOL may be a little different from those you are used to. A numeric constant in COBOL is from one to eighteen digits long. It may have a plus or minus sign in front of it; if it has no sign, it is assumed to be positive. It may also have a decimal point; if it has no decimal point, it is assumed to be an integer. Some examples of legal and illegal numeric constants are:

LEGAL NUMBERS	
3.141592	
+16	
−25	
100	

ILLEGAL NUMBERS	REASON FOR PROBLEM
123456789.0123456789	Too long
$1.98	Illegal character, $
25−	Minus sign on the right
1,000,000	Imbedded commas

The first number is illegal because it is too long, the second because it uses a dollar sign, the third because it has a negative sign on the right, and the fourth because it has imbedded commas.

A nonnumeric literal is simply a string of alphabetic characters between two quotation marks. Some examples are:

```
'NOW IS THE TIME FOR ALL GOOD MEN TO COME TO THE AID OF THE PARTY.'
'The time is 3:00 P.M.'
```

A nonnumeric literal may be used to print messages, table headings, or anything else that will not change. The second example may look a little strange to you. First, it contains numbers. A nonnumeric literal may contain any symbols in the computer's character set, even those not in the COBOL language character set. Second, it contains lower-case letters. The use of lower-case letters is possible on many machines, and there are even printers that will print them out. They are widely used for printing out letters and other types of text.

Figurative Constants

There is another type of constant unique to COBOL called a **figurative constant**. A figurative constant is a COBOL reserved word that may be used in place of certain literals. The figurative constants and their meanings are:

figurative constant

NAME	MEANING
ZERO ZEROES ZEROS	Represents the value 0. The number of places depends on the data field receiving the 0 value.

SPACE SPACES	One or more blanks or spaces.
HIGH-VALUE HIGH-VALUES	This represents the character that has the highest value in the computer's collating sequence. In sorting a group of characters in ascending order, this character would be last.
LOW-VALUE LOW-VALUES	This represents one or more occurrences of the character that has the lowest value in the computer's collating sequence. In sorting a group of characters in ascending order, this character would be first.
QUOTE QUOTES	This represents one or more occurrences of the quotation symbol. It cannot be used to define a nonnumeric literal.

Figurative constants are used in COBOL statements to enhance the readability of the language. One of the goals of the COBOL designers was to produce an Englishlike language, and the use of figurative constants helps make the language look more familiar.

Now that we have the basic COBOL elements down, we are ready to begin discussion of how to write a statement in COBOL. COBOL follows somewhat rigid spacing conventions. You can better understand the spacing conventions if you look at the COBOL coding form in Figure 2.5. A coding form is a preprinted form that helps the programmer observe the proper spacing rules and facilitates writing programs. The completed program can then be given to a keypunch operator.

The eighty-column computer card is divided up into different fields. The way in which these fields are used is:

COLUMNS	CONTENTS
1–6	These columns contain the sequence number of the card. Successive cards should have higher numbers. If they do not, the COBOL compiler will print a warning message, but it will allow your program to run.
7	The continuation column. If you have a nonnumeric literal that is too long to be contained on a single card, place a hyphen (minus sign) in column 7 and continue on another card.
8–11	Area A. Certain types of COBOL statements must begin in the area A columns. These include the names of divisions, sections, or paragraphs as well as file descriptions.

| 12–72 | Area B. All COBOL statements that cannot begin in area A must begin somewhere in area B. |
| 73–80 | Program identification columns. These contain the name of the program or some other identifying characters set up by the organization. The computer ignores them. |

Some explanation is needed to justify the way in which COBOL breaks up its cards into fields. The sequence numbers in columns 1 through 6 are very important. If a deck is ever dropped (as occasionally happens to large decks of cards), it can be put back in its original order very easily by sorting the cards using the sequence numbers in columns 1 through 6. You may decide not to put the sequence numbers in (the computer does not care whether you do or not), but you are taking your chances. A dropped deck can mean days or even weeks of work trying to restore the deck to its former condition.

FIGURE 2.5
Sample COBOL Coding
Form

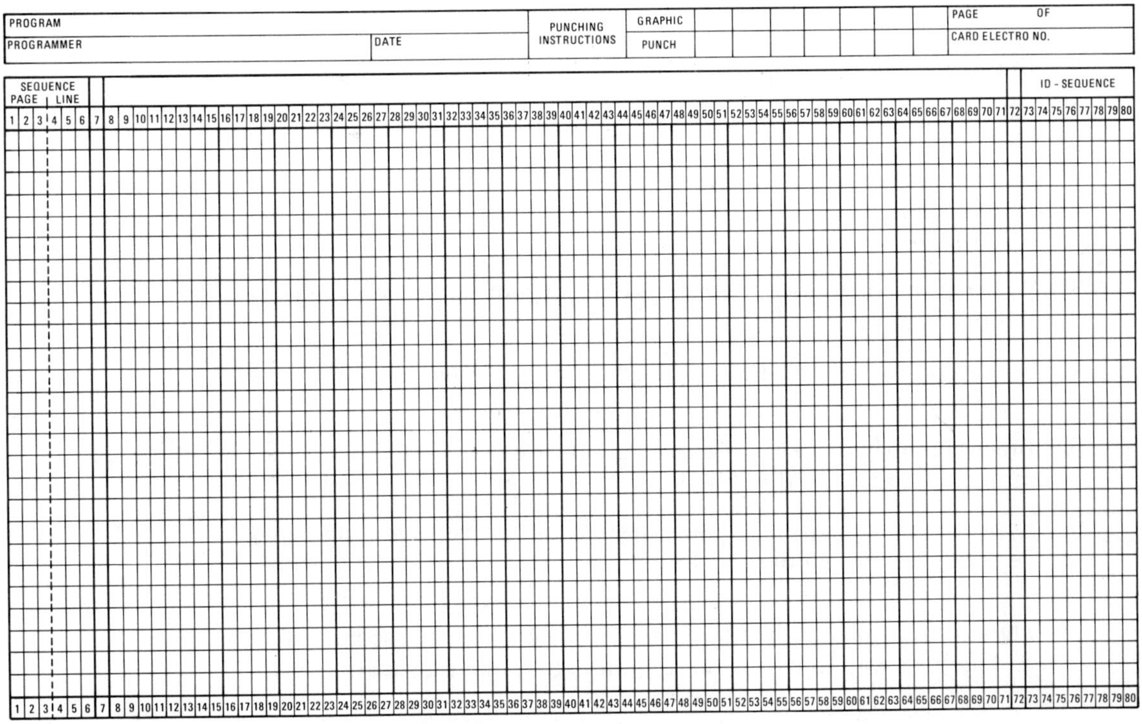

The area A and the area B restrictions are sometimes confusing to beginners in COBOL. These restrictions were added to force the programmer to use indenting in the program to make the structure clearer. In the PROCEDURE DIVISION, the only things beginning in area A are division names, section names, and paragraph names. When we discuss the DATA DIVISION in Chapter 8, you will also have to put file descriptions, record descriptions, and certain other data descriptions in area A. You will be told which these are. For the time being, you will be writing only PROCEDURE DIVISION statements, and you can assume that everything in the PROCEDURE DIVISION except the paragraph names will start in area B.

The program identification columns, columns 73 through 80, can usually be ignored. They provide additional information about the program for anybody who might be storing the program. You can put your own messages in these columns.

Now, we are ready to discuss the format we will use for describing COBOL statements. Like most computer languages, COBOL allows the programmer to write statements in different ways. It would be impossible to list all the possible ways to write a statement, so a notation for showing the general form of a statement has been developed. The rules for this notation are:

1. All words in capital letters are reserved words that can be used in the statement. If the word is underlined, it is a key word and must appear when a given option is selected. If the word is not underlined, it may be omitted without generating an error.

2. All punctuation given in a statement definition (except that in Appendix B, which reproduces the ANSI COBOL specifications) is required. Additional punctuation may be inserted in any statement to improve readability as long as you follow the rules for punctuation.

3. Words printed in lower-case letters represent names supplied by the programmer.

4. Square brackets ([and]) are used to indicate that a given clause may be omitted if desired.

5. Braces or curly brackets ({ and }) enclosing stacked COBOL lines indicate that one of the lines *must* appear in the statement.

6. Repeated periods (. . .) indicate that the preceding clause may be repeated any number of times.

These rules look fairly complicated, but they are not hard to use in practice. The best way to understand them is to look at a specific example. Consider the addition statement in COBOL. Specific addition statements might look like:

```
ADD A TO B
ADD A, B, C, D, TO X ROUNDED
ADD A GIVING B ON SIZE ERROR PERFORM CLEANUP
```

To determine the general form of an addition statement, we use our six rules to write a general definition for **COBOL addition**. It is:

COBOL addition

$$
\underline{\text{ADD}} \quad \begin{Bmatrix} \text{identifier-1} \\ \text{literal-1} \end{Bmatrix} \begin{bmatrix} \text{identifier-2} \\ \text{literal-2} \end{bmatrix} \ldots \underline{\text{TO}} \text{ identifier-m } [\underline{\text{ROUNDED}}]
$$

$$
[\text{ identifier-n } [\underline{\text{ROUNDED}}]]\ldots [\text{ ON } \underline{\text{SIZE ERROR}} \text{ imperative-statement }]
$$

The explanation of the definition is fairly easy to understand. The reserved word ADD is required (hence the underlining) to show the computer that this is an addition statement. ADD must be followed by either a numeric constant—that is, a number—or an identifier. Nonnumeric literals are not permitted. The fact that the identifier is given as identifier-1 indicates that it is distinct from other identifiers given in the definition (such as identifier-2, etc.). The repeated periods after the item in square brackets indicate that you may give as many identifiers or numbers as you like.* The braces indicate that you must have either an identifier or a constant in that position. It is not possible to leave this item out, and one or the other must be chosen. Similarly, the reserved word TO must appear in every COBOL addition statement of this format. The phrase ROUNDED is optional as is the phrase ON SIZE ERROR. Note that in the ON SIZE ERROR phase, only the words SIZE ERROR are underlined. This means that they must be included when the phrase is chosen. The word ON is optional and may be omitted.

This format for COBOL definitions will be used throughout this book. It is commonly used in other books and reference manuals for defining the language. It is a very concise way of expressing the options available to you in a COBOL statement, and you will become accustomed to it quickly. All of the definitions of 1974 ANSI COBOL statements are given in Appendix B of this book, and you can use the appendix as a quick, convenient reference for your questions about the syntax of specific COBOL statements. These definitions are generally similar to the ones used in the book. Sometimes the book examples have been shortened for illustration.

---

* Your COBOL compiler may limit the number of identifiers and numeric constants that may appear after ADD. Always make sure that what you intend to do is allowed by your COBOL.

2.2 COBOL STATEMENTS FOR INFORMATION RETRIEVAL

The first thing that we want to do with a computerized file is to retrieve information from it. In COBOL this can be a formidable task for a beginner. If you know nothing about the file other than the general layout of the data, it is necessary to write DATA DIVISION statements in COBOL to describe the data and its location. If you are learning COBOL on the job, the information retrieval task is usually somewhat simpler. Somebody else will have written the necessary file and environment descriptions, and all you have to do is borrow the descriptions and add your own code to do the information retrieval.

This is what has been done for you in the MASTER-FILE (described in Section 2.0) and the related programs. The field names have already been defined as have the file names. Remember that these names are not part of the COBOL language but, rather, are special names associated with this data base. Later when you learn how to define your own files, you can make up your own names for files and their fields. Your instructor will tell you how to gain access to the data needed to do your problems.

All you have to do at this point, is to write the PROCEDURE DIVISION. The PROCEDURE DIVISION is the fourth division of a COBOL program, which contains the statements telling the computer how to process the data. It is introduced by the reserved words PROCEDURE DIVISION beginning in area A. These two words (with a period following them) will be the first two words of every COBOL program you write for the first few chapters. They are required to introduce the statements to the computer.

You are also required to have a paragraph or procedure name following these two words. A procedure name follows the COBOL naming rules in Section 2.1. It is usually a good idea to make the name something indicative of the purpose of the procedure. The computer does not know or care what the name means, but you do. It will help jog your memory later if you (or somebody else) should come back to modify the program. This is good practice to observe when you work as a programmer or when you manage programmers. Programmers should be encouraged to use procedure and data names that are easy to remember, and they should be encouraged to provide meaningful comments with their programs.

This practice is intended not so much for the programmer who wrote the program, but for the programmers who later maintain the program. Program maintenance is one of the most expensive activities of any computer installation. Maintenance is the periodic updating of programs that have become obsolete for one reason or another. For example, changes in labor laws may render old payroll programs obsolete, and a maintenance programmer must be called in to make the necessary changes to the program. By carefully setting and following certain programming standards, managers can help make this a less expensive and time-consuming problem.

Statement Classification

In discussing the COBOL instructions in this and later chapters, we will use a number of terms to describe them. The first of these is **statement.** A statement is any COBOL verb or the word IF or ON followed by the appropriate operands. A statement may be an **imperative** statement or a **conditional** statement. An imperative statement directs the computer to take some action. It is always performed when the flow of control reaches it. Some examples are:

statement
imperative
conditional

```
ADD 1, 2, 3 GIVING X.
MOVE ZEROS TO TOTAL-SUM.
PERFORM CLEANUP.
```

A conditional statement directs the computer to take some action only if a specific condition is met. Some examples are:

```
IF A = 1 PERFORM CHECK-ROUTINE.
READ MASTER-FILE AT END MOVE 'NO' TO MORE-DATA.
```

The top conditional statement is called an IF statement. The imperative statement (PERFORM CHECK-ROUTINE) following the conditional is carried out only if the condition is true. The next statement is a READ statement with a conditional test to see if the file is out of data. This too is considered a type of conditional statement. Conditional statements may change the direction of the flow of control in a program.

Statements may be grouped together into **sentences.** A sentence is a statement or a group of statements terminated by a period (.). These statements may be separated by blanks, or they may be separated by commas or semicolons to enhance their readability. A sentence must start within the limits of area B. An example of a sentence is:

sentences

```
IF A = 1
     MOVE ZERO TO TOTAL
     ADD 1 TO COUNTER.
```

You will notice in the example above, we have an IF statement and two imperative statements. The period ends this block of statements and completes the sentence.

A **paragraph** is a logical entity consisting of one or more sentences. A paragraph must always be introduced by a paragraph name that conforms to the rules for names given in Section 2.0. Paragraph names should not be duplicated. If you do use duplicate names, the computer will not know which name you are referring to in later statements. You can see an example of a paragraph in the sample program given in Figure 2.2.

paragraph

This Englishlike structure of statements, sentences, and paragraphs provides COBOL programmers with a convenient way of segmenting programs into independent units. It allows them to concentrate on one unit at a time to ensure that the code in the unit is correct before proceeding to the next. It is very helpful to think of your program as composed of independent building blocks rather than to try to understand the entire program as a whole. Segmenting your programs into logical blocks will keep your computer code more manageable.

We now begin introducing some of the simple information retrieval instructions you will need. We will follow the conventions given for definitions in Section 2.1. Please note that some of the definitions given here are not the complete versions of the instruction, which will be given in your computer's specific COBOL reference manual and in Appendix B of this book. This is done to avoid confusion by introducing all possible options of each statement early in the book. The different options will be introduced as you are ready to use them.

Preparing Files

The first COBOL statement we will introduce is simply a housekeeping one. If you wish to retrieve information from a file, you must read the file. But before the computer can read a file it must be sure that the file is ready to be read. For example:

```
OPEN INPUT MASTER-FILE, REPORT-FILE.
```

The OPEN **statement** tells the computer to prepare the file for input–output. We will consider only the input version for now. Its syntax is:

OPEN statement

```
OPEN INPUT     file-name-1  [ file-name-2 ]  ...
```

The only file you will be dealing with in this chapter is the MASTER-FILE containing the student records, so your version of the statement will be:

```
OPEN INPUT MASTER-FILE.
```

This tells the computer to set the old master file up so your program can read it. It is possible to open any number of files in a single open statement. Suppose that we had files called FILEA, FILEB, and FILEC. Then we could write:

```
OPEN INPUT FILEA, FILEB, FILEC.
```

Preparing Variables

We have discussed the OPEN statement, which is used for preparing files for I/O activity. We have a corresponding statement that we can use to prepare variables for use. It is the MOVE statement, and it looks like this:

```
MOVE 1 TO COUNTER
MOVE ZEROS TO X1, X2, X3
MOVE 'YES' TO MORE-DATA
MOVE COUNTER TO X1, X2, X3, X4
```

As its name implies, the MOVE statement is used for moving data values from one variable to another or from a constant to a variable. The first MOVE statement above places a 1 in the variable called COUNTER. The second MOVE statement uses one of our figurative constants (zeros). It places the value 0 in each of the variables X1, X2, and X3. The third MOVE shows how the MOVE statement is used on nonnumeric (alphabetic) literals, and the fourth move shows the use of MOVE to move the value in a variable to the variables X1, X2, X3, and X4.

The general format of the MOVE **statement** is: MOVE statement

$$\text{MOVE} \begin{Bmatrix} \texttt{identifier-1} \\ \texttt{literal} \end{Bmatrix} \underline{\texttt{TO}} \texttt{ identifier-2 [identifier-3]} \ldots$$

Our most common use of the MOVE statement is to initialize the values in the variables before we use them. You should always initialize the variable values you use in a computer program. Some machines will do this for you automatically, but you should never assume that a variable has a particular value unless you have set it yourself.

Reading Information

The next statement to consider is the READ statement. After we have opened the file, we may begin to read data from it. Some examples of the READ statement are:

```
READ MASTER-FILE RECORD AT END MOVE 'NO' TO MORE DATA.
READ MASTER-FILE END STOP RUN.
READ ACCOUNT-DATA RECORD AT END PERFORM CLOSE-OUT.
```

In the READ statement we tell the computer from which file we wish to read data. We should have already executed an OPEN statement before reading, but we only have to execute *one* OPEN statement. We do not have to open the file every time we READ. We must tell the machine what we want to do if the file has no more data in it. This is the purpose of the AT END phrase in the READ. There is an imperative statement after the AT END that tells what is to be done next. In the first READ, we move the value 'NO' into the variable called MORE-DATA. We will be using the variable MORE-DATA as a flag to tell our programs when we are out of data. We can use any type of imperative statement after the AT END in a READ. The second and third reads in the example above use a STOP RUN and a PERFORM as their imperative statements.

The READ **statement** has the following format:

READ statement

```
READ file-name RECORD [AT END imperative-statement]
```

The READ statement reads a single record from the file into the data area associated with that file. In our initial work with COBOL, all the files you will use and their data areas are already defined for you. You will be using three files. Their names and associated data areas are:

FILE NAME	DATA AREA
MASTER-FILE	MASTER-RECORD
REPORT-FILE	REPORT-RECORD
SORT-FILE	SORT-RECORD

This means that if you read a record from the MASTER-FILE, the data goes into the record area called MASTER-RECORD. All of these file names are programmer-defined names and not **COBOL** reserved words. The record itself is broken down into fields named by individual variable names. These variable names are the ones given earlier in Figure 2.3.

The same variable names are used for the fields in all three record areas above. You might be asking yourself at this point how the computer is able to tell which data area we are talking about. The answer is that it has no way of knowing which one we mean unless we use the **fully qualified** data name. For instance, if we are talking about the FIRST-NAME, LAST-NAME, and PHONE fields in the MASTER-FILE, then the fully qualified names are:

fully qualified

```
FIRST-NAME OF MASTER-RECORD
LAST-NAME OF MASTER-RECORD
PHONE OF MASTER-RECORD
```

which instruct the computer to go to the definition of the MASTER-RECORD areas for the contents of these fields.

Printing Information

Once you have put data into your program, you will want to be able to print it out. COBOL has a number of statements for doing output, but for the time being, we will restrict ourselves to one, the DISPLAY statement. These are some examples:

```
DISPLAY FIRST-NAME OF MASTER-RECORD.
DISPLAY 'SUCCESSFUL END OF PROGRAM'.
DISPLAY FIRST-NAME OF MASTER-RECORD,
     LAST-NAME OF MASTER-RECORD,
     PHONE OF MASTER-RECORD.
DISPLAY MORE-DATA.
DISPLAY 'FIRST NAME:', FIRST-NAME OF MASTER-RECORD.
```

The DISPLAY statement can be used on both literals and variables. In the first example, we use the statement to print out only one variable, the FIRST-NAME OF MASTER-RECORD. Each DISPLAY statement causes a new line of printout to be generated, so if we executed all five statements above in order, we would get five lines of printout. The second DISPLAY statement is used to print out a literal. We might use a statement like this one in the paragraph that ends a program to show that we have reached a successful end of run. The third DISPLAY statement prints out several values on a line of output (if there is room).

The definition of the DISPLAY **statement** is: DISPLAY statement

$$\text{DISPLAY} \quad \begin{Bmatrix} \text{identifier-1} \\ \text{literal-1} \end{Bmatrix} \quad \begin{bmatrix} \text{identifier-2} \\ \text{literal-2} \end{bmatrix} \quad \dots$$

The DISPLAY statement is normally used for low-volume printing, but it will work quite well for any of the tasks we have for it in this chapter.

Transferring Control

The next statement we will discuss is the PERFORM statement, which transfers control to another paragraph and instructs the computer to execute the statements in that paragraph. After the computer has completed that, control is transferred back to the statement after the PERFORM. As an example, consider the following COBOL program:

```
PROCEDURE DIVISION.
CONTROL-ROUTINE.
     PERFORM INITIALIZE.
```

```
            PERFORM PRINT-READ UNTIL MORE-DATA = 'NO'.
            PERFORM CLEANUP.
            STOP RUN.
        INITIALIZE.
            OPEN INPUT MASTER-FILE.
            MOVE 'YES' TO MORE-DATA.
            READ MASTER-FILE AT END MOVE 'NO' TO MORE-DATA.
        PRINT-READ.
            DISPLAY FIRST-NAME OF MASTER-RECORD,
                LAST-NAME OF MASTER-RECORD.
            READ MASTER-FILE AT END MOVE 'NO' TO MORE-DATA.
        CLEANUP.
            DISPLAY 'SUCCESSFUL END OF PROGRAM'.
            CLOSE MASTER-FILE.
```

In this sample program, look at the paragraph called CONTROL-
ROUTINE. Notice that it is made up of only PERFORM statements and a
STOP RUN statement in a simple sequence. You can think of the
CONTROL-ROUTINE as the first block in the hierarchy diagram in Figure
2.6. The CONTROL-ROUTINE paragraph calls in all the other blocks in the
diagram, which are represented by the paragraphs INTIALIZE, PRINT-
READ, and CLEANUP. The program is well structured because it matches
our HIPO diagram in Figure 2.6 and uses only the structures we presented in the flowcharts in Chapter 1.

There are quite a number of options possible with the PERFORM
statement. It is one of the most flexible (and useful) statements in
COBOL. For the time being, we will consider only a few possibilities. In
Chapter 10 we will present a more detailed discussion of PERFORM. Our
initial definition of a PERFORM **statement** is: PERFORM statement

```
    PERFORM paragraph-name [ UNTIL MORE-DATA = 'NO' ]
```

In the first option we perform the paragraph only once. For instance, in:

```
    PERFORM INITIALIZE
```

we transfer control to the INITIALIZE paragraph and perform the state-
ments in that paragraph. When we hit the new paragraph name, PRINT-
READ, control is transferred back to the statement after the PERFORM
INITIALIZE.

The second PERFORM in our example is a bit different. This is the
one that reads:

```
    PERFORM PRINT-READ UNTIL MORE-DATA = 'NO'
```

In this version of PERFORM, control is transferred to the paragraph, PRINT-READ, until the variable MORE-DATA takes on the value 'NO'. MORE-DATA will eventually contain a 'NO' because a 'NO' is moved into it when we run out of data on the MASTER-FILE. If you forget to do this, then the computer will try to perform PRINT-READ forever. This is what is called an **infinite loop.** This means that the computer will keep executing the same code over and over with no way of stopping. Obviously, such a loop does not go on forever. Your computer program will run out of time or will generate too many print lines. Something will eventually bring it to a halt, but it may be expensive or embarrassing getting it to stop. Be careful of situations that potentially may generate infinite loops.

infinite loop

Additional Housekeeping

To run the program we need two more housekeeping statements. The first of these is the CLOSE statement. If we have an OPEN statement for files, then it stands to reason that we ought to have a CLOSE statement as well. Some examples are:

```
CLOSE MASTER-FILE.
CLOSE MASTER-FILE, REPORT-FILE.
```

A CLOSE **statement** is the word CLOSE followed by a list of the files you are closing. The syntax of the statement is:

CLOSE statement

```
CLOSE file-name-1 [ file-name-2 ]  ...
```

The CLOSE statement directs the computer to perform whatever end-of-file processing is needed on the files that you have given it. If you close a file, then you must give another OPEN statement if you want to use the file again. Normally, you will open and close a file only once during the run of a particular program.

The final statement we will discuss is STOP RUN, written:

```
STOP RUN
```

It must appear at least once in your COBOL program (usually at the end). When encountered, this statement stops the execution of your program.

Commentary Text

One final element of your COBOL programs that we should discuss is the **comment.** In COBOL you can make a line into a comment line

comment

by putting an asterisk (*) in column 7 of your program card. The computer then treats the rest of the card as a comment, which it prints with your program listing. You should make extensive use of comments in the programs you write. Treat these comments as notes to yourself on how your program works. This way, if you have to come back and redo it later, you will be better able to understand what is going on. This may sound silly, but you will be surprised to find out how quickly you forget the details of complicated programs when you are away from them. There is another reason for learning the use of comments now. It builds good programming habits for your professional work later. Programs are much easier to maintain if they are well documented. The effective use of comments can save you and your employer time and money.

2.3 PREPARING A COBOL PROGRAM

At this point, we have covered enough COBOL statements to write a simple information retrieval program. The program will be run using the simulated student file discussed in Section 2.0. All you have to do is write the PROCEDURE DIVISION statements to retrieve the information. It is also necessary to write cards with job information and job control language to call the COBOL compiler and set up all the necessary files. Your instructor will give you the format of the job control cards since they vary from computer to computer. It might also be helpful at this point to review the COBOL spacing conventions and the MASTER-FILE naming conventions covered in Section 2.0.

One of the first problems that a student encounters while learning a new computer language is how to arrange the statements together into a meaningful program. The definitions of the individual statements seem simple enough, but how do you put them all together? This problem is similar to the one encountered in learning a foreign language. It is easy enough to read the definitions and understand the syntax rules in a textbook, but it is quite another thing to apply these same definitions and rules in conversation. One must develop a speaking knowledge of the language, and whether it is COBOL or a foreign language, practice is the only thing that will help.

An excellent approach to this problem is to start with a program that works and is similar to the type you wish to write. After you understand this program, modify it until it meets your needs. As a first problem in COBOL, let us try printing out the names of all the students whose records are on the MASTER-FILE.

To start this problem, we will first prepare a hierarchy diagram giving the structure of the program. First, we will have a control routine that calls in the processes needed. The processes we will need are an initialization routine to set up our files and initialize our data variables, a routine to print out a name and then read a new name off the MASTER-FILE, and finally a cleanup routine to close the files and end. A hierarchy diagram for the program to read and print the names on the MASTER-FILE is given in Figure 2.6. As you can see, the program will have a very simple structure.

Now, let us do the flowcharts for each of the processes in the hierarchy diagram. These flowcharts are given in Figure 2.7. Flowchart a shows for the CONTROL-ROUTINE pictured in the hierarchy chart. It has a simple sequence structure. The sequence is to call each of the three routines that were subordinate to the CONTROL-ROUTINE on the hierarchy chart. After that, it is done. Flowchart b in Figure 2.7 shows the INITIALIZE routine. This routine opens the MASTER-FILE for input. It moves 'YES' into the flag MORE-DATA to let the program know that there is data available on the file. It then reads the first record from the MASTER-FILE. Remember that our READ is a type of conditional statement. If there is no data in the MASTER-FILE, the MORE-DATA flag is set to 'NO'. Finally, a header line is printed, and we exit from the procedure.

The next flowchart (c) is for the PRINT-READ routine. The first thing we do upon entering this routine is print out the first and last name of the student whose record we have just read from the MASTER-FILE. Then, we read another record from the MASTER-FILE. Because we used the

```
PERFORM PRINT-READ UNTIL MORE-DATA = 'NO'
```

version of the PERFORM to enter the PRINT-READ routine, we will never get into this paragraph if the MASTER-FILE is out of data. Any of the READ statements we use in this program will set the flag MORE-DATA to 'NO' if

FIGURE 2.6
Hierarchy Diagram of
MASTER-FILE Lister Program

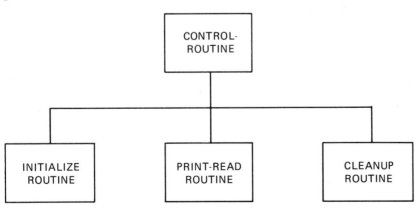

we run out of data. The final routine to be flowcharted is the CLEANUP routine (Figure 2.7d), which closes the MASTER-FILE and prints out a success message. The success message printed at the end is a reasonable thing to put into your programs. If you end your programs with a standard message when they terminate normally, it makes it easier to isolate an abnormal termination problem caused by an error in your program.

FIGURE 2.7
Flowchart of the *MASTER-FILE* Lister Program

FIGURE 2.7
(Continued)

a. CONTROL-ROUTINE

b. INITIALIZE Routine

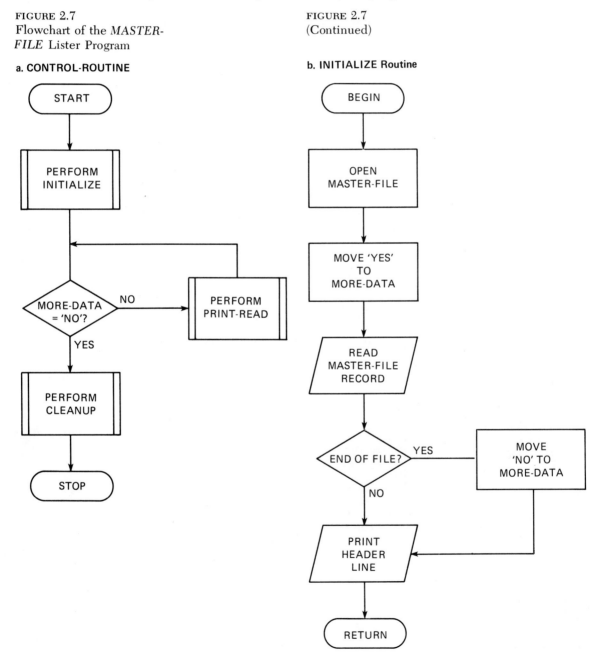

Now that we have the flowcharts of the program, we can begin to write the COBOL code directly from these flowcharts. The COBOL program for this problem is given in Figure 2.8. There are a number of points that you should notice about this program. First, the line numbers in the program start at 10000 and go up in steps of 10. We have done this because we are only writing the PROCEDURE DIVISION. The other three divisions of your COBOL program have been prepared for you and will be inserted ahead of this code. The COBOL compiler will perform a sequence check on the line numbers to see if they are in ascending order. If they are not, it will print out a warning message. You should try to keep your line numbers in ascending order because these warning messages are useful. They tell you that your cards are out of order, possibly because somebody dropped or shuffled your deck. We do our line numbering in steps of 10 because this gives us nine possible line numbers that we can insert between any given pair of lines. This means that you do not have to completely redo all the line numbers when you add a few new cards. On

FIGURE 2.7
(Continued)

c. PRINT-READ Routine

FIGURE 2.7
(Continued)

d. CLEANUP Routine

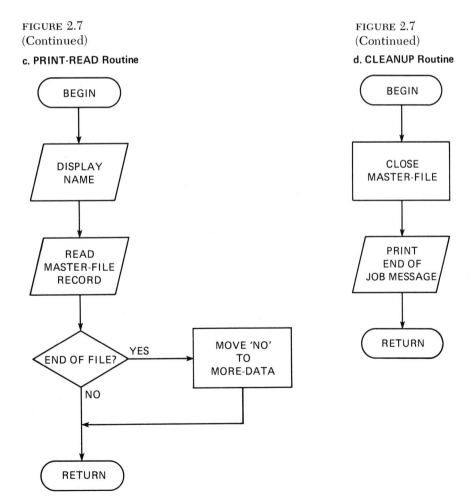

FIGURE 2.8
COBOL Program to Print
Names of Students on
MASTER-FILE

Program

```
010000 PROCEDURE DIVISION.
010010 PROGRAM-PURPOSE.
010020*    THIS PROGRAM PRODUCES A SIMPLE LISTING OF THE
010030*    NAMES OF THE STUDENTS ON THE MASTER-FILE. WHEN
010040*    IT RUNS OUT OF DATA, IT PRINTS OUT A MESSAGE AND
010050*    TERMINATES. IT IS AN EXAMPLE OF A STRUCTURED
010060*    COBOL INFORMATION RETRIEVAL PROGRAM.
010070 CONTROL-ROUTINE.
010080     PERFORM INITIALIZE.
010090     PERFORM PRINT-READ UNTIL MORE-DATA IS EQUAL TO 'NO'.
010100     PERFORM CLEANUP.
010110     STOP RUN.
010120 INITIALIZE.
010130     OPEN INPUT MASTER-FILE.
010140     MOVE 'YES' TO MORE-DATA.
010150     READ MASTER-FILE AT END MOVE 'NO' TO MORE-DATA.
010160     DISPLAY 'FIRST NAME  MID.INIT.  LAST NAME'.
010170     DISPLAY ' '.
010180 PRINT-READ.
010190     DISPLAY FIRST-NAME OF MASTER-RECORD,
010200         INIT OF MASTER-RECORD, '.         '
010210         LAST-NAME OF MASTER-RECORD.
010220     READ MASTER-FILE AT END MOVE 'NO' TO MORE-DATA.
010230 CLEANUP.
010240     CLOSE MASTER-FILE.
010250     DISPLAY 'END OF PROGRAM'.
```

Sample Output

FIRST NAME	MID. INIT.	LAST NAME
STEPHEN	L.	WILCOX
SHERRI	K.	GARLOCK
DANIEL	C.	AIRINGTON
ELAINE	S.	SHAFER
CHARLES	T.	MARTINI
LORI	D.	AVANT
ALAN	C.	GARLAND
MARY	C.	SPARKS
JAMES	D.	TRACY
KAREN	L.	BARCLAY
JOHN	P.	NEWCOMER
ANN	N.	FREITAG
MICHAEL	M.	ADDISON
BRENDA	D.	SETTLE
ELMER	L.	SAVAGE
MARTHA	S.	SALVINO
KENNETH	P.	CHAMBERLAIN
NANCY	B.	FELLERS
DEAN	N.	BARNETT

many on-line systems, the text editor will automatically line number your program for you, so numbering the lines may not be an issue.

In Figure 2.8, you will notice that the data appears to come out in a strange order. The names of the students on the MASTER-FILE appear to be all jumbled up and not in any possible logical order. This is because the MASTER-FILE is a sequential file, and it is kept in order by the student number field (STUDENT-NO) (see Figure 2.3). The printout of the records that you retrieved from the file comes out in the same order because your program prints the records as it encounters them. If you wish the printout to be in some other order, you must reorder the file yourself by sorting it on some other field.

You might ask why such a strange field was chosen as the key for ordering the file. Why not choose a field that makes a little more sense—for example, the LAST-NAME and FIRST-NAME fields? Then the file would be in alphabetical order. One reason for this will become painfully obvious when we begin updating files in Chapter 9. To change the contents of a record in a file, it is necessary to identify the record uniquely. An individual's name is not necessarily unique. Hence, managers of large data files usually choose some field that will always be unique, such as an identification number or social security number.

Another reason is that one field is no better than another for ordering the file. For example, suppose that we wish to mail an announcement to all the students. Then the best way to order the printout will be in zip code order so that the letters may be processed more quickly by the post office. Or suppose that we wish to choose students from the file to be considered for an honors program. Then, the most logical way to print out the file would be on basis of GPA. We could consider a large number of possible orderings of the file, and this leads us to the topic of sorting files to be considered in the next chapter.

STUDY EXERCISES

1. What are the four divisions that make up every COBOL program? What is the purpose of each?

2. What type of characters can be used in an alphabetic field? An alphanumeric field? A numeric field?

3. Should you print the contents of a numeric field? What steps should you take if you want to print the contents?

4. Which of the words below are legal COBOL programmer-defined names? (Check Appendix A when in doubt.)

```
PRINT-A-LINE
DISPLAY
READ-MASTER-FILE
READ-MASTER-FILE-RECORD-AT-END-STOP-RUN
WORKING STORAGE
```

5. Which of the numbers below are legal COBOL numeric constants?

```
7.99
+7.99
7.99CR
7.99-
7.99+
1234567890.12345678
12345678901234567890
$1.98
```

6. Where is area A on a COBOL program card? Area B?

7. The following is the definition of a DIVIDE statement in COBOL:

$$\underline{\text{DIVIDE}} \left\{ \begin{array}{c} \text{data-name-1} \\ \text{literal-1} \end{array} \right\} \left\{ \begin{array}{c} \underline{\text{BY}} \\ \underline{\text{INTO}} \end{array} \right\} \left\{ \begin{array}{c} \text{data-name-2} \\ \text{literal-2} \end{array} \right\}$$

$$\underline{\text{GIVING}} \text{ data-name-3}[\underline{\text{ROUNDED}}][\text{data-name-4}[\underline{\text{ROUNDED}}]] \ldots$$

$$[\underline{\text{ON}} \underline{\text{SIZE}} \underline{\text{ERROR}} \text{ imperative-statement}]$$

Which statements are legal DIVIDE statements according to this definition?

```
DIVIDE 4 BY 2 GIVING X ROUNDED
DIVIDE 4 BY 2 GIVING 2
DIVIDE X ROUNDED BY Y GIVING Z
DIVIDE X BY Y GIVING Z ROUNDED A B C
DIVIDE READ BY WRITE GIVING X
DIVIDE A INTO C GIVING D GIVING E
DIVIDE A B INTO C GIVING D
DIVIDE A INTO B GIVING C ROUNDED D SIZE ERROR
      PERFORM CHECK-DIV
DIVIDE A INTO B GIVING C ROUNDED ON SIZE ERROR
      PERFORM CHECK-DIV
DIVIDE A INTO B GIVING C ROUNDED ON SIZE ERROR
      PERFORM CHECK-DIV GIVING G ROUNDED ON
      SIZE ERROR PERFORM CHECK-DIV
```

8. What is wrong with the code below? Will it run? If yes, what will the output be? If no, why not?

```
PROCEDURE DIVISION.
CONTROL-ROUTINE.
      PERFORM INITIALIZE.
      PERFORM PRINT-READ UNTIL MORE-DATA = 'NO'.
      PERFORM CLEANUP.
      STOP RUN.
INITIALIZE.
      OPEN INPUT MASTER-FILE.
      MOVE 'YES' TO MORE-DATA.
      READ MASTER-FILE AT END MOVE 'NO' TO MORE-DATA.
PRINT-READ.
      DISPLAY 'FIRST NAME:', FIRST-NAME OF
      MASTER-RECORD.
      DISPLAY 'LAST NAME:', LAST-NAME OF
      MASTER-RECORD.
      READ MASTER-FILE AT END MOVE 'YES' TO
      MORE-DATA.
CLEANUP.
      CLOSE MASTER-FILE.
      DISPLAY 'SUCCESSFUL END OF PROGRAM'.
```

9. Why are comment lines important in a COBOL program? How are they written?

10. Write a program that will print out the names and addresses of all students on the MASTER-FILE.

SORTING AND INFORMATION RETRIEVAL

3.0 USES OF SORTING IN DATA PROCESSING

Sorting a data file into order is perhaps the commonest type of activity performed on digital computers. In his classic book, *The Art of Computer Programming*, Donald Knuth estimates that the computers of the world spend 25 percent of their time sorting. When one considers the billions invested in computing equipment, this percentage represents quite a bit of money spent on this simple activity.

Before we discuss some examples of the uses of sorting, we should look at the basic terminology. In most of our work in this book, we will be dealing with sequential data files. Sequential means that the records are stored one after another in sequence. Sequential files are kept in order by a **key field.** To keep the integrity of the data, this key field must uniquely   key field
identify the record in the file in the same way that the call number identifies a book in a library. This key field may not be very convenient for generating reports from the data file. After all, who wants a student directory printed out in order by social security number?

The way around this problem is to select the records from the file and then sort them into the desired order. Suppose, for example, that we are going to send out grade report forms. To do this, we read in the student records one at a time, calculate the grade for each record, and then sort the output in order by zip code for convenient mailing. If we did not do this operation by computer, then some postal clerk would have to do it by hand. This would be a lot more expensive and time-consuming than doing it by machine.

There are many different ways in which data might be sorted for use. Suppose that we are distributing paychecks written by computer in a large firm with many departments. The payroll file is probably kept in order by social security number. But the paychecks are likely to be printed in order by department. In this way, all the paychecks for a given department will be together, and they can be delivered to the department for distribution. In this case, the department name is used as a sort key although it is not the file key. It would also be helpful to have the paychecks in alphabetical order by last name within each department. This would save the department secretary a lot of time in distributing the paychecks. Thus, the department name is the **major key** because it is the key on which we sort first. The employee's last name is the **minor key**. We may have as many minor keys as we wish in a sorting operation.

major key

minor key

It is also convenient to sort data for input. Suppose that we were going to update the grades kept in the MASTER-FILE. The grade cards that we used to record the student grades could be punched from the student records already in the MASTER-FILE. These cards would be given to the instructors teaching each course. These cards would have the course number and the student name and number, and they would be sorted in order by course number when they were punched. The card deck for each course could be delivered to the instructor teaching the course. The instructor would mark the grades on the cards and return them to the registrar to have the grades punched from the hand-marked cards. The punched cards could be used to update the student records.

The cards returned by the faculty members would still be in order by course. (Actually, this is optimistic. After passing through so many hands, they would probably be in quite a jumble.) Before the grades could be added to the students' records, the grade input cards would have to be sorted by student number again. Then the machine could read a grade card and a student record. If the student number of the grade card matched the student number of the record, then the grade would be updated. If the student number of the grade card were greater than the student number on the input file record, the grade card would apply to a student record further along on the file, and a new student record would be read in for updating. This process would continue until all the grade cards and all the student records had been entered.

Normally, the use of the sort facility is not taught until much later in the learning sequence for COBOL. However, sorting is fundamental to good information retrieval programs, and it should be introduced and used as early as possible. The next sections of this chapter discuss how the sort feature is implemented in COBOL.

3.1   SORTING TECHNIQUES FOR SMALL COMPUTERS

Sorting data is handled differently on small computers than on larger machines. On the full-scale systems, there is a built-in COBOL verb that sorts, but this feature is sometimes absent from the smaller systems. This does not mean that sorting is not possible on these systems. A worthwhile data processing system of any size will have the ability to sort a data file.

In the smaller systems, sorting is usually done by an external program. This external program is called by control cards that are entered with your COBOL program. These control cards will tell the external program (which is usually referred to as a "sort utility") to sort your data in the order that you desire and write it out on some file. If your computer has such a system, your instructor will give you the control cards necessary to set up the sort for the exercises in this chapter. The file produced by the external sort program will be used as an input file by your program.

Let us consider an example. Suppose that we wished to print out the contents of the MASTER-FILE in alphabetical order by name. We would use sort control cards to read the MASTER-FILE, sort it in ascending alphabetical order by LAST-NAME (the major key), and FIRST-NAME, and INIT (the minor keys). We would call the external routine to sort the MASTER-FILE on these fields and then write the sorted output to some other file. For our work, we will use the REPORT-FILE for this. The REPORT-FILE can receive the sorted data from the MASTER-FILE. You will not have to worry about opening or closing files or reading the data while you are doing the sort. The computer will take care of all of this for you automatically.

One thing that you will have to know when you sort the file is where the data fields are on the file. External sort routines sort the files by specific character fields in the record. If we want to sort the MASTER-FILE on LAST-NAME, FIRST-NAME, and INIT, we have to know where these fields begin within the record and how long they are. To find this out, refer to Figure 2.3, which gives the layout of the MASTER-FILE. The fields in Figure 2.3 are presented in the order in which they occur on the MASTER-FILE. Add up the lengths of the fields before the one you are interested in and add one. This gives the starting position of your field.

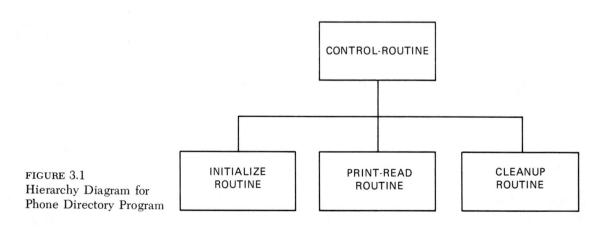

FIGURE 3.1
Hierarchy Diagram for
Phone Directory Program

From Figure 2.3, we can see that

FIELD	BEGIN	LENGTH
LAST-NAME	11	20
FIRST-NAME	31	20
INIT	51	1

FIGURE 3.2
Flowchart for Phone Directory Program

a. CONTROL-ROUTINE

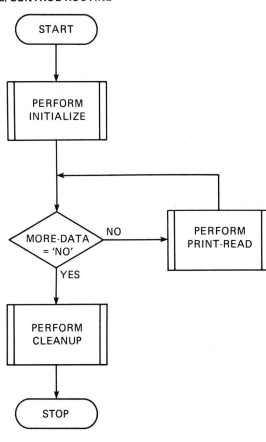

FIGURE 3.2
(Continued)

b. INITIALIZE Routine

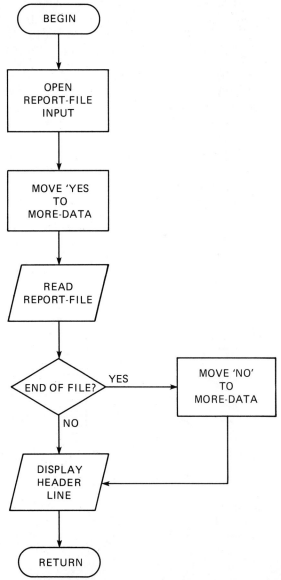

Ask your instructor about the setup of the sort cards for your computer. If your system has a SORT verb built into COBOL, it still might be worthwhile for you to learn how to use the external sort packages. They can be very handy in your work with other computer languages or simply to use by themselves.

Let's return to our earlier problem. Suppose that we wished to produce a phone directory of the students on the MASTER-FILE. As we learned earlier, the records on the MASTER-FILE are stored in order by student number. For our phone directory, we want the records printed out in alphabetical order as in the discussion above. As we discussed earlier, we will use the sort facility to sort the MASTER-FILE in the desired order and write the sorted data out on the REPORT-FILE. We will then write a COBOL program that will read in the sorted data from the REPORT-FILE and print out the FIRST-NAME, INIT, LAST-NAME, and PHONE fields to give us our phone directory.

FIGURE 3.2
(Continued)

FIGURE 3.2
(Continued)

c. PRINT-READ Routine

d. CLEANUP Routine

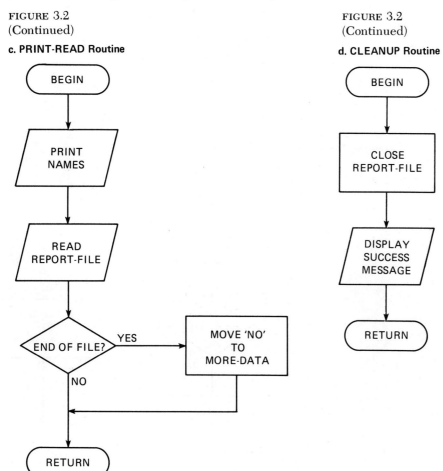

FIGURE 3.3
Program to Produce a Phone
Directory

```
010000 PROCEDURE DIVISION.
010010 PROGRAM-PURPOSE.
010020*    THIS PROGRAM GIVES AN EXAMPLE OF THE USE OF
010030*    THE SORT VERB TO PRODUCE A TELEPHONE LISTING
010040*    FROM THE MASTER-FILE. THE DATA IS SORTED
010050*    INTO THE PROPER ORDER AND WRITTEN ONTO THE
010060*    REPORT FILE. THE REPORT FILE IS THEN OPENED
010070*    FOR INPUT AND THE RECORDS ARE READ IN AND
010080*    PRINTED USING A DISPLAY COMMAND. WHEN THE PROGRAM
010090*    IS OUT OF DATA, IT TERMINATES WITH
010100*    A SUCCESS MESSAGE.
010110 CONTROL-ROUTINE.
010120     PERFORM INITIALIZE.
010130     PERFORM PRINT-READ UNTIL MORE-DATA IS EQUAL TO 'NO'.
010140     PERFORM CLEANUP.
010150     STOP RUN.
010160 INITIALIZE.
010170     OPEN INPUT REPORT-FILE.
010180     MOVE 'YES' TO MORE-DATA.
010190     READ REPORT-FILE AT END MOVE 'NO' TO MORE-DATA.
010200     DISPLAY 'FIRST NAME       LAST NAME       PHONE'.
010210     DISPLAY ' '.
010220 PRINT-READ.
010230     DISPLAY FIRST-NAME OF REPORT-RECORD,
010240         INIT OF REPORT-RECORD, '. ',
010250         LAST-NAME OF REPORT-RECORD,
010260         PHONE OF REPORT-RECORD.
010270     READ REPORT-FILE AT END MOVE 'NO' TO MORE-DATA.
010280 CLEANUP.
010290     CLOSE REPORT-FILE.
010300     DISPLAY 'END OF PROGRAM'.
```

Sample Output

FIRST NAME	LAST NAME	PHONE
CAMILLE	O. ABBE	1352102
MICHAEL	M. ADDISON	8855729
WILSON	S. ADDISON	4231723
DANIEL	C. AIRINGTON	3094205
JOANN	B. AIRINGTON	9387807
KENT	I. AIRINGTON	9077063
LOREN	U. ALDRICH	2332099
ANN	W. ALEXANDER	9880943
JEWELL	Q. ALEXANDER	2555526
LORI	F. ALEXANDER	4469572
LUCY	U. ALEXANDER	4761940
WALTER	M. ALEXANDER	9264374
DEBORAH	C. ALLDAY	1421507

END OF PROGRAM

The hierarchy diagram for this program is given in Figure 3.1. The flowcharts are given in Figure 3.2. Notice that the CONTROL-ROUTINE (Figure 3.1a) is much the same as the one we used for Chapter 2. About the only difference between this program and that of Chapter 2 is in the INITIALIZE routine (Figure 3.1b) where we read from the REPORT-FILE instead of the MASTER-FILE. Otherwise, the programs are much the same.

Figure 3.3 gives a listing of the program. Notice that we have a set of comment lines at the beginning of the program to describe its purpose. It is always a good idea to document the code. Then our COBOL paragraphs correspond to the blocks in the hierarchy diagram. We initialize the variables and the data files, print the data we have read in, read in a new record, and repeat this process until we run out of data. Afterwards, we close files and terminate with a success message. Figure 3.3 also shows some sample output from this run.

3.2 SORTING TECHNIQUES USING THE SORT VERB

For computer systems that include the SORT verb, sorting data is a little easier. You still have to supply most of the control cards you needed for the external sort routine, but the calling of the sort is done within the COBOL program. This means that the sort is part of the program rather than a separate system.

Let us suppose we wanted to sort the MASTER-FILE in order by zip code so that we could produce a list of our students who lived in the same general area. We could use this list, for example, to help form car pools. We will take data from the MASTER-FILE, pass it through the SORT-FILE, and write our output to the REPORT-FILE. The SORT verb in COBOL always makes use of an intermediate sort file. The COBOL statement to do this is:

```
SORT SORT-FILE ON ASCENDING KEY ZIP OF SORT-RECORD,
     USING MASTER-FILE,
     GIVING REPORT-FILE.
```

Remember that SORT-FILE is a programmer-defined name just as MASTER-FILE and REPORT-FILE are. All three files have the same length and contain the same data fields in the same order. This SORT statement tells COBOL to take the data on the MASTER-FILE and sort it in ascending order (lowest numbered zip codes first) and then write this sorted file out on the REPORT-FILE. All opening and closing of files as well as all the I/O activity necessary to accomplish this are taken care of by the sort routine itself. You do not have to do anything more. When you get control of the REPORT-FILE after the SORT statement has been executed, you still have to use the OPEN statement to open it for input. The commas and the periods in the statement above are just for clarity. COBOL does not require them.

The definition of the SORT **statement** is: SORT statement

```
SORT   sort-file-description-name

              ⎧ DESCENDING ⎫
        ON    ⎨ ASCENDING  ⎬     KEY   data-name-1 [data-name-2] ...
              ⎩           ⎭

              ⎧ DESCENDING ⎫
      [ ON    ⎨ ASCENDING  ⎬     KEY   data-name-3 [data-name-4] ... ] ...
              ⎩           ⎭

        USING file-name-1    GIVING file-name-2
```

Because you are using a predefined sort file, all of your SORT statements will start out with SORT SORT-FILE. In Chapter 9 you will learn how to define your own sort files that can have any legal COBOL name.

The definition above implies that it is possible to mix the ASCENDING and DESCENDING phrases and to give as many data names as you want for sorting. This feature can be very handy in allowing us to write fairly complicated sort routines. For example, suppose you were asked to write a program that would print out the names of all the students on the MASTER-FILE by college. All students who went to the same college would have their names printed together. Within each college, you would like the men's names printed first followed by the women's names. For each group of men or women, you would like to have the names in alphabetical order. This sounds like a difficult program, but it is not. All that we have to do is sort the MASTER-FILE into the proper order, write it to the REPORT-FILE, and then read and print the contents of the REPORT-FILE. The SORT statement that will sort the MASTER-FILE in the desired order is:

```
SORT SORT-FILE ON ASCENDING KEY COLLEGE OF
         SORT-RECORD,
      DESCENDING KEY SEX OF SORT-RECORD,
      ASCENDING KEY LAST-NAME OF SORT-RECORD,
         FIRST-NAME OF SORT-RECORD,
         INIT OF SORT-RECORD,
      USING MASTER-FILE,
      GIVING REPORT-FILE.
```

The first key that we give the SORT statement is SEX. The codes for SEX on our file are 'M' for men and 'F' for women. If we use SEX as our

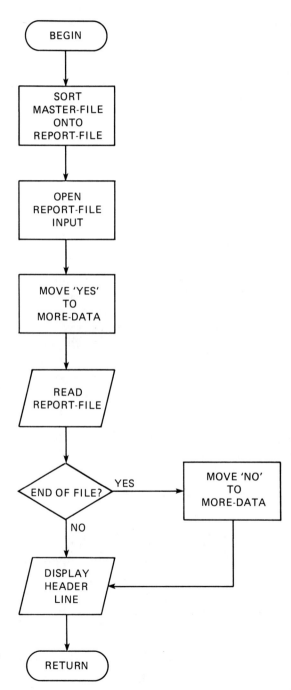

FIGURE 3.4
INITIALIZE Routine Flowchart Using *SORT* Verb

FIGURE 3.5
Program to Produce a Phone
Directory

```
010000 PROCEDURE DIVISION.
010010 PROGRAM-PURPOSE.
010020*    THIS PROGRAM GIVES AN EXAMPLE OF THE USE OF
010030*    THE SORT VERB TO PRODUCE A TELEPHONE LISTING
010040*    FROM THE MASTER-FILE. THE DATA IS SORTED
010050*    INTO THE PROPER ORDER AND WRITTEN ONTO THE
010060*    REPORT FILE. THE REPORT FILE IS THEN OPENED
010070*    FOR INPUT AND THE RECORDS ARE READ IN AND
010080*    PRINTED USING A DISPLAY COMMAND. WHEN THE PROGRAM
010090*    IS OUT OF DATA, IT TERMINATES WITH
010100*    A SUCCESS MESSAGE.
010110 CONTROL-ROUTINE.
010120     PERFORM INITIALIZE.
010130     PERFORM PRINT-READ UNTIL MORE-DATA IS EQUAL TO 'NO'.
010140     PERFORM CLEANUP.
010150     STOP RUN.
010160 INITIALIZE.
010170     SORT SORT-FILE ON ASCENDING KEY LAST-NAME OF SORT-RECORD,
010180         ASCENDING FIRST-NAME OF SORT-RECORD,
010190         ASCENDING INIT OF SORT-RECORD,
010200         USING MASTER-FILE,
010210         GIVING REPORT-FILE.
010220     OPEN INPUT REPORT-FILE.
010230     MOVE 'YES' TO MORE-DATA.
010240     READ REPORT-FILE AT END MOVE 'NO' TO MORE-DATA.
010250     DISPLAY 'FIRST NAME     LAST NAME      PHONE'.
010260     DISPLAY ' ' .
010270 PRINT-READ.
010280     DISPLAY FIRST-NAME OF REPORT-RECORD,
010290         INIT OF REPORT-RECORD, '. ',
010300         LAST-NAME OF REPORT-RECORD,
010310         PHONE OF REPORT-RECORD.
010320     READ REPORT-FILE AT END MOVE 'NO' TO MORE-DATA.
010330 CLEANUP.
010340     CLOSE REPORT-FILE.
010350     DISPLAY 'END OF PROGRAM'.
```

Sample Output

FIRST NAME	LAST NAME	PHONE
CAMILLE	O. ABBE	1352102
MICHAEL	M. ADDISON	8855729
WILSON	S. ADDISON	4231723
DANIEL	C. AIRINGTON	3094205
JOANN	B. AIRINGTON	9387807
KENT	I. AIRINGTON	9077063
LOREN	U. ALDRICH	2332099
ANN	W. ALEXANDER	9880943

major sort key and print it out in descending order (largest to smallest), we will have all the men's names first followed by all the women's names. The minor keys are our name fields, and these will cause alphabetical ordering by name for all the men and for all the women.

Notice in the data names we are giving in the SORT statements that we use the fully qualified name. Again, this is because all three of our data files have the same field names on them, and we must tell COBOL which file we are talking about. When we are sorting, the SORT verb always uses the sort file, so we qualify our data names with SORT-RECORD, the name of the record area associated with the SORT-FILE. The indentation of the parts of the statement above is only for the convenience of the programmer. COBOL does not require it.

As an example of the use of the SORT statement, let us do the same phone directory program that we did in Section 3.1. For this program, the hierarchy diagram is the same as it was in Figure 3.1. For the flowchart, the only thing different is the INITIALIZE routine. Its flowchart is given in Figure 3.4, and all we have done is to add a box for the SORT statement. The program is given in Figure 3.5. Again, it is the same program except that we have added a SORT statement.

We have introduced the SORT statement at a somewhat earlier point in your study of COBOL than is customary. This is because it is a very important statement, and it is difficult to get a real feel for the types of problems you have in data processing without using a sort. The use of the sort routine will differ somewhat from computer to computer, but on all of them, it is a relatively simple thing to use. You will find that your ability to use the computer effectively will increase greatly when you are able to use a sort.

STUDY EXERCISES

1. Suppose that we sorted the MASTER-FILE so that the output file contained all students from the same state. Within each state, all of the students from the same city would be listed together. We would be sorting on the CITY field and the STATE field. Which is the major key and which is the minor key?

2. Write a SORT statement to sort the MASTER-FILE in order by college.

3. Write a program to produce a list of all students by college. Within each college, the students should be listed by major, and within each major, the students should be listed alphabetically. Print out the college, major, and the student's full name.

4. Write a program to print out the names of all students listed in order by their GPA. List the men and the women separately.

5. Write a program to list the students on a college-by-college basis. List the men and the women separately, women first.

6. Write a program listing the names of all students in order by the number of credits they have received. List those with the most credits first. Print the names and the number of credits.

7. Write a program that will produce a list of students in order by their GPA. Print name and GPA.

COMPUTATIONS IN COBOL

```
4 4
 4 4
4 4
 4 4
4 4
 4 4
4 4
 4 4
4 4
 4 4
4 4
 4 4
```

4.0 INTRODUCTION

Although COBOL is not intended primarily for arithmetic, it does have a built-in mathematical capability because typical business data processing applications involve a great deal of computation. In a payroll program, for example, the computer is used to figure taxes, deductions for insurance, social security, and a wide variety of other calculations. Some of the calculations required in COBOL are fairly sophisticated, such as the formulas used to calculate compound interest tables and loan payments.

In this chapter we will discuss the five basic mathematical statements. The first four handle addition, subtraction, multiplication, and division. The fifth statement is the COMPUTE statement, and it handles more complicated formulas. The types of arithmetic operations that COBOL can handle may not seem particularly sophisticated compared to the mathematical capabilities of other languages such as FORTRAN and PL/I, but they are sufficient for the COBOL programming applications arising from business problems.

4.1 ADDITION AND SUBTRACTION

The first two arithmetic statements to be introduced are those for addition and subtraction. For example:

```
ADD AVERAGE OF MASTER-RECORD TO SUM-UP.
ADD ACCOUNT-BALANCE TO ACCOUNTS-TOTAL.
ADD PRICE, TAX, DISCOUNT TO TOTAL-BILL ROUNDED.
ADD TUITION, ROOM, FEES TO TOTAL-BILL ROUNDED
     ON SIZE-ERROR PERFORM ERROR-CHECK.
ADD 1 TO COUNTER-1, COUNTER-2.
SUBTRACT DISCOUNT FROM TOTAL-BILL.
SUBTRACT 1 FROM COUNTER-1, COUNTER-2, COUNTER-3.
```

```
SUBTRACT DISCOUNT1, DISCOUNT2 FROM TOTAL-BILL,
    MONTHLY-BILL.
SUBTRACT INSURANCE, UNION-DUES FROM SALARY ROUNDED.
SUBTRACT TOTAL-1, TOTAL-2 FROM BALANCE
    ON SIZE ERROR PERFORM CHECK-TOTALS.
SUBTRACT AMOUNT-1, AMOUNT-2 FROM MONTHLY-TOTAL
    ROUNDED,QUARTERLY-TOTAL ROUNDED, YEARLY-TOTAL
    ROUNDED, ON SIZE ERROR PERFORM DUMP-TOTALS.
```

Addition and subtraction statements have two formats. All the examples above are of the first format. As you can see, these COBOL statements have the usual English-like style. The formal definition for the ADD statement is:

ADD statement

FORMAT 1

$$\underline{\text{ADD}} \quad \left\{ \begin{matrix} \text{identifier-1} \\ \text{literal-1} \end{matrix} \right\} \quad \left[\begin{matrix} \text{identifier-2} \\ \text{literal-2} \end{matrix} \right] \quad \dots$$

$$\underline{\text{TO}} \text{ identifier-m [} \underline{\text{ROUNDED}} \text{]}$$

$$[\text{ identifier-n [} \underline{\text{ROUNDED}} \text{]] } \dots \text{ [ON } \underline{\text{SIZE}} \underline{\text{ERROR}} \text{ imperative-statement]}$$

For the SUBTRACT **statement,** the corresponding first form is:

SUBTRACT statement

FORMAT 1

$$\underline{\text{SUBTRACT}} \left\{ \begin{matrix} \text{identifier-1} \\ \text{literal-1} \end{matrix} \right\} \left[\begin{matrix} \text{identifier-2} \\ \text{literal-2} \end{matrix} \right] \dots \underline{\text{FROM}} \text{ identifier-m [} \underline{\text{ROUNDED}} \text{]}$$

$$[\text{ identifier-n } [\underline{\text{ROUNDED}} \text{]] } \dots \text{ [ON } \underline{\text{SIZE}} \underline{\text{ERROR}} \text{ imperative-statement]}$$

Both of these formats offer fairly flexible options to the programmer as you can see from our examples at the start of the section. In the addition and subtraction examples, the operand(s) before the TO phrase are added to the operand(s) after the TO phrase as the English structure implies. The result may be rounded if desired. For example, suppose that an addition generated the result:

999.017

to be stored in one of our scratch variables, X1. By the data definitions we set up in Figure 2.3, the variable X1 is a field with five places before the decimal and two after. Thus, this value will be truncated to:

999.01

If in our addition statement, we had used the ROUNDED phrase after the instruction to put the result in X1, the number would be stored as:

```
999.02
```

following the usual mathematical rules for rounding.

Truncating or rounding numbers on the right after the decimal point is not too serious a problem. A business data processing shop should establish which will be done in writing business code, however. It is actually possible for an unscrupulous programmer to steal the round off error that results from calculations and add it to a personal account. Of course, this would only average a half-cent per transaction, but if there are thousands of transactions (as there will be in almost any data processing system) the round-off error can amount to a lot of money. A more serious problem occurs when a number overflows a field on the left. Suppose that we ran this code as part of a COBOL program:

```
MOVE 99999 TO COUNTER-1, COUNTER-2.
ADD COUNTER-1 TO COUNTER-2.
DISPLAY COUNTER-2.
```

If we had defined the variables called COUNTER-1 and COUNTER-2 to be five places to the left of the decimal, we would have problems. The computer would print out this result from this program:

```
99998
```

but the correct answer is:

```
199998
```

This problem occurs because the fields we have defined are five places, whereas the two numbers added together give a six-place result. If this result represented dollars, then we would be $100,000 short. The solution to this problem is to use the SIZE ERROR option. We might have coded the addition statement as:

```
ADD COUNTER-1 TO COUNTER-2 ON SIZE ERROR PERFORM CHECK-UP.
```

The block of code named CHECK-UP could take some sort of corrective action. One possibility might be to print out the values of the variables that caused the problem along with an appropriate error message. For example:

```
CHECK-UP.
      DISPLAY '****SIZE ERROR 1'
      DISPLAY 'COUNTER-1 = ', COUNTER-1.
      DISPLAY 'COUNTER-2 = ', COUNTER-2.
```

We have used the asterisks in our first DISPLAY statement to set off the message and make it more noticeable to somebody reading the output. In this example, when a size error occurred, control would be transferred to the CHECK-UP routine. The clerks who monitored the data could be alerted to this type of message and handle the data problems when they occurred.

It is the responsibility of the system designer to anticipate errors that can occur in such processing and to design computer programs that check for them and even correct them if possible. It is much more costly to correct an error that has occurred in processing than it is to catch it before it is processed.

The second formats of the addition and subtraction statements are similar to the first except that the addition and subtraction is not done in one of the fields that contains a value. Instead, the operation is done and then the results are placed in a new variable that did not contain one of the original values. Some examples of the second formats are:

```
ADD BILL-AMOUNT, SALES-TAX GIVING BILL-TOTAL.
SUBTRACT SALES-TAX FROM BILL-TOTAL GIVING
      ADJUSTED-TOTAL.
ADD A, B, C, D GIVING E ROUNDED.
SUBTRACT A, B, C FROM D ROUNDED ON SIZE ERROR
      PERFORM CHECK-UP.
SUBTRACT A, B, C FROM D GIVING E
      ROUNDED ON SIZE ERROR PERFORM CHECK-UP.
```

The main difference between format 1 and format 2 is that you do not have to worry about initializing the result field which occurs after the GIVING phrase. The addition or subtraction is done and then the result replaces whatever was in the old field. For instance, in the first example above, BILL-AMOUNT and SALES-TAX are added together, and the sum replaces whatever was in BILL-TOTAL. As with our earlier examples of the addition and subtraction statements, it is possible to use ROUNDED and ON SIZE ERROR options. The general formats for these statements are:

FORMAT 2

ADD {identifier-1 / literal-1} {identifier-2 / literal-2} [identifier-3 / literal-3] ... GIVING

identifier-m[ROUNDED] [ON SIZE ERROR imperative-statement]

SUBTRACT {identifier-1 / literal-1} [identifier-2 / literal-2] ...FROM {identifier-m / literal-m}

GIVING identifier-n [ROUNDED] [ON SIZE ERROR imperative-statement]

In writing COBOL programs, make sure that you are using the correct format of the statement for the options you have chosen. The two forms are slightly different, which can cause confusion.

4.2   MULTIPLICATION AND DIVISION

As with the addition and subtraction statements, the multiplication and division statements have two formats. For example:

```
MULTIPLY A BY B.
MULTIPLY A BY B GIVING C.
MULTIPLY A BY B GIVING C ROUNDED.
MULTIPLY DISCOUNT-RATE BY BILL GIVING TOTAL-BILL.
MULTIPLY A BY B ROUNDED ON SIZE ERROR PERFORM
      CHECK-WORK.
DIVIDE A INTO B.
DIVIDE A INTO B GIVING C.
DIVIDE A BY B.
DIVIDE A BY B GIVING C ROUNDED.
DIVIDE A BY B GIVING C ROUNDED ON SIZE ERROR
      PERFORM CHECK-UP.
DIVIDE A BY B GIVING C ROUNDED REMAINDER D.
DIVIDE A BY B GIVING C ROUNDED REMAINDER D
      ON SIZE ERROR PERFORM CHECKUP.
```

Because of the Englishlike format of COBOL, it is fairly easy to see what these statements are doing. In the first example above, A is multiplied by B, and the result is stored in the variable A. In the second example above, A is again multiplied by B, but the result is stored in C. In the first case, the value in B is left unchanged while in the second, the values in both A and B are left unchanged. Thus,

```
MULTIPLY A BY B.
```

is an abbreviation for

```
MULTIPLY A BY B GIVING A.
```

In some of the other versions of the statements, you can see that we still have the options of using ROUNDED and SIZE ERROR to control the results of our computations. These statements are very similar to our earlier work with addition and subtraction. The general formats for the MULTIPLY **statement** are:

MULTIPLY statement

FORMAT 1

$$\underline{\text{MULTIPLY}} \quad \begin{Bmatrix} \text{identifier-1} \\ \text{literal-1} \end{Bmatrix} \quad \underline{\text{BY}} \quad \text{identifier-2} \ [\ \underline{\text{ROUNDED}} \ ]$$

$$[\ \text{ON} \ \underline{\text{SIZE}} \ \underline{\text{ERROR}} \ \text{imperative-statement} \ ]$$

FORMAT 2

$$\underline{\text{MULTIPLY}} \quad \begin{Bmatrix} \text{identifier-1} \\ \text{literal-1} \end{Bmatrix} \quad \underline{\text{BY}} \quad \begin{Bmatrix} \text{identifier-2} \\ \text{literal-2} \end{Bmatrix} \underline{\text{GIVING}} \ \text{identifier-3}$$

$$[\ \underline{\text{ROUNDED}} \ ] \ [\ \text{ON} \ \underline{\text{SIZE}} \ \underline{\text{ERROR}} \ \text{imperative-statement} \ ]$$

The corresponding definitions for the DIVIDE **statement** are:

DIVIDE statement

FORMAT 1

$$\underline{\text{DIVIDE}} \quad \begin{Bmatrix} \text{identifier-1} \\ \text{literal-1} \end{Bmatrix} \quad \underline{\text{INTO}} \quad \text{identifier-2} \ [\ \underline{\text{ROUNDED}} \ ]$$

$$[\ \text{ON} \ \underline{\text{SIZE}} \ \underline{\text{ERROR}} \ \text{imperative-statement} \ ]$$

FORMAT 2

$$\underline{\text{DIVIDE}} \quad \begin{Bmatrix} \text{identifier-1} \\ \text{literal-1} \end{Bmatrix} \begin{Bmatrix} \underline{\text{INTO}} \\ \underline{\text{BY}} \end{Bmatrix} \begin{Bmatrix} \text{identifier-2} \\ \text{literal-2} \end{Bmatrix} \underline{\text{GIVING}} \ \text{identifier-3}$$

$$[\ \underline{\text{ROUNDED}} \ ] \ [\ \underline{\text{REMAINDER}} \ \text{identifier-4} \ ]$$

$$[\ \text{ON} \ \underline{\text{SIZE}} \ \underline{\text{ERROR}} \ \text{imperative-statement} \ ]$$

In looking over the statements, probably the only thing that may seem strange to you is the REMAINDER option in the DIVIDE statement. In the last example above, we divide A by B, store the result in C and the remainder of the division operation in D. It may seem odd to want to save the remainder of a division operation, but there are a number of occasions in business data processing where this might prove useful.

Suppose that a business has assigned a four-digit part number to each item in its inventory file. To update the inventory records, the clerk must give the part number of the item being removed or added. But suppose that the clerk punched the wrong number into the card when updating the file. Then the wrong part will be shown as deleted from the inventory, and there will be two errors in the inventory file (a part removed from inventory will not be recorded, and a part not removed from inventory will be recorded as gone).

To handle this problem, we might add a fifth digit to the part number. We could establish the convention that the five digits in the part number should sum to a number divisible by 10. Then we could have the computer check each part number entered to see if the sum of the digits were divisible by 10. If it were not, the computer could print an error message and the clerk could enter the correct data. This procedure would not catch all of the errors, but it would cut down on most of the errors resulting from punching incorrect digits. To see how it works, suppose the original four-digit part number were:

4597

The sum of the digits in this number is:

$$4 + 5 + 9 + 7 = 25$$

This means that the fifth digit to be added to the part number should be a 5 to make the new part number:

45975

The sum of the digits is now:

$$4 + 5 + 9 + 7 + 5 = 30$$

Now, suppose that the clerk make an error in entering the new part number and gave it as **45875**. The sum of the digits in this part number is:

$$4 + 5 + 8 + 7 + 5 = 29$$

When we divide 29 by 10, we get a remainder of 9 instead of 0, which indicates that there is a data entry error in the part number. Only if there is a remainder of 0 can we be reasonably sure that the part number is correct. It is possible to have double errors that will give a correct check sum, but these will be rarer than the single errors.

Transposition is another common type of data entry error. When two digits are transposed, the check sum method above will not catch them. But this is no problem. All we have to do is extend the scheme above a little. Let us go back to our original part number of:

45975

We will add every other digit of the original number like this:

4<u>5</u>9<u>7</u>5

4 + 9 + 5 = 18

and add a new digit to obtain a number divisible by 10. So, in this case the new digit will be a 2, which added to 18 gives us 20. We place the new digit at the end of our original number, and our new part number will be:

459752

This way, we can use the computer to automatically check for errors in our data entry operation. This is much easier than having a clerk check the records by hand, and it will catch a high proportion of the data entry errors.

4.3 THE COMPUTE STATEMENT

In the examples to this point, we have given simple English-like sentences to perform arithmetic operations. This approach is all right for simple calculations, but it is inadequate for more complicated operations. Complicated operations might have to be expressed as long sequences of ADD, SUBTRACT, MULTIPLY, and DIVIDE verbs. This would tend to obscure rather than clarify what was going on. You may have also noticed that the statements introduced so far provide no more mathematical capability than a simple four-function calculator. For many types of processing, more capability than that is needed, and COBOL provides it through the COMPUTE verb. Some examples are:

```
COMPUTE A = B + C + D
COMPUTE DISCOUNT ROUNDED = RATE * TOTAL-BILL
COMPUTE TOTAL = 24 * 1.06 ** 354
```

In the COMPUTE statement, we evaluate formula definition on the right-hand side of an equals sign. The computed value is placed in the variable on the left-hand side of the equals sign. Do not confuse the COMPUTE statement with an algebraic equation. It is possible to write a COMPUTE statement that looks like this:

```
COMPUTE A = A + 1
```

This does not make sense as an equation, but it does make sense as a COMPUTE statement. What it says is to take the old value of A, add 1 to it, and place the result back in A.

The formal definition of the COMPUTE statement is: COMPUTE statement

$$\text{COMPUTE identifier-1 [\underline{ROUNDED}] = } \left\{ \begin{array}{l} \text{identifier-2} \\ \text{literal-1} \\ \text{arithmetic-expression} \end{array} \right\}$$

[ON <u>SIZE</u> <u>ERROR</u> imperative-statement]

As an example of how to use the compute statement, let us consider a situation that requires it. Suppose that you are going to take out an automobile loan. You wish to borrow some amount of money from the bank and pay it back over a specified period in equal monthly installments. Such an arrangement is called a "level payment," and to figure out the amount of the monthly installments, we have to use a formula called the level-payment formula. If the amount of money borrowed is denoted by A, the interest rate per period is denoted by r, and the number of periods is denoted by n, then the level payment is given by:

$$\frac{Ar}{[1 - (1 + r)^{-n}]}$$

It would be very difficult to evaluate this formula using the ADD, SUBTRACT, MULTIPLY, and DIVIDE verbs because it contains an exponent, or power. Before we can evaluate this formula, we need some arithmetic operators for writing formulas. The basic operators we will use are:

```
**    Exponentiation
*     Multiplication
/     Division
+     Addition
-     Subtraction
```

We can also use parentheses as needed in writing formulas. Some spacing rules should also be considered:

1. Each operator and the equals sign in a COMPUTE statement must be preceded by a space and followed by a space (this rule is followed to avoid confusion between the minus sign and the hyphen). The exception is a unary minus sign.

2. There should be no space immediately after a left parenthesis.

3. There should be no space immediately before a right parenthesis.

With these rules, we can write the COMPUTE statement for the level-payment formula as:

```
COMPUTE PAYMENT ROUNDED = A * R / (1 - (1 + R) ** (-N))
```

The formula on the right will be evaluated, the result will be rounded, and the result will be stored in the variable PAYMENT. This formula assumes, of course, that the variables called PAYMENT, A, R, and N have been defined previously by the programmer. (This is not the case in our student record system.)

Suppose now that we had this piece of a COBOL program that used the scratch variables we have defined to go with our system:

```
COMPUTE X1 = 1.
COMPUTE X2 = 2.
COMPUTE X3 = 4.
COMPUTE X4 = 5.
COMPUTE X5 = X1 + X2 * X3 / X2 + X4 ** 2 + X1.
MOVE X5 TO XP5.
DISPLAY XP5.
```

To test your understanding of COBOL, you should try to determine what would be printed out by this code. If you assume that the arithmetic operations in the formula are done in order, from left to right, then the answer would be 122.

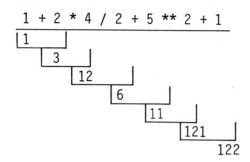

This answer is not correct, however, because arithmetic operations are not simply carried out from left to right. Rather, a priority of evaluation must be followed. All exponentiations are performed first, followed by multiplications and divisions, finally followed by additions and subtractions. This order of evaluation is summarized as follows:

Priority	Operation
1	Exponentiation
2	Multiplication and division
3	Addition and subtraction

When you see a COMPUTE statement like the one for X5 in the COBOL code above, you can use these priority rules to evaluate it. Just go through the statement and do all of the exponentiations first. Then go back through, from left to right and do all the multiplications and divisions. Finally, go back through again and do the additions and subtractions. From these rules, you should have no trouble figuring out that the correct answer above is 31. To help yourself see this, use parentheses to force the order of evaluation to that given by the rules. Rewrite the line as:

```
COMPUTE X5 = X1 + ((X2 * X3) / X2) + (X4 ** 2) + X1.
```

The parentheses show the correct order as imposed by the hierarchy rules. If we wish to force a different order, we may use the parentheses to do that, too. This was done in our level-payment formula.

To test your understanding of COMPUTE statements, you should try using them to evaluate some simple formulas (such as the quadratic equation formulas you had back in high school algebra). Because COMPUTE statements have such a free format, there is much more of a chance for error in using them than there is in the other arithmetic statements, so you should learn the rules well and use them carefully.

4.4 PROGRAMMING EXAMPLE

As an example of how we can use the arithmetic statements presented in this chapter, let us write a computer program to analyze the GPAs of the students on the MASTER-FILE. We would like to write a program to compute the average GPA and the standard deviation of the GPAs. The average is usually called the mean, and it is found by summing all the GPAs and dividing by the number of students. The standard deviation is a little more complicated. We find it by squaring the GPAs of the students and then summing all the squared GPAs and using the following formula:

$$\sqrt{\frac{\text{Sum of GPA}^2}{\text{number of students}} - \text{Mean}^2}$$

The standard deviation gives us a measure of the "spread" of the GPAs on either side of the average or mean value.

Figure 4.1 gives us the hierarchy diagram of the program to perform this calculation. There will be four processes in addition to the control routine: one to initialize the system, one to read the GPAs and sum them and their squares, one to compute the desired results, and one to do the cleanup.

Figure 4.2 gives the flowchart of the processes that make up the hierarchy chart. Some comments are in order on how we will be doing the computation. We will be using our scratch variables to store the intermediate values of the variables. The variable X1 will be used to

FIGURE 4.1
Hierarchy Diagram for GPA
Program

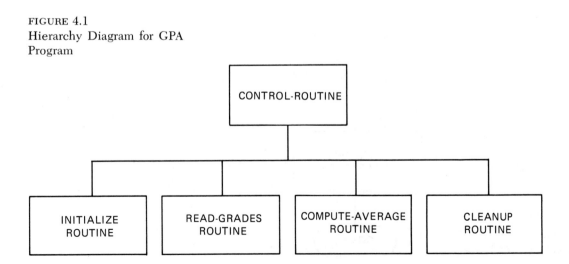

store the running sum of the student GPAs; the variable X2 will be used to store the running sum of the squares of the GPAs; and the variable X3 will be used to store the count of the number of students. To print out these variables, we will use the display variables XP1, XP2, and XP3.

We begin our initialization (Figure 4-2b) by moving zero values to X1, X2, and X3. This is necessary and important. If we did not do this, we could not be sure of the values stored in these variables, and the program might use whatever was stored in memory at that location for the computation of the average and standard deviation. After this, we open the

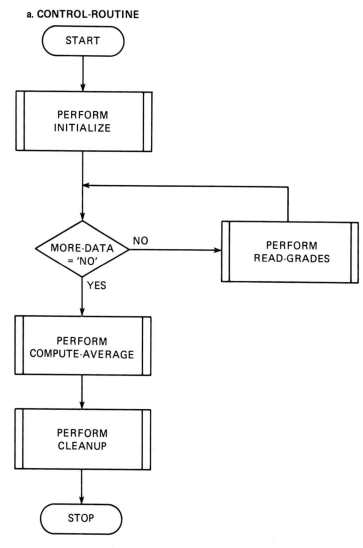

FIGURE 4.2
Flowchart of GPA Program

MASTER-FILE to input and read in the first record. It is not necessary to sort the data on the MASTER-FILE; the order of the date does not make any difference for the computation of an average.

In the READ-GRADES routine (Figure 4.2c), we add the GPA of the

FIGURE 4.2
(Continued)

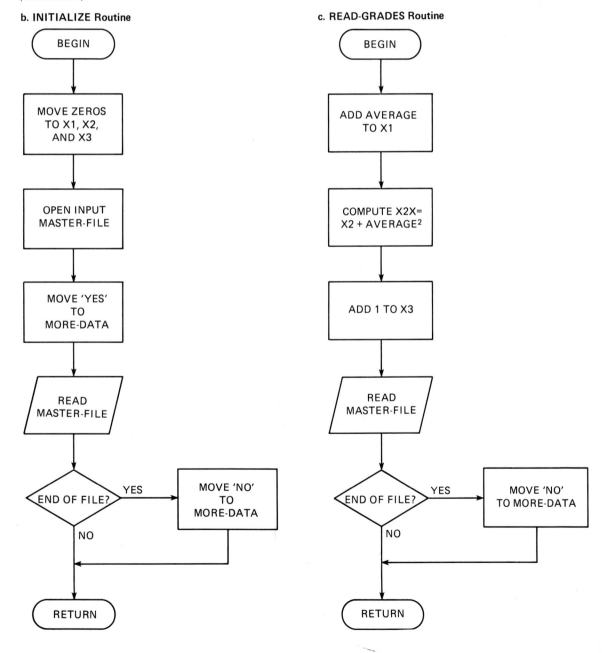

b. INITIALIZE Routine

c. READ-GRADES Routine

current student to X1, the square of the GPA of the current student to X2, and add one to the counter. Then we read in a new student record from the MASTER-FILE, which cleans out the old record. After we run out of data on the MASTER-FILE, control is transferred to COMPUTE-AVERAGE, which does the actual computations and prints the results (Figure 4-2d). Then we transfer to CLEANUP, print a success message, and terminate

FIGURE 4.2
(Continued)

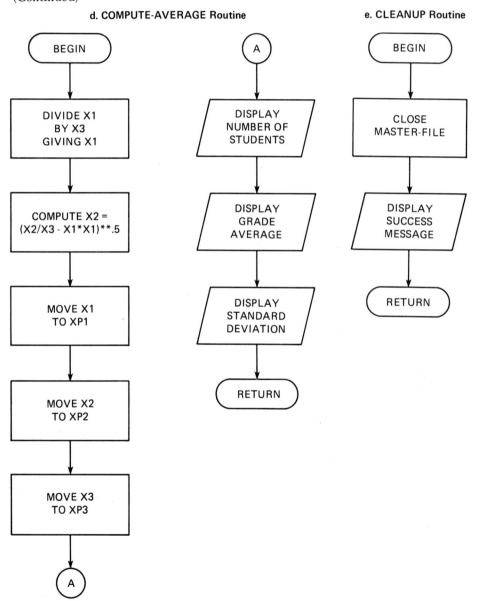

d. COMPUTE-AVERAGE Routine

e. CLEANUP Routine

FIGURE 4.3
Grade Average Program
Listing

```
010000 PROCEDURE DIVISION.
010010 PROGRAM-PURPOSE.
010020*      THIS PROGRAM COMPUTES THE AVERAGE AND
010030*      STANDARD DEVIATION OF THE GPA'S OF THE
010040*      STUDENTS ON THE MASTER-FILE. THE VARIABLES
010050*      USED ARE:
010060*          X1  CONTAINS THE AVERAGE.  DURING THE
010070*              INPUT OF THE DATA, IT CONTAINS
010080*              THE RUNNING SUM OF THE GPA'S.
010090*          X2  CONTAINS THE STANDARD DEVIATION.  DURING
010100*              THE INPUT OF THE DATA, IT CONTAINS
010110*              THE RUNNING SUM OF SQUARES OF THE GPA'S.
010120*          X3  CONTAINS THE COUNT OF THE NUMBER OF STUDENTS.
010130*      WHEN THE RESULTS ARE PRINTED, XP1, XP2, AND XP3 ARE
010140*      USED FOR THE CORRESPONDING X VARIABLES.
010150 CONTROL-ROUTINE.
010160      PERFORM INITIALIZE.
010170      PERFORM READ-GRADES UNTIL MORE-DATA IS EQUAL TO 'NO'.
010180      PERFORM COMPUTE-AVERAGE.
010190      PERFORM CLEANUP.
010200      STOP RUN.
010210 INITIALIZE.
010220    MOVE ZEROS TO X1, X2, X3.
010230    OPEN INPUT MASTER-FILE.
010240    MOVE 'YES' TO MORE-DATA.
010250    READ MASTER-FILE AT END MOVE 'NO' TO MORE-DATA.
010260 READ-GRADES.
010270    ADD AVERAGE OF MASTER-RECORD TO X1.
010280    COMPUTE X2 = X2 + AVERAGE OF MASTER-RECORD *
010290       AVERAGE OF MASTER-RECORD.
010300    ADD 1 TO X3.
010310    READ MASTER-FILE AT END MOVE 'NO' TO MORE-DATA.
010320 COMPUTE-AVERAGE.
010330    DIVIDE X1 BY X3 GIVING X1.
010340    COMPUTE X2 = (X2 / X3 - X1 * X1) ** .5.
010350    MOVE X1 TO XP1.
010360    MOVE X2 TO XP2.
010370    MOVE X3 TO XP3.
010380    DISPLAY 'NUMBER OF STUDENTS:  ', XP3.
010390    DISPLAY 'GRADE AVERAGE:       ', XP1.
010400    DISPLAY 'STANDARD DEVIATION:  ', XP2.
010410 CLEANUP.
010420    CLOSE MASTER-FILE.
010430    DISPLAY 'END OF PROGRAM'.
```

```
                    Sample Output

          NUMBER OF STUDENTS:    201.00
          GRADE AVERAGE:           2.71
          STANDARD DEVIATION:      0.51
          END OF PROGRAM
```

(Figure 4-2e). Figure 4.3 shows the COBOL program to do this and the results it generates.

STUDY EXERCISES

1. Which of the addition and subtraction statements below are illegal and why? Rewrite them correctly.

```
ADD 1, 2, 3 TO 4.
ADD X, Y, Z GIVING A.
ADD X ROUNDED TO Y.
SUBTRACT 1, 2, 3 FROM FOUR.
ADD PRICE, TAX GIVING TOTAL-BILL
      ON SIZE ERROR PERFORM CHECK-UP.
SUBTRACT DISCOUNT FROM TOTAL-BILL.
```

2. Assume that the definition of the scratch variables is as given in Chapter 2. What will this COBOL code print out?

```
MOVE 98765 TO X1, X2.
ADD X1 TO X2.
MOVE X2 TO XP2.
DISPLAY XP2.
```

3. Which of the multiplication and division statements below are illegal and why? Rewrite them correctly.

```
MULTIPLY RATE BY PRICE GIVING COMMISSION.
DIVIDE SHARE BY TOTAL-BILL ROUNDED GIVING PERCENT.
MULTIPLY A INTO B GIVING C ROUNDED.
DIVIDE X BY Y ROUNDED.
MULTIPLY A BY B GIVING C ON SIZE ERROR PERFORM
      CHECK-UP ROUNDED.
MULTIPLY A BY B GIVING C REMAINDER D.
```

4. Which of the COMPUTE statements below are illegal and why? Rewrite them correctly.

```
COMPUTE A = B * C + D ** E / F.
COMPUTE A ROUNDED = ((B + C) * D * E) (F + C).
COMPUTE X = B ROUNDED + C.
COMPUTE X = (A + (B + C * (D * E + F * (C + 1)))).
```

5. What is printed by the COBOL code below?

```
MOVE 1 TO X1.
MOVE 2 TO X2.
MOVE 3 TO X3.
MOVE 4 TO X4.
MOVE 5 TO X5.
COMPUTE X5 = X1 *X2 ** X3 - X4 / X5.
MOVE X5 TO XP5.
DISPLAY XP5.
```

6. Write a COBOL program that will add the numbers from one to ten and print out the result.

7. Write a COBOL program that will count the number of students on the MASTER-FILE.

8. Write a COBOL program that will total up all the student bills on the MASTER-FILE.

9. Write a COBOL program that will find the average total bill for the students on the MASTER-FILE.

5 5
  5 5
5 5
  5 5
5 5
  5 5
5 5
  5 5
5 5
  5 5
5 5
  5 5
CONDITIONAL STATEMENTS

5.0 INTRODUCTION

In the previous chapters we saw how to retrieve information from a file and how to sort that information in any order we wished, using the sort facility. Suppose we do not want to retrieve the whole file; we want to look at only a portion of it. We have some criterion for selecting records from the file, and we want to retrieve only records that meet that criterion. To do this, we must have a way of saying "If this record meets our selection criterion, retrieve the fields we want." We need such statements frequently when dealing with a data base. Some examples might be:

1. Retrieve the names of all women students from the MASTER-FILE.

2. Print the names of all engineering students whose GPA is greater than 3.5 and who have senior standing in the college.

3. Produce a student directory for those students registered in the College of Agriculture.

4. Print out the GPA for John Jones this semester.

5. Print out the amount of money owed by Mary Smith on her room and board bill.

All of these examples are alike in that they deal with only a portion of the whole MASTER-FILE. The types of examples that we discussed in Chapters 2 and 3 where we print the entire contents of the MASTER-FILE are really rather unusual. Normally, we write programs that select only a portion of the file. The first three examples above are the more common type. They deal with large portions of the file, and the output they generate would likely be sizable. The last two requests would likely be found as "one-shot" programs. These requests ask for information on a single record in the file. It is much more likely that these requests would be "batched" or included with other requests for information. Suppose, for example, that the MASTER-FILE were on magnetic tape, and the records were stored sequentially. Then, the computer might have to read all the way through the tape before it got to John Smith's record so that it could print his GPA. It would be much more efficient to do this request with a set of other requests of the same type in a batch. It is generally better to try to make only one pass through the MASTER-FILE and to handle as many individual requests for information as possible on that pass.

The statement in COBOL used for these tasks is the IF statement. All computer languages have some version of the IF statement. It is the ability to ask what-if questions that distinguishes a computer from a calculator. A calculator simply has the ability to do computations in a straight line sequence, one after another. A computer can ask IF questions and modify its flow of control based on the answers it receives. The IF statement in COBOL is one of a general class of statements called **conditional statements.** You have already been introduced to some conditional statements, namely the READ statement and the ON SIZE ERROR option in the arithmetic statements. Both of these statements are able to change the flow of control in the program based on some event that occurs. With an IF statement, we do not have to wait for a specific event. We can set up our own conditions to change the flow of control. As an example, consider the IF statements we might use to handle the problems at the beginning of this section.

conditional statements

```
IF SEX OF MASTER-RECORD = 'F'
     DISPLAY FIRST-NAME OF MASTER-RECORD,
          LAST-NAME OF MASTER-RECORD.

IF COLLEGE OF MASTER-RECORD = 'ENGINEERING' AND
     AVERAGE OF MASTER-RECORD IS GREATER THAN 3.5
     AND CREDITS OF MASTER-RECORD IS GREATER THAN 90
     DISPLAY FIRST-NAME OF MASTER-RECORD,
          LAST-NAME OF MASTER-RECORD.

IF COLLEGE OF REPORT-RECORD = 'AGRICULTURE'
     DISPLAY FIRST-NAME OF REPORT-RECORD,
          LAST-NAME OF REPORT-RECORD.

IF FIRST-NAME OF MASTER-RECORD = 'JOHN' AND
     LAST-NAME OF MASTER-RECORD = 'JONES'
     MOVE AVERAGE OF MASTER-RECORD TO XP1
     DISPLAY 'AVERAGE = ', XP1.

IF FIRST-NAME OF MASTER-RECORD = 'MARY' AND
     LAST-NAME OF MASTER-RECORD = 'SMITH'
     MOVE TOTAL-BAL TO XP1
     DISPLAY 'TOTAL BALANCE = ', XP1.
```

These examples should be fairly easy to understand. COBOL's English-like structure makes them quite readable. Notice that we are using the fully qualified names of the fields in the records for the student files. Although the computer does not require it, the indentation shown in these examples improves readability. From these brief examples, we could not expect you to begin writing IF statements. The rest of this chapter explains the syntax and rules for IF statements in detail and presents a pair of programming examples using IF statements.

5.1 CONDITIONAL EXPRESSIONS

The basic structure of IF statements is very simple, but the different forms of their parts can get quite complicated. The basic definition of the IF **statement** is:

IF statement

$$\underline{\text{IF}} \text{ condition } \left\{ \begin{matrix} \text{statement-1} \\ \underline{\text{NEXT}}\ \underline{\text{SENTENCE}} \end{matrix} \right\} \left[\underline{\text{ELSE}} \left\{ \begin{matrix} \text{statement-2} \\ \underline{\text{NEXT}}\ \underline{\text{SENTENCE}} \end{matrix} \right\} \right]$$

As an example of how this might be used in practice, suppose we wished to consider for membership in an honor society all students whose GPAs were better than 3.2. We might use the IF statement:

```
IF AVERAGE OF MASTER-RECORD IS GREATER THAN 3.2
      PERFORM HONORS.
```

If the condition AVERAGE OF MASTER-RECORD IS GREATER THAN 3.2 is true, then control is transferred to the paragraph called HONORS.

We will discuss the use of the IF statement fully in Section 5.2. In this section we want to focus on only one portion of it—namely the *condition*. The condition has a truth value; it can be either *true* or *false*. If it is true, then COBOL will execute statement-1. If it is false, COBOL will either execute statement-2 (if there is one), or it will go on to the next sentence.

There are several types of conditions. The first conditional test is called the **relation test**. This type of test simply tests the relationship between one value and another. Some examples are:

relation test

```
AVERAGE OF MASTER-RECORD IS GREATER THAN 3.0
X = 2
X + Y IS GREATER THAN A + B + C
B ** 2 - 4 * A * C IS GREATER THAN 0
X NOT = 0
Y NOT GREATER THAN X
```

The general format of the relation test is:

```
⎧ identifier-1              ⎫           ⎧ >           ⎫   ⎧ identifier-2              ⎫
⎨ literal-1                 ⎬ IS [ NOT ] ⎨ <           ⎬   ⎨ literal-2                 ⎬
⎪ arithmetic-expression-1  ⎪           ⎪ =           ⎪   ⎪ arithmetic-expression-2  ⎪
⎩ figurative-constant-1    ⎭           ⎪ GREATER THAN⎪   ⎩ figurative-constant-2    ⎭
                                        ⎪ LESS THAN   ⎪
                                        ⎩ EQUAL TO    ⎭
```

The relations used in the example are reasonably easy to understand. You should notice that it is also possible to use arithmetic expressions in a relation. For instance, in the fourth relation, we are using the portion of the quadratic formula known as the discriminant to see if it is possible to solve the quadratic equation. This ability to use arithmetic expressions in a relation can sometimes save us work, but such expressions should be used carefully because by using them, it is easy to write relations that may be difficult to understand.

Tests like the next to last one should also be used carefully in relations. In this test, X is compared to 0 to see if it is equal. If the value in X came from computation, then there might be a slight round-off error that leaves a value in X that is not exactly zero. This can sometimes generate strange results and confusion. Depending on the application, it might be safer to use an X that has been rounded before the test.

Notice in all of the examples how both the English forms of the relation (GREATER THAN, LESS THAN, EQUAL TO) and the mathematical forms ($>$, $<$, $=$) can be used interchangeably. This is another example of COBOL's attempt to provide readability.

These relations have shown how comparisons can be used for numeric values. They can also be used for nonnumeric identifiers and literals. For example:

```
LAST-NAME IS EQUAL TO 'JONES'
LAST-NAME IS GREATER THAN 'J'
FIRST-NAME IS EQUAL TO SPACES
```

When we are comparing two alphabetic fields, the comparison takes place from left to right. If one of the fields is shorter than the other, then the shorter field is automatically padded with spaces on the right until it is the same length as the longer field.

The second comparison above may look a little strange. We are not used to thinking of character strings as being greater than other character strings. Yet this type of comparison is done all the time in sorting, insertion, and merge operations. A collating sequence is established for the characters used by the computer. On all computers, the letter A is less than B, B is less than C, and so on. The order of the collating sequence for the other characters may vary from machine to machine, so check the manual for your particular machine. On IBM machines this collating sequence taken in ascending order is

```
Space(blank)
 .      (period)
 <      (less than symbol)
 (      (left parenthesis)
 +      (plus sign)
 $      (dollar sign)
 *      (asterisk)
 )      (right parenthesis)
 ;      (semicolon)
 -      (hyphen or minus sign)
 /      (slash or division sign)
 ,      (comma)
 >      (greater than symbol)
 '      (single quote or apostrophe)
 =      (equals sign)
 "      (double quotes)
 a-z    (lower-case letters)
 A-Z    (upper-case letters)
 0-9    (numbers)
```

This collating sequence applies only to IBM machines, although those of other machines will be similar.

In our second example, suppose that the LAST-NAME were Jones. The comparison for GREATER THAN would be done character by character against the character J, padding it on the right with blanks until it was the same length as the other string. Let the symbol ¢ represent a blank. Then, the two fields to be compared would contain:

```
Jøøøø
```

```
JONES
```

On the first character, the letter J is equal to the letter J, so the relation is not proved true. But, on the second character, O is greater than a blank, so the relation:

```
LAST-NAME IS GREATER THAN 'J'
```

is true when the LAST-NAME is Jones.

The next type of test in a conditional expression is the **class test,** class test which tests to see if a variable belongs to a specific class. Some examples are:

```
ACCOUNT-NUMBER IS NOT NUMERIC
LAST-NAME IS ALPHABETIC
AGE IS NUMERIC
```

The definition of the class test is:

$$\text{identifier-1} \quad \text{IS [} \underline{\text{NOT}} \text{]} \quad \left\{ \begin{array}{l} \underline{\text{NUMERIC}} \\ \underline{\text{ALPHABETIC}} \end{array} \right\}$$

The class test is a simple test of the data stored in identifier-1 to see what class it belongs to. If the data contains only the characters 0 through 9, then the data is NUMERIC. If it contains only the characters A through Z or a space, then it is alphabetic. This may seem like a strange type of test, but it can be very useful. Suppose a certain field in a data card (for example, the social security number) is supposed to be numeric. This test could be used in a condition like

```
SOCIAL-SECURITY-NUMBER IS NOT NUMERIC
```

to test for problems in reporting the number. A social security number written with hyphens as 585-01-7942 instead of as one long number might cause problems for the program if it tried to process the number, and a class test could be used to edit out bad data before it was processed.

The final type of condition that will be discussed in this chapter is the **sign test,** which is used on numeric items only. As its name implies, sign test the sign test is used for testing the sign of a variable. Some examples are:

```
AVERAGE OF MASTER-RECORD IS NOT ZERO
ACCOUNT-BALANCE IS POSITIVE
ACTIVITY-COUNT IS NOT NEGATIVE
B ** 2 - 4 * A * C IS NOT NEGATIVE
```

The syntax of the sign test is:

$$\left\{ \begin{array}{l} \text{identifier-1} \\ \text{arithmetic-expression} \end{array} \right\} \quad \text{IS [} \underline{\text{NOT}} \text{]} \quad \left\{ \begin{array}{l} \underline{\text{POSITIVE}} \\ \underline{\text{ZERO}} \\ \underline{\text{NEGATIVE}} \end{array} \right\}$$

The sign test is simply used as a way of checking the sign of an arithmetic or numeric item. It could be done using a relation test, but the code would not be quite as Englishlike.

Sometimes it might be desirable to check more than one condition when using an IF statement. Suppose we wanted to display a student's record only if he were a male in the College of Arts and Sciences. This gives us two conditions to be tested simultaneously. We could do it using two IF statements, but an easier way to do it would be to use a **logical operator.** A logical operator is a sort of connector used to join two or more relations together into a compound condition that also has truth value. The three logical operators are:

logical operator

```
NOT
AND
OR
```

These look like standard English words, and sometimes we are tempted to use them the same way. For instance, beginners sometimes write statements like

```
MOVE 1 TO A AND ADD 3 TO B
```

This is not correct. The AND (and the other logical operators) cannot be used to join statements together. They can only be used to join relations together in IF statements and UNTIL phrases in PERFORM statements. Suppose that P and Q are two conditions that can be either true or false. Then the result of joining P and Q using our logical operators is shown by the table.

Truth Table for Logical
Operators

P	Q	NOT P	P AND Q	P OR Q	NOT (P AND Q)	NOT (P OR Q)
T	T	F	T	T	F	F
T	F	F	F	T	T	F
F	T	T	F	T	T	F
F	F	T	F	F	T	T

You may read the truth value for each expression's combination of variables under the expression. For example, when P is true, Q is false, the P OR Q is true. Notice that NOT reverses the truth value of anything it is applied to. It can be applied to a single condition as it is in the third column, or it can be applied to a compound condition made up of both simple conditions and logical operators. The result is the same in either case. For an expression using AND to be true, both parts of it must be true. In the case of OR, only one of the two conditions need be true to make the whole expression true. This is not the way we use *or* in colloquial English. We usually use what is called the "exclusive or" to say that either one or the other is true, but not both. Note the difference. Here are some examples of compound conditions:

```
AVERAGE IS GREATER THAN 3.2 AND SEX = 'F'
AGE IS GREATER THAN 21 OR AGE IS LESS THAN 25
AGE IS GREATER THAN 21 AND LESS THAN 25
NOT (AGE IS LESS THAN 21 AND SEX = 'F')
```

Study these examples carefully. When you start stringing conditions together to form compound conditions, the possibilities for errors increase greatly. Look at the second compound statement above, for example. One or the other of the conditions will always be true. This means that since the two conditions are joined by OR, the whole statement will always be true. There is nothing wrong with this from the point of view of COBOL syntax, but it is probably not what you intended. The third line above illustrates one of the possible variations on the syntax of these logical operators. The first operand has been deleted in the condition after the AND. COBOL automatically assumes that you mean the same one that was used in the previous condition. Since this corresponds to the way we speak, it adds clarity to the language.

A final point should be made about mixing logical operators in one compound condition. Suppose you were faced with this compound conditional statement:

```
A = 3 AND B = 2 OR C GREATER THAN D OR LESS THAN D
    AND X NOT = 1
```

How should you go about evaluating this? The logical operators have rules of hierarchy just as the arithmetic operators do. When you have several in a single conditional statement, the hierarchy is:

1. First evaluate all the NOT operators.

2. Evaluate all the AND operators.

3. Evaluate all the OR operators.

As in the arithmetic statements, parentheses can be used to change the order of evaluation. An even better approach is to keep your conditional statements as simple as possible. A compound conditional statement like the one above is difficult to evaluate mentally. You should be able to write compound conditional statements with a single logical operator. Then you will not have to bother about rules of hierarchy for logical operators at all, and your programs will be much more simple and readable.

5.2   IF STATEMENTS

Now that we have introduced the idea of a condition, we can begin to practice the use of these conditions in IF statements. To refresh your memory, refer to the definition of IF statements in Section 5.1 then consider some of the following examples:

```
IF SEX OF MASTER-RECORD IS EQUAL TO 'F'
      ADD 1 TO X1
      ADD AVERAGE OF MASTER-RECORD TO X2.
```

The first example is an IF statement that might be used in computing the average grade for all female students. The scratch variable X1 contains a count of the women, and scratch variable X2 holds the running sum of their grade averages. This is a simple IF statement. If the SEX field is equal to 'F', then the next two statements are performed. If not, they are ignored. In an IF statement, the statement after the condition includes everything up to the next period ending the sentence.

Now, let us look at another form of the IF statement. Suppose that a company gives quantity discounts of 10 percent on orders of 1,000 or more. This could be handled by an IF statement that looked like this:

```
IF AMOUNT-ORDERED IS LESS THAN 1000
      MULTIPLY AMOUNT-ORDERED BY PRICE GIVING TOTAL-PRICE
      ELSE
      COMPUTE TOTAL-PRICE = PRICE * AMOUNT-ORDERED * .9.
```

In this IF statement, if the condition AMOUNT-ORDERED IS LESS THAN 1000 is true, then the TOTAL-PRICE is computed by multiplying the amount and the price together. If this condition is not true, then the amount must be greater than or equal to 1000 items, and the order qualifies for the 10 percent quantity discount. In this event, the first MULTIPLY statement is bypassed, and the COMPUTE statement after the ELSE is performed instead.

Notice some points about the examples used so far. First, if possible the conditions should be kept simple. From the material in the previous section, we know how to write very complex compound conditions using the logical operators. Avoid this if you can, but realize that it is not always possible to avoid it. Second, we have tried to make the statements readable by using indentation of the statements to be performed if the condition is true. It is generally a good idea to indent logically subordinate clauses in a computer program in the same way you would in an outline. It makes your work much easier for other programmers to understand.

We did not say anything in the definition of the IF statement about what type of statements could be used in the statement-1 and statement-2 positions in the definition. These statements could be IF statements, in which case we would have something called a "nested" IF statement. Nested IF statements can be very complicated, and it is a good idea to avoid them as much as possible. They do provide a good way of testing your understanding of computers and of COBOL, however, so they are worth considering. Suppose you were confronted with the following COBOL code:

```
MOVE 2 TO X1.
IF X1 > 1 MOVE 1 TO XP2 IF X1 > 2 IF X1 > 3
MOVE 2 TO XP2 ELSE MOVE 3 TO XP2 ELSE MOVE 4 TO XP2.
DISPLAY XP2.
```

Most likely, your first reaction is to say that the mess that comprises the IF statement cannot be COBOL. But, it is COBOL and it is syntactically correct. One of the things that makes this statement look so formidable is that we have completely forgotten about indentation.

Since this statement is so complicated, let us set up some special rules for indentation.

1. When you come to the subordinate statement(s) after an IF phrase, indent them five spaces to the right.

2. When you come to the ELSE phrase, indent it back five spaces to the left.

IF we use these rules on our previous example, it looks like this:

```
MOVE 2 TO X1.
IF X1 > 1
     MOVE 1 TO XP2
     IF X1 > 2
        IF X1 > 3
             MOVE 2 TO XP2
        ELSE MOVE 3 TO XP2
     ELSE MOVE 4 TO XP2.
DISPLAY XP2.
```

When we follow the rules and write the IF statement this way, we now have the IF phrases lined up directly over their associated ELSE phrases. The first IF has no ELSE associated with it. Let us now examine this example line by line. The variable X1 initially has the value 2 from the first MOVE statement. The condition in the first IF is true, and the computer then performs the statements after the IF. The first statement moves a 1 into XP2. The second statement asks if X1 is greater than 2. This is not true, so control passes to the ELSE phrase associated with that IF. The statement in the ELSE phrase moves a 4 into XP2, and this is what is printed by the DISPLAY statement. Because the IF phrases and the ELSE phrases line up, it is easy to get the proper ones linked together. To further help your understanding of this IF statement, Figure 5.1 gives a flow chart of the control sequence for this statement.

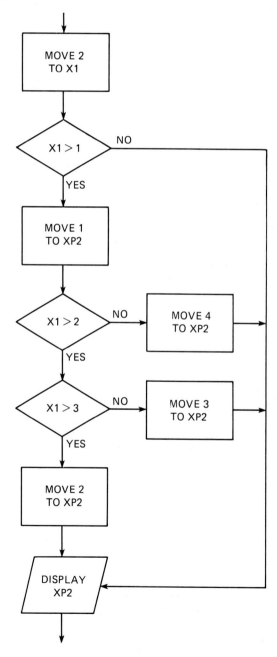

FIGURE 5.1
Flow of Control in a Nested
IF Statement

5.3   PROGRAMMING EXAMPLES USING IF

In the previous chapters we have had examples of reports printed out using data from our student MASTER-FILE. In each of these reports we have had to print out the whole record. Now that we have the ability to make decisions using the IF statement, we can generate a much wider variety of reports than was possible before.

Suppose, for example, that we would like to print out a list of students who were in academic difficulty. We would like to send this list to the advisors of the students who were in trouble. For our purposes, academic difficulty may be defined as a GPA of less than 2.0. We would like the printout to be ordered alphabetically by advisor and each advisor's students to be printed out in ascending order by grades. This way, the advisors see the names of their worst students first. We would also like to print out the GPA of each student.

Figure 5.2 gives the hierarchy diagram of this program. The flow-charts are shown in Figure 5.3. In order to perform this program, we have to sort the data into the order in which we wish to print it out. This means that we will use ADVISOR as our major key and sort it in ascending order. We will use AVERAGE, as our minor key and sort it in ascending order also.

We are going to do something a little different in the way in which we print out the advisor's name. We will only print out the ADVISOR OF STUDENT field when the value in that field changes. This way, we do not print out the advisor's name for every student. We only print it out once for each batch of advisees. This procedure produces a neater-looking print-out. When we use a field in this way, it is called a **control break.** To find out when the value in the advisor field changes, we will store the ad-

control break

FIGURE 5.2
Hierarchy Diagram for Program to Print Out Names of Students in Academic Difficulty

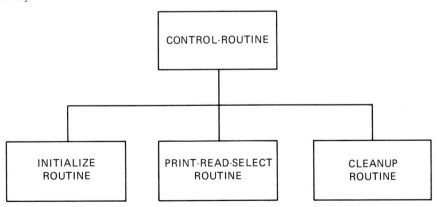

visor's name in the display scratch field, D1. Initially, D1 will have spaces in it, and we initialize it to spaces in the INITIALIZE paragraph (Figure 5.3b). In this same paragraph, we also open the REPORT-FILE to INPUT (it is the file that contains the sorted data), and we print out a header and a space for the listing we will generate. After that, we read in an initial data record.

The PRINT-READ-SELECT routine (Figure 5.3c) handles the printing of the names of the students who have been selected. If the AVERAGE OF REPORT-RECORD for that record is greater than 2.0, we do nothing with it and go back to read another record. If the average is less than 2.0, this means that we have a student in academic difficulty. We then check to see if the advisor's name is the same as the one stored in D1. If it is not, we have a new advisor, and we must print out his or her name. We print the new advisor's name and then print out the student name. If we still have the same advisor, then we merely print the student's name. We printed the advisor's name already at the control break. After this, we read in a

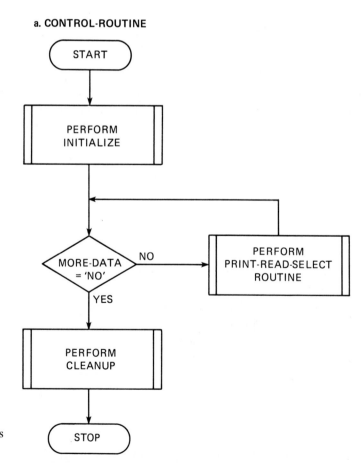

a. CONTROL-ROUTINE

FIGURE 5.3
Flowchart for Program to
Print Out Names of Students
in Academic Difficulty

FIGURE 5.3
(Continued)

b. INITIALIZE Routine

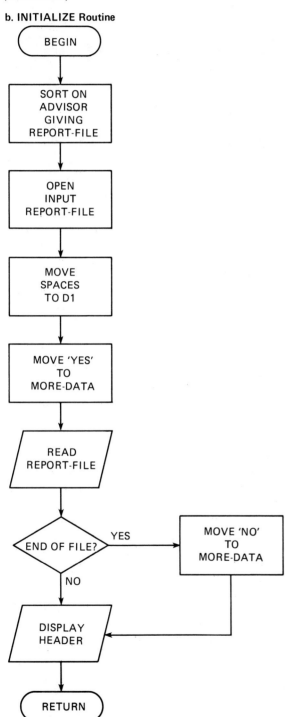

FIGURE 5.3
(Continued)

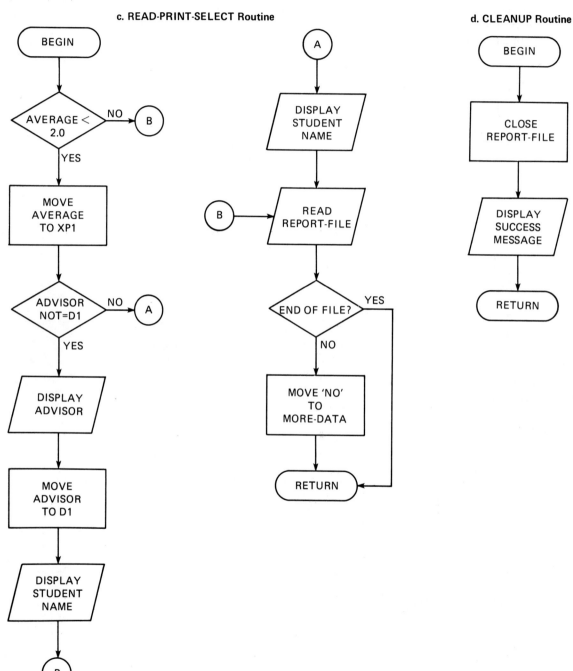

c. READ-PRINT-SELECT Routine

d. CLEANUP Routine

new record from the REPORT-FILE and start the process over. The CLEANUP routine (Figure 5.3d) handles the end of program processing as usual. The COBOL program for performing this task is shown in Figure 5.4.

FIGURE 5.4
COBOL Program to Print Out
Names of Students in Aca-
demic Difficulty.

```
010000 PROCEDURE DIVISION.
010010 PROGRAM-PURPOSE.
010020*       THIS PROGRAM PRINTS OUT THE NAMES OF ALL STUDENTS
010030*       WHO ARE IN ACADEMIC DIFFICULTY (STUDENTS WHOSE
010040*       GRADE AVERAGE IS LESS THAN 2.0). THE PRINTOUT IS
010050*       ORDERED ALPHABETICALLY BY ADVISOR. FOR A
010060*       PARTICULAR ADVISOR, THE STUDENTS ARE ORDERED
010070*       BY GRADE IN ASCENDING ORDER. THE ADVISOR'S NAME IS
010080*       PRINTED ONLY ONCE FOR A GIVEN GROUP OF STUDENTS.
010090 CONTROL-ROUTINE.
010100     PERFORM INITIALIZE.
010110     PERFORM PRINT-READ-SELECT UNTIL MORE-DATA IS EQUAL TO 'NO'.
010120     PERFORM CLEANUP.
010130     STOP RUN.
010140 INITIALIZE.
010150     SORT SORT-FILE ON ASCENDING KEY ADVISOR OF SORT-RECORD,
010160         ASCENDING KEY AVERAGE OF SORT-RECORD,
010170         USING MASTER-FILE,
010180         GIVING REPORT-FILE.
010190     OPEN INPUT REPORT-FILE.
010200     MOVE SPACES TO D1.
010210     MOVE 'YES' TO MORE-DATA.
010220     READ REPORT-FILE AT END MOVE 'NO' TO MORE-DATA.
010230     DISPLAY '               ACADEMIC DIFFICULTY LIST'.
010240 PRINT-READ-SELECT.
010250     IF AVERAGE OF REPORT-RECORD IS LESS THAN 2.0
010260         MOVE AVERAGE OF REPORT-RECORD TO XP1
010270         IF ADVISOR OF REPORT-RECORD IS NOT EQUAL TO D1
010280             DISPLAY ' '
010290             DISPLAY ADVISOR OF REPORT-RECORD
010300             MOVE ADVISOR OF REPORT-RECORD TO D1
010310             DISPLAY '            ',
010320             FIRST-NAME OF REPORT-RECORD,
010330                 LAST-NAME OF REPORT-RECORD, '    ', XP1
010340         ELSE
010350             DISPLAY '                ',
010360             FIRST-NAME OF REPORT-RECORD,
010370                 LAST-NAME OF REPORT-RECORD, '   ', XP1.
010380     READ REPORT-FILE AT END MOVE 'NO' TO MORE-DATA.
010390 CLEANUP.
010400     CLOSE REPORT-FILE.
010410     DISPLAY 'END OF PROGRAM'.
```

Our next programming example is a little more complicated. This program is designed to print out the names of probable graduating seniors. A student whose GPA is at least 1.3 and who has accumulated at least 90 credits is considered a possible graduating senior. We want this list printed on a college-by-college basis, and we want the names of the individuals printed alphabetically within each college. We would also like to compute the GPA for all students in the colleges (not just the graduating seniors) and print this average out with our lists.

The hierarchy diagram for this program is shown in Figure 5.5 and the flowcharts in Figure 5.6. This program is similar to the earlier one in that we will be using a control break. This time, the field COLLEGE OF REPORT-RECORD will be used as the break. The INITIALIZE routine (Fig-

FIGURE 5.4
(Continued)

Sample Output

ACADEMIC DIFFICULTY LIST

ANDREWS, DOUGLAS

| | TONY | COKER | 1.93 |

BOWLIN, O.D.

| | WILLIAM | KING | 1.74 |
| | BRUCE | EUBANKS | 1.96 |

CHENEY, PAUL

| | JOANN | CARRERA | 1.71 |
| | LILLY | JAMES | 1.76 |

DALE, CHARLES

| | KELLY | COLE | 1.90 |

DUNNE, PATRICK

| | BRAD | SPEIGHT | 1.81 |

FINN, DAVID

| | JON | THOMPSON | 1.71 |

GOODWIN, JACK

| | DEBORAH | EUBANKS | 1.94 |

HOOVER, DUANE

| | ALICIA | ESTES | 1.89 |

MALLOY, JOHN

| | KENNETH | CARTWRIGHT | 1.09 |

WATT, JAMES

| | MARLA | FLOYD | 1.99 |

END OF PROGRAM

ure 5.6b) begins by sorting our file in ascending order by college name and then in ascending order by the names of the students in the college as our minor key. We then open the REPORT-FILE to input and initialize the variables we will be using to spaces (for alphabetic display variables) and zero (for numeric compute variables). After this, we read our first record and print out the header.

The SELECT-PRINT-READ routine (Figure 5.6c) handles the selection and printing of the graduating seniors. First, we must check to see if D1 still has the same college name stored in it. If it does not, we have hit a control break and must compute the old college average and print a header for the new college. After we have checked this, we add the average to X1, count the student in X2, and then use our compound IF condition to see whether the student is a graduating senior. If so, we display the student's name. Notice that we have moved the name over several spaces in the DISPLAY output (see Figure 5.7). This serves to set off our control break headers (the college name) a little better. After we have checked this, we read a new record from the REPORT-FILE.

The CLEANUP routine (Figure 5.6e) handles the end of job processing. Notice that in the CLEANUP routine, it is necessary to call the PRINT-COLLEGE-AV routine one last time to print out the average for the last college. Then, we close our files and terminate normally.

FIGURE 5.5
Hierarchy Diagram for Program to List Graduating Seniors

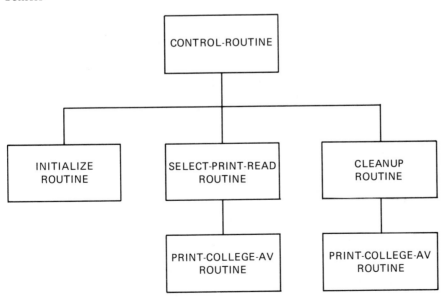

This program may seem quite a bit more complicated than anything we have done to this point. But, do not let this apparent complication worry you. Think of the program as a sequence of pieces of code, and try first to understand how each of the pieces works. Then try to understand how the pieces fit together into a system, and you will have no problem understanding the whole program.

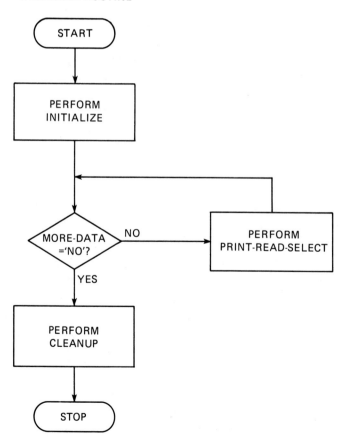

a. CONTROL-ROUTINE

FIGURE 5.6
Flowchart for Program to
List Graduating Seniors

FIGURE 5.6
(Continued)

b. INITIALIZE Routine

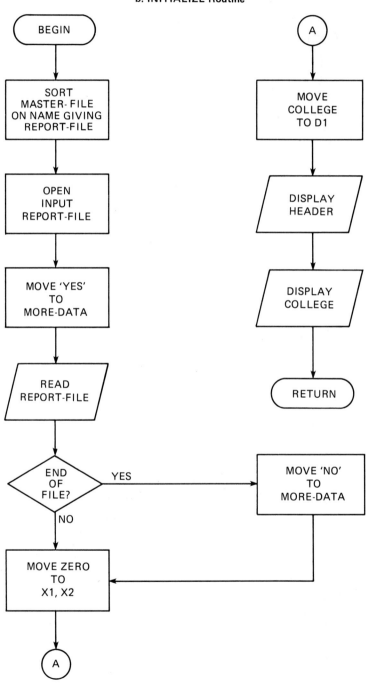

FIGURE 5.6
(Continued)

c. SELECT-PRINT-READ Routine

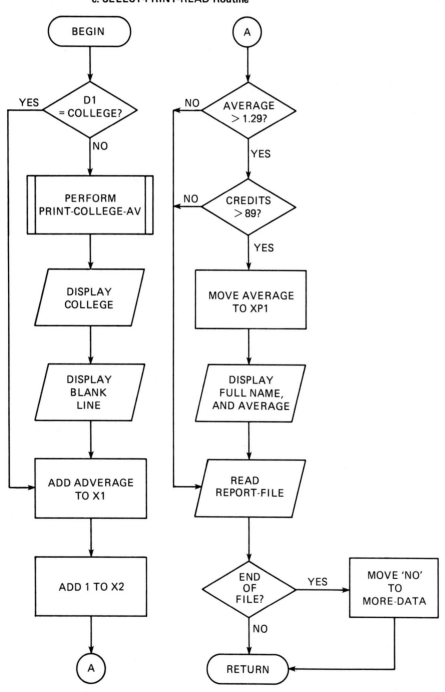

FIGURE 5.6
(Continued)

d. PRINT-COLLEGE-AV Routine

e. CLEANUP Routine

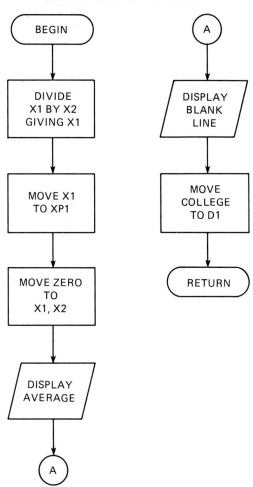

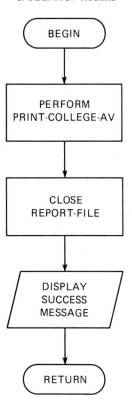

FIGURE 5.7

COBOL Program to Print Out
Names of Graduating Seniors

```
010000 PROCEDURE DIVISION.
010010 PROGRAM-PURPOSE.
010020*       THIS PROGRAM PRINTS OUT THE NAMES OF PROBABLE
010030*       GRADUATING SENIORS. A PERSON IS DEFINED AS A
010040*       POSSIBLE GRADUATING SENIOR IF HE HAS AT LEAST 90
010050*       CREDIT HOURS AND HIS GRADE AVERAGE IS AT LEAST 1.3.
010060*       THE NAMES AND AVERAGES ARE PRINTED OUT ALPHABETICALLY
010070*       BY COLLEGE. IN ADDITION, THE AVERAGE (OF ALL STUDENTS)
010080*       IS COMPUTED ON A COLLEGE BY COLLEGE BASIS. THE
010090*       FOLLOWING VARIABLES ARE USED:
010100*           X1    HOLDS THE SUM OF THE GRADE AVERAGES.
010110*           X2    HOLDS THE COUNT OF STUDENTS.
010120*           D1    HOLDS THE NAME OF THE COLLEGE.
010130 CONTROL-ROUTINE.
010140     PERFORM INITIALIZE.
010150     PERFORM SELECT-PRINT-READ UNTIL MORE-DATA IS EQUAL TO 'NO'.
010160     PERFORM CLEANUP.
010170     STOP RUN.
010180 INITIALIZE.
010190     SORT SORT-FILE ON ASCENDING KEY COLLEGE OF SORT-RECORD,
010200         ASCENDING LAST-NAME OF SORT-RECORD,
010210         ASCENDING FIRST-NAME OF SORT-RECORD,
010220         ASCENDING INIT OF SORT-RECORD,
010230         USING MASTER-FILE,
010240         GIVING REPORT-FILE.
010250     OPEN INPUT REPORT-FILE.
010260     MOVE 'YES' TO MORE-DATA.
010270     READ REPORT-FILE AT END MOVE 'NO' TO MORE-DATA.
010280     MOVE ZEROES TO X1, X2.
010290     MOVE COLLEGE OF REPORT-RECORD TO D1.
010300     DISPLAY '                 PROBABLE GRADUATING SENIORS'.
010310     DISPLAY ' '.
010320     DISPLAY COLLEGE OF REPORT-RECORD.
010330     DISPLAY ' '.
010340 SELECT-PRINT-READ.
010350     IF D1 IS NOT EQUAL TO COLLEGE OF REPORT-RECORD
010360         PERFORM PRINT-COLLEGE-AV
010370         DISPLAY COLLEGE OF REPORT-RECORD
010380         DISPLAY ' '.
010390     ADD AVERAGE OF REPORT-RECORD TO X1.
010400     ADD 1 TO X2.
010410     IF AVERAGE OF REPORT-RECORD IS GREATER THAN 1.29 AND
010420         CREDITS OF REPORT-RECORD IS GREATER THAN 89
010430         MOVE AVERAGE OF REPORT-RECORD TO XP1
010440         DISPLAY '            ', FIRST-NAME OF REPORT-RECORD,
010450             INIT OF REPORT-RECORD, '. ',
010460             LAST-NAME OF REPORT-RECORD, XP1.
010470     READ REPORT-FILE AT END MOVE 'NO' TO MORE-DATA.
010480 PRINT-COLLEGE-AV.
010490     DIVIDE X1 BY X2 GIVING X1.
010500     MOVE X1 TO XP1.
010510     MOVE ZEROES TO X1, X2.
010520     DISPLAY ' '.
010530     DISPLAY 'COLLEGE AVERAGE: ', XP1.
```

FIGURE 5.7
(Continued)

```
010540      DISPLAY ' '.
010550      MOVE COLLEGE OF REPORT-RECORD TO D1.
010560 CLEANUP.
010570      PERFORM PRINT-COLLEGE-AV.
010580      CLOSE REPORT-FILE.
010590      DISPLAY ' '.
010600      DISPLAY 'SUCCESSFUL END OF PROGRAM'.
```

Sample Output

POSSIBLE GRADUATING SENIORS

AGRICULTURE

TOBY	V. AVANT	3.16
DORIS	Y. PATRICK	2.33
MARTHA	S. SALVINO	2.28
MARILYN	A. SPENCER	3.91

COLLEGE AVERAGE: 2.73

ARTS AND SCIENCES

ANN	W. ALEXANDER	3.23
KEVIN	T. AYLOR	2.67
RODNEY	I. AYLOR	2.61
LAWRENCE	T. BATES	2.06
CASEY	J. BETTZ	2.23
RICHARD	Q. CAINS	2.40
ELLEN	O. CAMERON	2.97
SARA	W. CAMERON	2.94
DEBRA	Y. CHAMBERS	2.86
SANDRA	D. CHAMBERS	2.73
DANIEL	B. COKER	2.13
GEORGE	F. ELLIS	2.03
DEBORAH	F. EUBANKS	1.94
JACKIE	D. GLEASON	2.32
BARRY	Z. HERRERA	2.03
JOEL	R. HERRERA	2.31
MARK	A. HERRERA	3.34
MARTHA	C. JARVIS	2.95
BERT	V. LAING	2.57
BENJAMIN	M. LAND	3.22
ELBERT	K. PURCELL	3.26
JON	J. THOMPSON	1.71
EUGENIA	E. WILCOX	2.68
JILL	E. WILLIAMS	2.56

COLLEGE AVERAGE: 2.67

BUSINESS

LUCY	U. ALEXANDER	2.76
RUBY	C. BETTZ	2.54
LUPE	O. CRAWFORD	2.49

FIGURE 5.7
(Continued)

```
        PATRICK       Z. FELLERS        2.37
        DONALD        J. JAMES          2.44
        LILLY         F. JAMES          1.76
        WILLIAM       F. KING           1.74
        HAROLD        R. NEWCOMER       2.63
        HERMAN        Z. REED           2.41

COLLEGE AVERAGE:      2.58

EDUCATION

        ANTHONY       R. BROWN          2.83
        VICTORIA      I. FULLER         2.70
        JOSEPH        D. GARLOCK        3.26
        SCOTT         V. MAHAN          2.75
        POLLY         Q. PATRICK        2.44
        GEORGE        N. RAYMER         3.23
        TIMOTHY       E. WHATLEY        2.06

COLLEGE AVERAGE:      2.86

ENGINEERING

        KELLY         E. BARCLAY        2.79
        KENNETH       P. CHAMBERLAIN    2.53
        RICHARD       O. CRAIG          2.62
        CONNIE        K. DAVIS          3.42
        MICHAEL       Z. MCALLISTER     3.12
        CHARLES       Z. SPEIGHT        3.01
        BRENDA        K. TURNER         2.50

COLLEGE AVERAGE:      2.83

SUCCESSFUL END OF PROGRAM
```

STUDY EXERCISES

1. Suppose that the variable A equals 1, B equals 2, C equals 3, D equals 4, and E equals 5. Tell whether the conditions below are true or false.

```
A IS ALPHABETIC
A IS LESS THAN OR EQUAL TO 1.5
A IS GREATER THAN B
A + B IS LESS THAN C
A + B * C IS EQUAL TO 7
A + B + C IS GREATER THAN A + D + E - 8
A = B OR B IS GREATER THAN A
A IS LESS THAN 20 OR GREATER THAN 15
A IS GREATER THAN 20 OR GREATER THAN 2
A IS ALPHABETIC
A IS POSITIVE
E - A + B IS NEGATIVE
```

2. Suppose that the variable A is alphanumeric and its value is 'SMITH'. Tell whether the conditions below are true or false.

```
A IS EQUAL TO 'SMITH' OR EQUAL TO 'JONES'
A IS GREATER THAN 'SMYTHE'
A IS LESS THAN '3CPO'
A IS ALPHABETIC
A IS EQUAL TO 'SMITH' AND EQUAL TO 'JONES'
A IS NOT NUMERIC
```

3. Write an IF statement that will print out the names of all women on the MASTER-FILE who are under 25 years old.

4. Write an IF statement that will print the names of all students on the MASTER-FILE who owe the college more than $1,000.

5. Write IF statement that will print the names of all male engineers on the MASTER-FILE.

6. What will the COBOL code below print out?

```
MOVE 1 TO A.
IF A IS POSITIVE IF A IS GREATER THAN 0 MOVE 2 TO A
ADD 1 TO A IF A IS GREATER THAN 7 ELSE IF A IS LESS
THAN 5 MOVE 10 TO A ELSE MOVE 7 TO A.
DISPLAY A.
```

7. Write a COBOL program that will print out a telephone directory of the men on the MASTER-FILE. The directory should be in alphabetical order.

8. Write a COBOL program that will compute the average GPA for men and the average GPA for women.

9. Write a COBOL program that will print out an alphabetical list of all advisors and their advisees. The advisor names should be used as a control break, and the names should be in alphabetical order. For a given advisor, the names of his advisees should also be in alphabetical order.

10. Write a COBOL program that will print out the names of honor students on a college-by-college basis. The colleges should be in alphabetical order, and the college name should be used as a control break. Within a college, the names of the students should be in descending order by grades. An honor student is defined as any student whose GPA is greater than 3.3.

11. Print out the name of the man with the highest GPA and the woman with the highest GPA on the MASTER-FILE.

12. Rewrite the COBOL program that prints out the students in academic difficulty by providing appropriate headers, such as ADVISOR, STUDENT, and GPA.

6 6
6 6 DATA REPRESENTATIONS
6 6
6 6
6 6
6 6
6 6
6 6
6 6
6 6
6 6
6 6

6.0 INTRODUCTION

Thus far, we have dealt with many different types of data. We have used alphabetic data to represent names and addresses, numeric data to represent dollar amounts or GPAs, and edited versions of numeric data to display that data in some specific format (with leading blanks, plus signs, dollar signs, etc.). You are probably wondering how the computer really does store this data internally, and how it keeps all the data straight.

The purpose of this chapter is to answer some of these questions for you. The answers have little to do with the COBOL language, but they will help you understand how the type of data with which you may be working is processed within the computer. Although the explanations in this chapter are generally for IBM and IBM-compatible computers, the principles should apply to any machine. An understanding of the material in this chapter is essential for any professional work you will do with computers. In analyzing errors, it is always helpful to know how the machine handles your data. If you know something about the machine's internal data processing, you will be able to avoid most problem-causing situations.

To begin with, any digital computer has only one way of representing data, that is as a string of 0s and 1s. The computer has only these two numbers in its vocabulary. Any other symbols it uses must be built up from these two symbols using a specific number system or code. You can think of these two symbols—0 and 1—as corresponding to no and yes or to the off and on positions of a switch.

To understand why a computer has to deal with a variety of number and coding systems, consider some of the demands for computation that are placed on a computer. Suppose that we are performing a simple count of the number of employees of a firm. The result might be:

972

This number could be represented as a simple integer (a number with no places to the right of the decimal) since we may not be dealing with fractional people.* It can also be a fairly small number since (if we are like most companies) we are not likely to be dealing with millions or even hundreds of thousands of employees. The fact that the number is relatively small allows us to save some storage space in the machine.

A scientist may require a computer that is able to represent numbers like:

$$6.023 \times 10^{23}$$

This number is 6.023 with the decimal point moved twenty-three places to the right, and this type of notation is called scientific notation. In it we can represent numbers of either very large or very small magnitude. We are not concerned about the precision of the number (the number of significant digits), and we are only slightly worried about round-off error. We will be doing very little work in scientific notation in COBOL. It is possible to work in scientific notation on most machines, but the type of problem for which COBOL is used has very little need for this kind of processing.

An accountant preparing a balance sheet for a large firm may want to be able to compute with such numbers as:

```
200492769.36
```

This number has eleven significant digits, and from the accountant's point of view, all of them must be carried in calculations. Business applications demand numbers of smaller magnitude than do scientific applications, but business applications require a great deal of precision.

In addition the computer also must be able to edit the numbers to produce readable output or specialized output for certain business purposes. The number above might also be represented as:

```
$200492769.36
$**********200,492,769.36
+200,492,769.36
$200,492,769.36CR
```

In one case, we have a dollar sign "floated in" to the beginning of the number. In the second, we have both a dollar sign and a check protection symbol. In addition, the number is separated into groups of three digits

---

* Although the term *fractional people* may strike you as very funny, whether or not you have to deal with fractional people depends on how you will count them. A typical way of counting, for example, is by "full-time equivalents" in which case those who work part-time or overtime will contribute fractions to your count.

by commas. None of these edited numbers would be particularly important for scientific or mathematical applications, but they are very important in business. COBOL gives us the capability to represent these forms of data.

The final type of data is alphabetic data. We want to be able to print out names, addresses, item descriptions, and so forth in readable English. We also want to be able to have the letters ordered into a standard collating sequence so that we can sort alphabetically. COBOL also gives us internal data representations for doing this.

All this may seem like a lot to demand of a system that can only use the symbols 0 and 1, but it is fairly easy to represent all these different types of data. The remainder of this chapter will discuss the different internal representations for data in COBOL, and the next chapter will discuss the way in which we describe data to the machine using the COBOL language.

6.1 OTHER NUMBER SYSTEMS

Before we can begin to understand how the computer stores its data, we must understand the number system used by computers, and we must understand numbers in general. For example, in our conventional decimal or base 10 number system the number

1,944

really means

$$1 \times 10^3 + 9 \times 10^2 + 4 \times 10^1 + 4 \times 10^0$$

Each of the places in the number 1,944 represents a number times a power of 10. Recall from algebra that 10 to the 0th power (or any number to the 0th power) is 1. The number 10 is called the **base,** and all other numbers in the base 10 or decimal system are expressed as one of ten symbols (0, 1, 2, 3, 4, 5, 6, 7, 8, and 9) times a power of the base.

base

In expressing numbers, we can use any base that is convenient. The fact that we use base 10 is probably the result of an anatomical accident—we have ten fingers. People can and do use other number bases. One example is the system we use to tell time. For this, we use a sort of modified base 60 with 60 minutes in an hour and 60 seconds in a minute. This is probably a result of early Babylonian attempts to make the lunar and solar calendars coincide.

Because computers have only two symbols (0 and 1), we find that we must depend on the base 2 or **binary** number system. In the decimal number system, the individual numbers are called digits. In the binary

binary

number system, the individual symbols that make up a number are called **bits,** which stands for *bi*nary dig*its*. Binary notation is also an exponential notation, but this time the base that we are raising to a power is the number 2. Consider the binary number

10110

This really means

$$1 \times 2^4 + 0 \times 2^3 + 1 \times 2^2 + 1 \times 2^1 + 0 \times 2^0$$

If you compute the number above, you find that you have

$$22_{10}$$

The subscript 10 means that 22 is written in the base 10 or decimal system. We often use subscripts to make sure that our meaning is clear when we are talking about numbers in different bases. After all, wouldn't you rather receive a check for $10110 rather than a check for $22? Unless, of course, we made it clear that the number 10110 is in binary form.

Converting a number from the binary system to the decimal system is easy. All you have to do is refer to the definition of a binary number and compute its decimal equivalent. Converting a number from the decimal system to the binary system is a little harder, but not too much. It requires elementary division. For example;

5 divided by 2 = 2 remainder 1

We will use the remainders we get to form the binary equivalent of a base 10 number. To do this, we successively divide by 2. Let us try converting the number 87 from the base 10 to base 2.

```
87 divided by 2 = 43 remainder 1
43 divided by 2 = 21 remainder 1
21 divided by 2 = 10 remainder 1
10 divided by 2 =  5 remainder 0
 5 divided by 2 =  2 remainder 1
 2 divided by 2 =  1 remainder 0
 1 divided by 2 =  0 remainder 1
```

When we get a 0 dividend, we are done. Read up the list of remainders from the bottom to get the binary number

$$1010111_2 = 87_{10}$$

From this example, we can see that working with the binary system would be fairly tedious because small numbers such as 87 convert into lengthy binary numbers. Therefore, computer engineers and programmers make extensive use of the base 8 or **octal** system and the base 16 or **hexadecimal** system. The word *hexadecimal* is sometimes shortened to **hex.** Figure 6.1 shows equivalent numbers in the four number systems we have discussed so far. In these number systems, the concept of a number as a symbol times a power of the base still holds. Consider these definitions:

octal

hexadecimal

hex

$$67_8 = 6 \times 8^1 + 7 \times 8^0 = 56_{10}$$

$$2A_x = 2 \times 16^1 + 10 \times 16^0 = 42_{10}$$

FIGURE 6.1
Equivalent Numbers in
Different Bases.

BASE 10 *Decimal*	BASE 2 *Binary*	BASE 8 *Octal*	BASE 16 *Hexadecimal*
0	0000	0	0
1	0001	1	1
2	0010	2	2
3	0011	3	3
4	0100	4	4
5	0101	5	5
6	0110	6	6
7	0111	7	7
8	1000	10	8
9	1001	11	9
10	1010	12	A
11	1011	13	B
12	1100	14	C
13	1101	15	D
14	1110	16	E
15	1111	17	F
16	10000	20	10

Notice that we use A, B, C, D, E, and F as digits in the hexadecimal system. The reason is that the hexadecimal system needs sixteen distinct symbols, and the base 10 system has only ten. So, we use the first six letters of the alphabet as the remaining six symbols. You should keep in mind that even though the numbers are represented differently in each system, the numbers themselves represent the same objects regardless of how they are expressed.

You are probably wondering why we need the octal and hexadecimal systems. After all, computers use base 2 and people use base 10, so why complicate things by introducing two new bases? The answer lies in the fact that 8 and 16 are powers of 2. Therefore, these bases give us a convenient shorthand notation for the binary numbers inside the machine. Suppose that we have the binary number

$$11011101110111011$$

and we wish to convert this number to the base 8. Arrange the number in groups of three from the right. Add leading zeros on the left if necessary to fill out the last group of three numbers. Then, under each group of three bits, write the equivalent of those three bits in the octal number system. This gives us

011	011	101	110	111	011
3	3	5	6	7	3

which can be read as 335673_8.

Conversion to base 16 is similar. This time, arrange the number in groups of four from the right adding leading zeros if necessary. Then, under each group of four, write the hexadecimal equivalent. This gives us

0001	1011	1011	1011	1011
1	B	B	B	B

which can be read as $1BBBB_x$.

Conversion back from octal and hexadecimal to binary is equally simple. This time, you write the binary equivalent under each digit. Use three bits when you are converting from octal to binary and use four bits when you are converting from hexadecimal to binary. Study the following examples.

$$742_8 = \underset{111}{7} \quad \underset{100}{4} \quad \underset{010}{2} = 111100010_2$$

$$ABC2_X = \underset{1010}{A} \quad \underset{1011}{B} \quad \underset{1100}{C} \quad \underset{0010}{2} = 1010101111000010_2$$

These octal and hexadecimal numbers can be used to give the exact bit patterns that are set in the machine. These bit patterns can be used by engineers and programmers to find locations in core (most computers address their memory in binary). It is also useful for printing out **core dumps.** A core dump is a printout of everything in the computer's memory.

core dumps

The material in this section forms a necessary foundation for your understanding of how the computer handles data. If you understand different number systems and their uses, you will have a much easier time understanding computer basics.

6.2 INTERNAL CODE FOR ALPHABETIC CHARACTERS

In the previous section, we saw how the binary number system is used in the computer and how the octal and hexadecimal systems could be used to represent the binary number system. But this still does not tell us how data is organized in the machine. The bits in a computer can be organized into **words.** A word in the computer memory is a standard-sized group of contiguous bits that can be treated as a single unit for computational purposes. On an IBM 360/370 series computer, the word size is thirty-two bits. This means that the largest number that can be represented in a single word is $2^{32} - 1$. A word is usually used to store certain types of numbers.

words

For many purposes, the word is too large a unit. We also use the term **byte,** which means some group of contiguous bits. When programmers talk about a byte, they usually mean eight contiguous bits aligned on a full- or half-word boundary. Eight bits is also the number of bits required to represent an alphabetic character in IBM's coding system. For all practical purposes, you can use the terms *byte* and *character* interchangeably on an IBM machine. People usually measure the size of a computer by the number of bytes of information that can be stored in its core memory. If somebody says that a computer is a 64K machine, the person usually means that it is possible to store $64 \times 1,024 = 65,536$ characters or bytes of information in the machine. The capital letter K represents by convention the number 1,024 or 2^{10}, which is used because computers address their internal memory in binary. It is more convenient to sell memory in increments of a power of 2.

byte

A variety of different types of character codes have been used in computers. One of the earliest was the **BCD** (Binary Coded Decimal) code. There were a number of versions of this code, which was popular in computers in the 1960s. The BCD code was a six-bit code, which meant that $2^6 = 64$ different characters could be represented. This was

BCD

sufficient for twenty-six upper-case letters, ten digits, and twenty-eight of punctuation and special symbols.

Sixty-four symbols were not really enough to process lower-case letters or any special control symbols, and other codes were developed. One very common code is the ASCII (American Standard Code for Information Interchange) code, usually pronounced *ass-key*. It is a seven-bit code and is usually augmented to eight bits for use in computers that use an eight-bit character size. It is widely used on non-IBM communications hardware and computers. The third common character code is EBCDIC (Extended Binary Coded Decimal Interchange Code—usually pronounced ib-see-dick), which IBM developed for use on the 360/370 series of computers. It is an eight-bit code and can represent $2^8 = 256$ different symbols.

Figure 6.2 gives the internal bit patterns for some common characters in BCD, ASCII, and EBCDIC codes. Notice that all the codes are arranged so that the alphabetic is numbered from smaller to larger binary numbers. This arrangement makes it possible to compare one letter to another to see which is "greater." In this way, simple numeric comparison of letters can be used in sort routines for alphabetization.

Notice also that a single EBCDIC character can be represented by two hexadecimal digits. For example the bit pattern for an A is

$$11000001 = C1_x$$

whereas in BCD, the bit pattern for an A is

$$010001 = 21_8$$

Hexadecimal, then, is a very convenient shorthand notation for the bit patterns in EBCDIC machines, whereas octal is a convenient notation for the bit patterns in BCD machines.

6.3 NUMBERS IN COBOL

In the previous section we saw how alphanumeric data is stored in COBOL. We can store numbers simply by storing the character code representation of the number, but this is not always done for a variety of reasons. The character code representation contains more bits than are needed to represent the number, and internally the computer does not do arithmetic on these character strings. Before arithmetic can be performed on a character string representing a number, it must be converted to some other internal representation. After the arithmetic has been performed,

FIGURE 6.2
Internal Bit Patterns for
BCD, ASCII and EBCDIC.

CHARACTER	BCD CODE	ASCII CODE	EBCDIC CODE
blank	110 000	0100 0000	0100 0000
.	011 011	0100 1110	0100 1011
,	111 011	0100 1111	0110 1011
A	010 001	1010 0001	1100 0001
B	010 010	1010 0010	1100 0010
C	010 011	1010 0011	1100 0011
D	010 100	1010 0100	1100 0100
E	010 101	1010 0101	1100 0101
F	010 110	1010 0110	1100 0110
G	010 111	1010 0111	1100 0111
H	011 000	1010 1000	1100 1000
I	011 001	1010 1001	1100 1001
J	100 001	1010 1010	1101 0001
K	100 010	1010 1011	1101 0010
L	100 011	1010 1100	1101 0011
M	100 100	1010 1101	1101 0100
N	100 101	1010 1110	1101 0101
O	100 110	1010 1111	1101 0110
P	100 111	1011 0000	1101 0111
Q	101 000	1011 0001	1101 1000
R	101 001	1101 0010	1101 1001
S	110 010	1101 0011	1011 0011
T	110 011	1101 0100	1011 0100
U	110 100	1101 0101	1011 0101
V	110 101	1101 0110	1011 0110
W	110 110	1101 0111	1011 0111
X	110 111	1101 1000	1011 1000
Y	111 000	1101 1001	1011 1001
Z	111 001	1101 1010	1011 1010
0	000 000	0101 0000	1111 0000
1	000 001	0101 0001	1111 0001
2	000 010	0101 0010	1111 0010
3	000 011	0101 0011	1111 0011
4	000 100	0101 0100	1111 0100
5	000 101	0101 0101	1111 0101
6	000 110	0101 0110	1111 0110
7	000 111	0101 0111	1111 0111
8	001 000	0101 1000	1111 1000
9	001 001	0101 1001	1111 1001

we must convert the number back from the internal representation to the character string representation if we wish to print it out.

Binary Representation

The simplest type of number representation is a pure binary number, which is represented by the bit pattern stored in the word. On IBM systems, there is a COBOL reserved word to describe this type of COBOL data item. It is called COMPUTATIONAL or COMPUTATIONAL-4. If you are using a system different from IBM, check your system's manuals to see what COMPUTATIONAL variables the system contains. This definition will vary from system to system, but they are probably pure binary numbers.

To see how the numbers are represented, suppose we had a half-word on an IBM system to represent the number 1. The internal representation would be

$$0000000000000001 \ = \ 0001_X$$

The first bit in this string is the sign bit. If it is zero, this means that the number is positive. If it is a 1, then the number is negative. But there is more to the representation of negative numbers than a simple bit change for a sign. Negative numbers are usually represented in some form of **complement notation.** There are two types. The first is called the **1s complement.** In this notation, a negative number is formed from the corresponding positive number by changing the 0s to 1s and the 1s to 0s in the positive number. For example, the 1s complement representation of -1 is

complement notation

1s complement

$$1111111111111110 \ = \ FFFE_X$$

The use of complement notation allows us to use addition logic for both addition and subtraction. If one adds the values for $+1$ and -1 together, the result is

$$
\begin{aligned}
&0000000000000001 \\
+\,&1111111111111110 \\
\hline
&1111111111111111 \ = \ FFFF_X \ = \ -0
\end{aligned}
$$

If the bit pattern had been all 0s, it would represent a $+0$. There is one problem with this. In ordinary mathematical usage, -0 is a meaningless concept. It should be the same as an ordinary 0. But to a computer operating in 1s complement mode, -0 and $+0$ are two different numbers. The possibility of having two different values that mean zero can cause a great deal of confusion.

Therefore, 1s complement mode is seldom used for the internal arithmetic in machines. Instead, the mode called **2s complement** is used. The 2s complement takes the 1s complement and adds 1 to it to form the desired negative number. For example, suppose that we wanted to write the 2s complement internal representation of a -1. This would be

2s complement

$$-1 = 1111111111111110 + 1 = 1111111111111111 = FFFF_X$$

Now, when we add 1 and -1 in 2s complement notation, we get

```
  0000000000000001

+ 1111111111111111
  ─────────────────
 10000000000000000 = 0000000000000000 = 0
```

because the one bit on the far left is dropped. Under 2s complement mode, there is no problem with $+0$ and -0.

This discussion of internal binary representation of computational numbers may seem too technical for some readers. After all, we were able to do arithmetic quite effectively in Chapter 4 without worrying about how the data was represented inside the machine. But a thorough understanding of the internal number system of a computer will help you in later work if you should ever have to worry about interpreting a core dump or similar type of raw data.

Other Notation

The binary number system is the fastest for the computer to use internally, but there are a number of reasons why we might not want to use it. Fractions, for example, can present problems. There are a number of fractions in the binary system (one-tenth, for example) that repeat digits in the same way that one-third generates a repeating decimal in the base 10 system. In the base 2 system, when we are dealing with binary fractions representing tenths or hundredths, part of the fraction will be truncated. So, it might be desirable to be able to represent the base 10 system directly in the machine rather than to use the base 2 representation for numbers.

Zoned Decimal

The first way in which this can be done is through the use of **zoned decimal.** Zoned decimal notation uses the EBCDIC representations of the numbers with some minor modifications. If the number has a decimal

zoned decimal

point, COBOL keeps track of the decimal point without actually inserting a decimal point in the internal representation. If the number has a sign, it is represented by changing the right-most digit of the number. The upper four bits (called the **zone bits**) of any EBCDIC representation of a number are F_x. The upper four bits of the last digit of a zoned decimal number will be changed to C_x if the number is positive and D_x if the number is negative. Consider the following examples of zoned decimal internal representation:

zone bits

$$12.34 = F1F2F3C4_x$$
$$-12.34 = F1F2F3D4_x$$

This is why you were discouraged from printing out an unedited numeric field. The inclusion of the sign as a change to the zone bits of the last digit of a number changes the character code. If we tried to print out the zoned decimal representation of the number +199, we would be trying to print out something with an internal representation of $F1F9C9_x$. If you check Figure 6.2, you will see that a bit pattern of $C9_x$ is the EBCDIC representation of the letter I. This means that our number would print out as 19I instead of +199.

Packed Decimal

Internally, IBM equipment cannot compute with zoned decimal. A zoned decimal number must be converted to **packed decimal** or **internal decimal** before it can be used in computation. In packed decimal format, the zone bits of each zoned decimal digit are stripped off. The hex digit representing the sign is moved to the end of the number. Consider these packed decimal representations:

packed decimal

internal decimal

$$12.34 = 1234C_x$$
$$-12.34 = 1234D_x$$

The advantage of packed decimal numbers is that they may be stored in about half the space of zoned decimal numbers. In both, we get true base 10 arithmetic. Zoned decimal is called COMPUTATIONAL-3 on IBM systems.

Floating Point

The final type of notation we will consider is the internal representation of scientific notation called **floating point**. Floating point numbers are seldom used in COBOL, and they will not be used in this book at all.

floating point

They are handy if you have to do statistical processing on some data or if you have to use COBOL on a data file constructed in another language that uses floating point more heavily.

Recall that a number in scientific notation is in the form

```
mantissa x base exponent
```

Thus, for the number 6.023×10^{23}, the mantissa is 6.023, the base is 10, and the exponent is 23. Computers handle scientific notation by breaking up a computer word as follows:

S	Exponent	Mantissa

A certain portion of the computer word is set aside for the exponent, and a certain portion for the mantissa. Usually the first bit of the word represents the sign of the number. On an IBM 360/370 computer, the exponent is seven bits long, and the mantissa is twenty-four bits long for a **single-precision** floating point number. A second word can be joined to the first word, and the mantissa can be extended to another thirty-two bits for a **double-precision** word. On IBM systems, single-precision floating point is called COMPUTATIONAL-1, and double precision floating point is called COMPUTATIONAL-2.

single-precision

double-precision

It is difficult to discuss how computing equipment processes data without referring to some specific machine. Therefore this discussion of the internal representation of numbers in COBOL has generally been for IBM computers. IBM equipment is so widely used that it is worthwhile for you to understand the systems and machinery. Whatever equipment you will work on will be similar in many ways, and understanding these processes will help you in later work.

STUDY EXERCISES

1. Write out the first fifteen numbers in the base 5 number system.

2. Why do computers use the base 2 number system?

3. Convert the numbers below from binary to decimal.

11011	110110	110
11011101	1110111	11011
100000	1011101	10001

4. Convert the numbers below from decimal to binary.

17	325	1024
5	512	1195
81	65	8721

5. Why are the octal and hexadecimal number systems important in computer applications?

6. Convert the decimal numbers below to octal and hexadecimal.

75	512	64
98	87	25

7. Convert the binary numbers below to octal and hexadecimal.

1011	110111	10111
101101	10110111	110111

8. Convert the octal numbers below to binary and decimal.

765	66	777
51	751	101

9. Convert the hexadecimal numbers below to binary and decimal.

1A	ABC	75A
75	101	BAC

10. What do BCD, ASCII, and EBCDIC stand for and what do they mean?

11. Why do computers use complement notation to represent negative numbers?

12. Write the hexadecimal representation of the bit patterns set in the machine for the numbers below when they are represented as zoned decimal numbers.

+125	+8.372
+175.25	−975.21

13. Write the hexadecimal representation of the bit patterns set in the machine for the numbers below when they are represented as packed decimal numbers.

+125	+8.372
−175.25	−975.21

14. What advantages does packed decimal have over zoned decimal?

15. Why is floating point not commonly used in COBOL?

THE IDENTIFICATION AND ENVIRONMENT DIVISIONS

7.0 INTRODUCTION

The IDENTIFICATION and ENVIRONMENT divisions are the first of the four divisions into which every COBOL program is divided. The material they contain is important in that it serves to introduce a program to the computer and to future users. They do not contain any commands for the computer to execute. This is left to the PROCEDURE DIVISION, which we have already used extensively in the earlier chapters of this book.

The IDENTIFICATION DIVISION gives information about the program and the individual who wrote it. It is possible to omit the material in this division almost entirely, but omitting it is not a good practice. The computer treats the documentation in this division as comments, but it is very helpful in providing basic record information about the program, its author, and its purpose. You should make full use of the capabilities of the IDENTIFICATION DIVISION in your professional work. You will be surprised how quickly it is possible to forget the details of a program you spent weeks designing. Well thought-out comments in the IDENTIFICA-TION DIVISION can make matters much easier when it comes time to modify the program.

The ENVIRONMENT DIVISION provides information on the relationship between your program and the external I/O devices that your program uses. For instance, we have been using a file called MASTER-FILE. The ENVIRONMENT DIVISION of our program contains code to tell the computer what external device has the file called MASTER-FILE and what this device looks like. The ENVIRONMENT DIVISION is the one area of a COBOL program that is most likely to have to be changed when transferring a program from one machine to another. Different machines, even those by the same manufacturer, have different conventions in naming files and I/O devices. Most of these differences will show up in the ENVIRONMENT DIVISION.

7.1 THE IDENTIFICATION DIVISION

Most of the material in the IDENTIFICATION DIVISION consists of comments that introduce the program to future users who will have to maintain it. A sample IDENTIFICATION DIVISION is:

```
000010 IDENTIFICATION DIVISION.
000020 PROGRAM-ID.  PAYROLL.
000030 AUTHOR. CHARLES ALLEN.
000040 INSTALLATION.  MENLO ELECTRONICS.
000050 DATE-WRITTEN.  FEBRUARY, 1980.
000060 DATE-COMPILED. FEBRUARY, 1980.
000070 SECURITY.  PERSONNEL DEPARTMENT USE ONLY.
000080*********VERSION 2.1 LAST MODIFIED APRIL, 1980********
000090*    THE PAYROLL PROGRAM COMPUTES THE PAYROLL         *
000100*    FOR THE HOURLY WORKERS AT THE MENLO PARK PLANT.  *
000110*    SEE THE COMMENTS IN THE DATA DIVISION FOR DETAILS*
000120*    ON THE USE OF THE VARIABLES IN THE PROGRAM.      *
000130****************************************************
```

A quick glance at the IDENTIFICATION DIVISION tells us who wrote the program and what it is used for. The programmer's name is available in case we wish to contact him for further information about the program.

The basic format of the material in the IDENTIFICATION DIVISION is:

IDENTIFICATION DIVISION.

PROGRAM-ID. program-name

[AUTHOR. [comment-entry]]

[INSTALLATION. [comment-entry]]

[DATE-WRITTEN. [comment-entry]]

[DATE-COMPILED. [comment-entry]]

[SECURITY. [comment-entry]]

Most of the statements in the IDENTIFICATION DIVISION are a series of comments that describe the program. Only the first two lines are absolutely necessary. The first introduces the division, and the second names the program. The other lines may be omitted, but this is not good programming practice. The comments supplied by the other statements in this division are valuable documentation for others who will use the program after you, and they should be included.

You will notice in the above example that all of the reserved words in the division must begin in area A. The comment entries themselves begin in area B, and they may be continued to subsequent cards if necessary. The entries for a continued comment must also begin in area B.

The statements in the IDENTIFICATION DIVISION should appear in the order that is given above, although some COBOL compilers (such as IBM's) will accept them in any order. All the comment entries are printed out as they appear with one exception. The entry after DATE-COMPILED is replaced on the listing by the actual date on which your COBOL program is run.

There is one final minor point that you should notice in the IDEN-TIFICATION DIVISION. The reserved words PROGRAM-ID, DATE-COMPILED, and DATE-WRITTEN are written with hyphens between the two parts of the word. It is a very common mistake for beginners to omit these hyphens. When they do, the COBOL compiler cannot recognize the reserved word, and it will generate an error message. The error message usually looks very strange to a beginner. Aside from this minor error, however, you should have no trouble with the IDENTIFICATION DIVISION.

7.2 THE ENVIRONMENT DIVISION—CONFIGURATION SECTION

The ENVIRONMENT DIVISION describes the physical environment in which your COBOL program will be executed. It is that part of a COBOL program most likely to have to be changed when the program is taken from one machine to another. In this section and the next, we will emphasize IBM equipment. However, not all the options available in this division will be discussed. For your work in this book, you will not need all the available features. Consult your system reference manual if you are not using IBM equipment; it will tell you your computer's ENVI-RONMENT DIVISION rules and how they differ from those of other equipment.

The ENVIRONMENT DIVISION consists of a CONFIGURATION SEC-TION and an INPUT—OUTPUT SECTION. To see what the CONFIGURA-TION SECTION looks like let us start with a sample:

```
000200 ENVIRONMENT DIVISION.
000210 CONFIGURATION SECTION.
000220 SOURCE-COMPUTER. IBM-370-168.
000230 OBJECT-COMPUTER. IBM-370-145.
000240     MEMORY SIZE 256000 CHARACTERS.
000250 SPECIAL-NAMES.  SYSPUNCH IS PUNCH.
```

The CONFIGURATION SECTION is the portion of the ENVIRONMENT DIVISION that describes the machine on which the job has been created, the machine for which it is intended, and it gives us some information about the names used in the program. As in the IDENTIFICATION DIVISION, the reserved words begin in area A and the entries making up the statement begin in area B.

The general format for the CONFIGURATION SECTION of the ENVIRONMENT DIVISION is:

```
ENVIRONMENT DIVISION.

CONFIGURATION SECTION.

SOURCE-COMPUTER paragraph

OBJECT-COMPUTER paragraph

[ SPECIAL-NAMES paragraph ]
```

The format of the first entry in the CONFIGURATION SECTION is:

```
SOURCE-COMPUTER.   computer-name.
```

An example would be:

```
SOURCE-COMPUTER. IBM-370-145.
```

This entry is simply treated as a comment.

The next entry in this section is:

```
OBJECT-COMPUTER. computer-name.
```

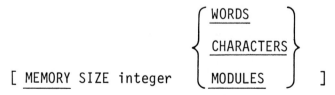

```
                            ⎧ WORDS      ⎫
                            ⎨ CHARACTERS ⎬
[ MEMORY SIZE integer       ⎩ MODULES    ⎭   ]
```

The computer may treat this material as comments. If you are operating IBM equipment and specify that the OBJECT-COMPUTER is an IBM 370, then the object program that the COBOL compiler produces will be in IBM 370 machine language and can only be run on an IBM 370. A sample entry for this section might be:

```
OBJECT-COMPUTER.   IBM-370-145
        MEMORY SIZE 256000 CHARACTERS.
```

The final paragraph in this section is the SPECIAL-NAMES paragraph. The format of the SPECIAL-NAMES **paragraph** is:

SPECIAL-NAMES.

    [function-name IS mnemonic-name]

    [CURRENCY SIGN IS literal]

    [DECIMAL-POINT IS COMMA].

The main purpose of the SPECIAL-NAMES paragraph is to equate system-defined function names with mnemonic names defined by the author of the program. This feature can be used to make it easier to transfer a COBOL job from one machine to another. Suppose, for example, we had a COBOL program that did a great deal of punched card output to the standard system punch file. If the program had been written for an IBM System 360 operating under the system called DOS, the system punch would have been referred to as SYSPCH. If we wished to take it to an IBM System 370 operating under OS, the system punch would have to be referred to as SYSPUNCH. To convert the COBOL program from one machine to another, we would have to find every place in the program where the word SYSPCH occurs and replace it by SYS-PUNCH. This is not difficult, just tedious. It is also likely that you will not find every SYSPCH and that you will have to run the job more than once to eliminate all the errors.

Suppose, however, that we had used the SPECIAL-NAMES paragraph in this way:

SYSPCH IS PUNCH

Then, every place in our program where we want to refer to SYSPCH, we refer to PUNCH instead. Then when the time comes to convert the program from one system to another, we replace the first card with one that reads:

SYSPUNCH IS PUNCH

This is the only change that has to be made because it tells our program that every time it refers to a file called PUNCH, it is talking about SYS-PUNCH.

The CURRENCY SIGN sentence is used to change the printer character used to print the currency sign. This is useful if your COBOL program is for use in a country where a currency symbol other than $ is used. You may redefine the currency symbol as any printer character *except* 0–9, A–Z, or the special characters * – , . ; ( ) + " or '.

The DECIMAL-POINT IS COMMA sentence is used to cause COBOL to replace the decimal point with the comma and vice versa when doing edited numeric output. For instance, the American form used to represent one hundred thousand dollars is:

$100,000.00

But in European usage the period is used as a separator and the comma is used as we use the decimal point. If we had done this, we would have:

$100.000,00

and COBOL would handle this automatically.

7.3 THE ENVIRONMENT DIVISION—INPUT—OUTPUT SECTION

The INPUT–OUTPUT SECTION is the most important section of the ENVIRONMENT DIVISION. It handles the linkage between the internal names given to a file and the external names and devices provided by the computer. For instance, in this book, we have been dealing with a file called the MASTER-FILE. However, in the programs we have written so far, we have not said just what type of device the MASTER-FILE is stored on or what the name given to this device by the computer might be. The answers to these questions are supplied in the INPUT–OUTPUT SECTION of the ENVIRONMENT DIVISION.

Consider this example of the INPUT–OUTPUT SECTION:

```
000300 INPUT-OUTPUT SECTION.
000310 FILE-CONTROL.
000320     SELECT MASTER-FILE ASSIGN TO UT-S-OLDMAST.
000330     SELECT SORT-FILE ASSIGN TO UT-S-SORTIN.
000340     SELECT REPORT-FILE ASSIGN TO UT-S-SORTOUT.
```

This INPUT–OUTPUT SECTION has been used with the file definitions in every program you have run so far. The definitions in these SELECT statements establish the link between the internal file names, such as MASTER-FILE, and the external names. Each computer system will have its own conventions for the external names. If you take your COBOL program to a different machine, then you have to change the SELECT statements to fit the format in use on that particular machine. If your instructor is having you run your programs on a computer other than an

IBM 370 operating under OS/VS, check the SELECT statements that appear in one of your old programs. They may be different from the ones given above.

The general format of the INPUT—OUTPUT SECTION is:

```
INPUT-OUTPUT SECTION.

FILE-CONTROL.

    SELECT [ OPTIONAL ] file-name

    ASSIGN TO system-name-1.
```

As with the other ENVIRONMENT DIVISION reserved words, you must be careful to include the required hyphens. The file name referred to in the SELECT phrase is the internal file name used by your COBOL program. It is up to you to choose this name within the limitations imposed by COBOL. The word OPTIONAL means that the file may occasionally be missing when the program is run. In this case, COBOL will treat any reading of this file as if there were an end of data on that particular unit.

It may seem odd to you that a file may be missing, but there are a number of occasions when this might be useful. Suppose we had a file that was to contain error corrections to the MASTER-FILE, but on a particular run of our program, there were no errors. If the file were declared OPTIONAL, then there would be no problem. On some systems, such as IBM 370 OS systems, the operating system handles the assignment of files, and the word OPTIONAL is treated as a comment. Check your own system's COBOL manual for details as to how your computer will handle this situation.

The system-name-1 in the ASSIGN phrase will be handled differently by different computer systems and different operating systems. IBM 370 OS systems have adopted external file names of the format:

```
dev-org-name
```

In this format, the word *dev* stands for device type. The device types are:

```
DA (Direct Access) for mass storage devices
UT (UTility) for utility devices
UR (Unit Record) for unit record devices
```

A direct access device is a disk file, access to which can be gained either sequentially or by going directly to the desired record. A unit record device is a device such as a card reader or a line printer. It is unlikely that you will use a UT device directly on a large machine. A large computer does not usually allow user's programs to read directly or print directly on such devices. The reading and printing is handled by the operating system of the machine, which schedules such activity at a convenient time. In your programs you will generally use files that are utility devices, which refers to any sequentially accessed device.

The word *org* stands for data organization. There are two types possible.

```
S   sequential organization
D   direct organization
```

Sequential organization means that access to the data must be gained sequentially, one record after another. Direct organization means that it is possible to go directly to the desired record without first going through all of the records in front of it. In this book, we will be using mostly sequential organization.

The word *name* refers to the name you have put on your data definition card (DD card in the job control language for IBM systems) to define the file. Some examples of SELECT statements are:

```
SELECT MASTER-FILE ASSIGN TO UT-S-OLDMAST.
SELECT ACCOUNT ASSIGN TO DA-D-CUSTOM.
```

These statements begin in area B.

7.4 IDENTIFICATION AND ENVIRONMENT PROGRAM EXAMPLE

In this section we present a use of the IDENTIFICATION and ENVIRONMENT divisions. This will not be a complete program like the others we have had to this point. The IDENTIFICATION and ENVIRONMENT divisions only present definitions for the rest of the program, and we would need a PROCEDURE DIVISION to accompany them.

The code used with the definitions for the top of the deck supplied by your instructor to run your programs (at least if he is using an IBM machine) is:

```
000010 IDENTIFICATION DIVISION.
000020 PROGRAM-ID.  FILEDEF.
000030 AUTHOR.  NORMAN LYONS.
000040 DATE-WRITTEN. JANUARY, 1980.
000050 DATE-COMPILED.  JANUARY, 1980.
000060 SECURITY.  NONE.
000070******VERSION 1.0 - LAST MODIFIED JANUARY,  1980******************
000080*    THE FILEDEF PROGRAM PROVIDES THE BASIC FILE DEFINITIONS     *
000090*    AND RECORD DEFINITIONS FOR INFORMATION RETRIEVAL USE OF THE *
```

```
000100*    STUDENT FILE.  IN THIS WAY, INEXPERIENCED COBOL USERS DO NOT*
000110*    HAVE TO WRITE THEIR OWN DEFINITIONS, BUT CAN              *
000120*    USE THOSE PROVIDED BY THEIR INSTRUCTOR.                   *
000130*************************************************************************
000140 ENVIRONMENT DIVISION.
000150 CONFIGURATION SECTION.
000160 SOURCE-COMPUTER.  IBM-370-145.
000170 OBJECT-COMPUTER.  IBM-370-145.
000180 INPUT-OUTPUT SECTION.
000190 FILE-CONTROL.
000200     SELECT MASTER-FILE ASSIGN TO UT-S-OLDMAST.
000210     SELECT REPORT-FILE ASSIGN TO UT-S-SORTOUT.
000220     SELECT SORT-FILE ASSIGN TO UT-S-SORTIN.
```

The coding above is mostly self-explanatory. Notice in the FILE-CONTROL section the choice of names assigned for the external names for the REPORT-FILE and the SORT-FILE. These were not arbitrarily chosen by the programmer, but they are the names required by the IBM sort package. You may find this type of restriction placed on your freedom to choose the names in the ENVIRONMENT DIVISION.

The material in the ENVIRONMENT DIVISION is very dependent on the particular machine with which you are working. Be sure to consult the manual for your machine and perhaps seek help from knowledgeable programmers. The material in this section is not difficult to master, although it may look a little confusing at first. In your programs, you will probably find that you pay very little attention to this part of your code. You will adopt a few standard techniques and use them for most of your programs without reference to any manuals at all.

STUDY EXERCISES

1. Why is it important to make full use of the comment facilities allowed in the IDENTIFICATION DIVISION and the ENVIRONMENT DIVISION?

2. Which statements are absolutely necessary in the IDENTIFICATION DIVISION?

3. Which statements are absolutely necessary in the ENVIRONMENT DIVISION?

4. What is the function of the SELECT statements?

5. Write the IDENTIFICATION DIVISION for a program to print a student directory for Balboa Junior College.

6. Why is the SPECIAL-NAMES paragraph useful?

7. Write a FILE-CONTROL section for your computer system that has three files called AUDIT-FILE, MASTER-FILE, and TRANSACTION-FILE.

8. What is an OPTIONAL file?

8 8
8 8 THE DATA DIVISION
8 8
 8 8
8 8
 8 8
8 8
 8 8
8 8
 8 8
8 8
 8 8

8.0 INTRODUCTION

The DATA DIVISION gives the descriptions of the files and the data used by your COBOL program. It is one of the most difficult parts of COBOL for a beginner to master, and it is very important because no COBOL program can be run without a DATA DIVISION of some kind. Because of the difficulty that beginners have in dealing with this section, we have saved it until a relatively late stage in your study of COBOL. By now, you have run enough programs and gained enough maturity in programming to be able to handle the concepts in the DATA DIVISION without major problems.

The DATA DIVISION has several purposes. First, it describes the structure of the data records used by your program. The computer must know the names of the variables you are using and the order in which they appear within a record. It must also know what type of data (alphabetic, numeric, etc.) these fields contain. In addition to describing the structure of the records we use, it is also possible to set up temporary fields that we can use to hold intermediate results. Finally, it is also possible to set up special output reports in the DATA DIVISION that we may want to produce.

The DATA DIVISION appears immediately after the IDENTIFICATION and ENVIRONMENT divisions in your COBOL program. For example, look at the DATA DIVISION that follows. It describes two files, an account card file and a sort file, which is used as an intermediate file for the sorting of data. It also contains a WORKING-STORAGE SECTION, which defines variables used for temporary purposes such as counters and intermediate results of computation. Unlike some computer languages, COBOL requires that every variable you use be explicitly defined.

SAMPLE DATA DIVISION

```
000500 DATA DIVISION.
000510 FILE SECTION.
000520 FD   ACCOUNT LABEL RECORDS ARE OMITTED.
000530 01   ACCOUNT-CARD.
000540      02   CUSTOMER-NUMBER          PICTURE X(10).
000550      02   CUSTOMER-NAME            PICTURE X(20).
000560      02   BILL-DATE.
000570           03   MM                  PICTURE 99.
000580           03   DD                  PICTURE 99.
000590           03   YY                  PICTURE 99.
000600      02   FILLER                   PICTURE XXXX.
000610      02   AMOUNT                   PICTURE 99999V99.
000620 SD   SORT-FILE DATA RECORDS ARE SORT-RECORDS.
000630 01   SORT-RECORDS.
000640      02   CUSTOMER-NUMBER          PICTURE X(10).
000650      02   FILLER                   PICTURE X(37).
000660 WORKING-STORAGE SECTION.
000670 77   COUNTER                       PICTURE 99.
```

As you can see from the example, the DATA DIVISION takes the form of an outline with the structure of the data records presented in outline format. This chapter will tell you in detail how to prepare the DATA DIVISION.

The DATA DIVISION is divided into three sections, and each of the three sections has its own special type of definitions. The general layout of the DATA DIVISION is:

```
DATA DIVISION.

FILE SECTION.

file-section-entries

WORKING-STORAGE SECTION.

working-storage-section-entries

REPORT SECTION.

report-section-entries
```

The FILE SECTION contains the descriptions of the data files and the sort files used by your program. Each description begins with a header describing the file itself, and then the structure of the record or records associated with the file is given. Each file used by your COBOL program must be defined in the FILE SECTION.

The WORKING-STORAGE SECTION sets up temporary field and record definitions that do not necessarily correspond to any data stored on an external device. This material is used to hold the intermediate results of computation and to build records for later movement to files in the FILE SECTION. The variables that we used for computation in Chapter 4 (the X1, X2, etc.) were all variables defined in the WORKING-STORAGE SECTION of the DATA DIVISION.

Finally, the REPORT SECTION contains the definitions of reports we may want to print out using the report writer feature of COBOL. This material will not be covered in this chapter but will be covered in Chapter 12. The report writer is a very useful feature of COBOL. It allows us to avoid a great deal of data movement and testing in the PROCEDURE DIVISION by defining the data to be printed and the format to be used in the DATA DIVISION.

These three sections make up the DATA DIVISION. They do not all have to be present, but if they do appear, they must be in the order given above. In the rest of the chapter, we will work on the contents of the entries in the individual sections.

8.1 THE WORKING-STORAGE SECTION

We will begin our discussion of the DATA DIVISION with the WORKING-STORAGE SECTION because it is easier to understand than the FILE SECTION and is a more convenient way to introduce the same concepts that we will use later. In this section you can only define temporary fields and record definitions that your program will use. These fields are not representations of data stored on some input–output device but exist only while your program is in the memory of the computer.

Here is an example of a WORKING-STORAGE SECTION:

```
001000 WORKING-STORAGE SECTION.
001010 77  CARD-COUNT          PICTURE 9999 VALUE IS ZERO.
001020 77  SUCCESS-MESSAGE     PICTURE X(20) VALUE IS 'END OF PROGRAM'.
001030 01  DATA-CARD.
001040     02  ACCOUNT-NUMBER PICTURE X(10).
001050     02  BILL-DATE.
001060         03   MM         PICTURE 99.
001070         03   DD         PICTURE 99.
001080         03   YY         PICTURE 99.
001090     02  FILLER         PICTURE X(10).
001100     02  BILL-AMOUNT    PICTURE 9999V99.
```

In this example, we have defined a number of variables. Some of them (CARD-COUNT and SUCCESS-MESSAGE) represent simple data items;

whereas DATA-CARD represents a record, and BILL-DATE represents a group of data items. This example should give you some idea how a WORKING-STORAGE SECTION is written, but you should study the definitions in this chapter to make sure you really understand how to put one together.

The WORKING-STORAGE SECTION is made up of **data description entries** that define the format of the data you will use. The general format of the data description entries we will use in this chapter is:

data description
entries

$$
\text{level-number}
\left\{
\begin{array}{c}
\text{data-name} \\
\underline{\text{FILLER}}
\end{array}
\right\}
$$

[<u>PICTURE</u> clause]

[<u>VALUE</u> clause]

[<u>BLANK</u> WHEN <u>ZERO</u> clause]

[<u>OCCURS</u> clause]

[<u>REDEFINES</u> clause]

There are a number of other options possible in this statement, but we will not discuss them until later. Even the ones here look formidable enough, but do not be intimidated. Generally, you will use only the PICTURE clause and occasionally the VALUE clause. However, you should understand the others and know when they can be useful.

The level number may be a difficult concept for beginners. In the WORKING-STORAGE SECTION we will generally use the level number 77, which means that we are defining a simple field that contains a single data item. The level numbers 1 through 49 are used to refer to a group or record structure, and are used in the same way as the numbers in an outline. A group is a set of data items that is treated as a single data item; it is referred to by its group name. The level numbers 77 and 1 must begin in area A; the level numbers 2 through 49 must begin in area B.

The data name referred to in the definition may be any legal COBOL name not already in use in the program. This data name is the variable name that we have been using in our arithmetic and I/O statements. The reserved word FILLER—used in place of the data name—has a special meaning. It means that we will not have to refer to this particular field by name. FILLER can be used to skip over certain fields in a record or to fill out the length of a data area.

8.2   THE PICTURE CLAUSE

Of the possible options after the data name, the PICTURE **clause** is   PICTURE clause
the most important. Its general format is

$$\left\{ \begin{array}{c} \underline{PICTURE} \\ \underline{PIC} \end{array} \right\} \qquad \underline{IS} \quad \texttt{character-string}$$

The character string that follows this statement describes the type and
the length of the data to be stored in the data name. To understand the
options available here, we first have to understand the types of data that
COBOL can use. There are five types:

1. Alphabetic

2. Alphanumeric

3. Numeric

4. Alphanumeric edited

5. Numeric edited

For **alphabetic** data items, the character string in the PICTURE   alphabetic
statement is made up of the letter A. For example:

```
77   FIRST-NAME   PICTURE A(20).
77   MIDDLE-INIT  PIC A.
77   ITEM-NAME PICTURE AAAAA.
```

In the first example, we see that the character string is A(20). The inclusion of the number in parentheses after the A is the same as repeating the
letter A twenty times. That means that the FIRST-NAME field can contain
up to twenty alphabetic characters. If it is shorter than this, it will be
padded on the right with blanks. Unless you specify something different,
alphabetic data items are always left justified. In the second example, we
have abbreviated the reserved word PICTURE to PIC. According to the
definition, both are legal and have the same meaning. In this example,
we only use the letter A once, which means that the MIDDLE-INIT field
can hold only a single character. In the final example, ITEM-NAME can be
up to five characters long. We could have said A(5) for its picture instead
of AAAAA if we had wished. In all of these examples, the value stored in
the variables can contain only the letters A through Z or a blank. Any
other characters are illegal in an alphabetic data item.

If we want the field to hold any characters (numbers, letters, or special characters such as punctuation), then we must define it as an **alphanumeric** item. Although we can store numbers in an alphanumeric item, the number should not be used for computation, only for display purposes. The character used in the PICTURE clause to indicate an alphanumeric item is the letter X. Consider these examples:

alphanumeric

```
77   CLASS-NAME  IS PICTURE X(10).
77   PART-NO PIC XXXXX.
```

The alphanumeric data items are also stored left-justified, and they may include any legal character in your computer's character set.

For storing **numeric** data items, our options are more complicated. We have to allow for signs and decimal points in the data. For numeric items, we can use four symbols in making up the PICTURE character string. They are:

numeric

```
S   Must appear as the first symbol if it is used.
    It means that the number is signed.  It is
    not used in figuring the length of the data item.

9   Indicates a digit position.

V   Indicates an implied decimal point. The decimal
    point does not actually appear in the data,
    and it is not used in computing the length of
    the item.

P   Represents trailing or leading zeros after the
    decimal point. It is used to change the
    magnitude of the number.
```

To see how these PICTURE items work, consider these examples:

```
77   A  IS PICTURE 999.
77   B  IS PIC S999.
77   C  PICTURE 9V99.
77   D  PICTURE S9V99.
77   E  PICTURE PPP999.
77   F  PICTURE S999PPP.
```

All the numbers have only three significant figures. The different variables are stored internally in zoned decimal format. The variable A can store any number from 0 to 999. It has no sign. The variable B can be used to store numbers from −999 to 999 because the sign is allowed. The variable C has no sign but has a decimal point; it can be used for storing numbers from 0.00 to 9.99. The variable D has both a sign and a decimal point. It can be used for storing numbers from −9.99 to 9.99. The variable E makes use of the P editing symbol to move the decimal point three places to the left. It can be used to store values from .000000 to .000999. In the variable F, we have moved the decimal point in the other direction. It can be used to store numbers ranging from −999000 to 999000.

You should avoid printing out the values stored in these numeric pictures because the data is stored in zoned decimal. The sign that appears on the last digit of the number will make the printout look rather strange (go back to Chapter 6 and see the discussion on the sign in zoned decimal). The decimal point also does not appear in the number itself and will not appear in the printout of a numeric item.

It is also possible to use the parentheses after the editing characters to cause them to be repeated. For example, we might write:

```
77  G  PIC 9(3)V9(3).
77  H  PICTURE SP(4)99.
```

The first of these means that we have three places before the decimal point and three after. We may store numbers in G ranging from 000.000 to 999.999 because G has no sign. The variable H has a sign and a scaling factor. We may store values in it ranging from −0.000099 to +0.000099.

8.3 EDITING VARIABLES IN COBOL

The alphanumeric and numeric pictures we have discussed are for the internal storage of data. They are used to specify the way the data would look inside the machine. But we also would like to be able to print the data, and for this purpose, we have a number of other editing options. To edit variables in COBOL you must move the data stored in one variable into another variable with a different PICTURE. The first edit item we will discuss is **alphanumeric edited.** For alphanumeric edited pictures, we may use these characters:

alphanumeric edited

A   Represents a position for a single alphabetic character.

X   Represents a position for any character.

9   Represents a position for a single numeric character.

B   Represents a blank inserted in the string.

0   Represents a zero inserted in the string.

Some examples of alphanumeric edited items are:

```
77  A  PICTURE XXXBXXX.
77  B  PIC 00XXX00.
77  C  X(5)BA(7).
```

The first item, A, represents a character string six characters long with a blank inserted in the middle. If we executed the following piece of COBOL code in our program:

```
MOVE  'HOTDOG'  TO A.
DISPLAY A.
```

the result would be:

```
HOT DOG
```

The PICTURE given for the variable A causes the insertion of a blank in the middle of the printout. This type of editing is sometimes called **insertion editing** because material is inserted into the data item. If we executed the following code:

insertion editing

```
MOVE 'HOTDOG' TO B.
DISPLAY B.
```

the result would be:

```
00HOT00
```

In this case, the variable B has room for only three character positions. In an alphanumeric item these three positions are counted from the left and the characters following them are dropped. In addition, the PICTURE for B causes two zeros to be placed before and after the printout. Finally, if we executed this code:

```
MOVE 'HOTDOG' TO C.
DISPLAY C.
```

the result would be:

```
HOTDO G
```

In this example we have five spaces for characters before the blank is inserted and seven after. The seven spaces after the first blank are not entirely filled, and they are padded on the right with blanks.

The alphanumeric editing capability is primarily useful for inserting blanks in character strings to improve readability. We might use it in printing out the PHONE field in the MASTER-FILE to insert a blank between the exchange number and the rest of the telephone number.

The final type of picture is the **numeric edited** picture. As with the numeric picture, there are several possible options. The characters used in describing edited numeric pictures are:

numeric edited

+ - CR DB	All of these symbols are used to indicate the sign of the item. If + is used, it means that a + is printed if the number is positive and a - is printed if the number is negative. The other signs appear only if the number is negative.
B	Means a blank is inserted.
P	Used for scaling the decimal point as in numeric.
V	Indicates an implied decimal point as in numeric.
.	Used to show the position of the decimal.
,	Used as a separator between groups of numbers.
0	Causes a 0 to be printed.
9	Represents a place for a number to be printed.
Z	Represents a place for a number to be printed. If the number is a leading zero, the position is blank.
$	Represents a dollar sign. If it is repeated, only a single $ is "floated" into the beginning of the number.
*	The check protection symbol. If it is repeated, *s are "floated" into the beginning of the number.

To see how these are used, consider these sample pictures:

```
77  A  PIC  +9999.99.
77  B  PIC  -9999.99.
77  C  PIC  +ZZZ9.99.
77  D  PIC  ZZZ9.99CR.
77  E  PIC  ZZZ9.99DB.
77  F  PIC  $9999.99.
77  G  PIC  $$$$$9.99DB.
77  H  PIC  $*****9.99
77  I  PIC  $$$$,$$$,$$9.99CR.
77  J  PIC  $999,000.00.
```

Suppose that we moved the number −1.99 to the variable A and displayed the result. The printout would be −0001.99. To test your understanding, you should try to predict what printout would result from moving data to other variables above and displaying the results. Check Fig-

FIGURE 8.1
DISPLAY Results Using
Edited Numeric Data.

DATA ITEM	PICTURE	DISPLAY RESULT
-1.99	+9999.99	-0001.99
1.99	+9999.99	+0001.99
-1.99	-9999.99	-0001.99
1.99	-9999.99	0001.99
-1.99	+ZZZ9.99	- 1.99
1.99	+ZZZ9.99	+ 1.99
.01	+ZZZ9.99	+ 0.01
-1.99	-ZZZ9.99	- 1.99
1.99	-ZZZ9.99	1.99
-1.99	ZZZ9.99CR	1.99CR
1.99	ZZZ9.99CR	1.99
-1.99	ZZZ9.99DB	1.99DB
1.99	ZZZ9.99DB	1.99
-1.99	$$$$9.99CR	$1.99CR
1000	$$$$9.99CR	$1000.00
.01	$$$$9.99CR	$0.01
11.99	$***9.99CR	$**11.99
-10.25	$***9.99CR	$**10.25CR
1.99	$$$$,$$$,$$9.99	$1.99
1000000	$$$$,$$$,$$9.99	$1,000,000.00
123	$999,000.00	$123,000.00

ure 8.1 for some results that would be printed by typical MOVE and
DISPLAY sequences.

From Figure 8.1, you should be able to see how different types of
printout can be achieved using edited numeric PICTURE statements in
COBOL. If you want the number to be printed with a sign, you should
use the + in front of the picture. If the sign is to be printed only in the
event that the number is negative, then the characters −, CR, or DB may
be used instead. Figure 8.1 also shows some examples of **floating inser-**   floating insertion
tion editing. In this type of editing, certain characters may be "floated"   editing
into the beginning of the first significant digits of the number. We can see

FIGURE 8.2
Summary of PICTURE
Codes.

CODE	MEANING
A	Alphabetic data item.
B	Causes insertion of a blank.
P	Causes scaling of the decimal point in a numeric item.
S	Indicates the presence of a sign in a numeric item.
V	Indicates the location of a decimal point in a numeric item. The decimal point is implied. It does not actually occupy a space in the number.
X	Alphanumeric editing symbol. It may contain any allowable character from the character set.
Z	Used in numeric editing. It represents either a position for a number, or a blank if that position is occupied by a leading zero.
9	Used in numeric or alphanumeric editing. Represents a digit position.
0	Used in numeric and alphanumeric editing. Causes insertion of a zero.
,	Used to insert commas into numeric character strings to improve readability.
.	Represents the decimal point in edited numeric items.
+ − CR DB	These are sign characters. They are mutually exclusive. If the data item is positive, the last three sign characters will not be printed if used. They represent negative amounts. If a + is used as an editing character and the item is negative, then a negative sign will be printed.
*	The check protection symbol.
$	The currency symbol.

where dollar signs and the check protection symbol, *, have been floated in. In COBOL, it is also quite easy to insert commas into a digit string. We can see an example near the bottom of Figure 8.1 where the number 1000000 is edited to produce $1,000,000.00. If the number is of smaller magnitude, the commas will not be printed, but the field for the number will still take up the same width on the print line. This is to ensure decimal point alignment when columns of numbers of different magnitudes are printed under this PICTURE. Study Figure 8.1 carefully and run a few programs of your own to test the different edited numeric pictures.

The material on edited numeric pictures gives you some idea of the way in which we can use the PICTURE phrase to describe and alter data. This topic will be discussed more fully in the section on editing techniques in COBOL. Figure 8.2 summarizes the principal COBOL PICTURE editing symbols and explains their meanings. You may want to use this list as a handy reference for your later work in COBOL.

8.4 RECORDS AND GROUPS

All the data we have discussed so far has made use of the level number 77. This means that we are dealing with simple data items. It would also be convenient to be able to deal with several data items at once by referring to them under a single name in a group or record. Let us suppose that we wanted to set up the record structure for a data card that would allow us to change the address of a student in our student record file. A possible example for such a card is:

COLUMNS	CONTENT
1–10	Student number
11–30	Student's full name
31–50	Student's street address
51–70	Student's city of residence
71–72	Student's state of residence using the post office's standard two-letter state name abbreviations
73–77	Zip code of the student's residence
78–80	A special three-character card code

In COBOL the record description for the format of this card might be written in this fashion:

```
01   ADDRESS-CHANGE.
     02   STUDENT-NO        PIC X(10).
     02   FULL-NAME         PIC X(20).
     02   ADDRESS.
          03   STREET            PIC X(20).
          03   CITY              PIC X(20).
          03   STATE             PIC X(2).
          03   ZIP               PIC X(5).
     02   CARD-CODE         PIC X(3).
```

This example uses three different level numbers. Only the first level, 01, begins in area A. The others may begin anywhere in area B, but we have used indentation to make the subordinate relationships clearer. The whole record structure may be referred to by the variable ADDRESS-CHANGE. We may also refer to individual fields by their data names. If we wish to use STUDENT-NO in a COBOL statement in our program, it is possible to do so. Remember that if there are other variables with the data name STUDENT-NO in our program (as there are in the file definitions that go with the MASTER-FILE), then you must use the fully qualified name, STUDENT-NO OF ADDRESS-CHANGE.

Within the record ADDRESS-CHANGE, there is also a group called ADDRESS. When we refer to ADDRESS, we are referring to all four of the data names that are subordinate to it. The fact that CARD-CODE has a level number of 02 indicates that this field is not part of the group AD-DRESS since it has the same level number as ADDRESS. The idea of level numbers may seem a little strange at first, but just think of them as representing the numbers in an outline that give the structure of the record. The indenting in an outline shows which topics are subordinate to a heading. In the same way, level numbers in a COBOL record or group show which data items can be referred to by a single name because they are subordinate to that name.

If the record ADDRESS-CHANGE referred to a data card, it would show us the positioning of the fields on the data card. In the first ten columns of the card, we would expect to find the student number. In the next twenty columns, we would find the full name and so on. In this example, the next field begins where the last one left off. This is not always the case when we are dealing with a record. Suppose we had a card format for a card that looked like this:

COLUMNS	CONTENT
1–10	Student number
11–30	Full name
40–41	Age
51–56	Birthday in mmddyy format

We would like to write the definition for a record structure to describe this card in the same way we did for ADDRESS-CHANGE. But now we have a problem. One field does not begin where another leaves off. We could get around this by defining the fields like the age field to be eleven characters long, but this could cause problems in other ways. We have no guarantee that there will not be other characters on the card in columns 31 to 39. We can get around this problem by using FILLER. A sample record structure for this information might be:

```
01   AGE-DATA.
     02   STUDENT-NO      PIC X(10).
     02   FULL-NAME       PIC X(20).
     02   FILLER          PIC X(9).
     02   AGE             PIC 99.
     02   FILLER          PIC X(9).
     02   BIRTHDAY.
          03   MM         PIC 99.
          03   DD         PIC 99.
          03   YY         PIC 99.
```

The reserved word FILLER may be repeated as many times as desired in a record or group to align the fields properly. The PICTURE with the FILLER tells the computer how long the field is. The use of FILLER does not necessarily mean that the field is blank. We can also use FILLER to skip over fields which are of no interest to us. This can save a lot of time and space in writing out record definitions.

8.5   ADDITIONAL DATA DESCRIPTION ENTRIES

The PICTURE clause has required a great deal of discussion because there are so many options associated with it. The only way to really understand its use, however, is to practice with it. The rest of the discussion of data description entries is much easier. The next item is the BLANK WHEN ZERO **clause** which is simply defined as:

BLANK WHEN ZERO
clause

```
BLANK WHEN ZERO
```

This clause is used with numeric edited items as in this example:

```
77 BILL-AMOUNT      PIC $$$$,$$9.99 BLANK WHEN ZERO.
```

This means that if this data field contains a zero value, then the data field is blank. This is useful when printing large tables of data when zero values are frequent. It allows the zero values to be blanked out, and it highlights the nonzero values.

Another useful item is the VALUE **clause.** Its definition is: VALUE clause

```
VALUE IS literal
```

The VALUE clause allows us to assign initial values to a data name when the program is first loaded into the computer. Do not confuse this with a MOVE statement. A MOVE statement is performed when the PROCEDURE DIVISION of your program is executed. The VALUE clause assigns a value even before your program is executed. If some code in your program changes the initial value you assigned to this variable, then the original value is lost for the duration of this particular computer run. Here is an example of the use of the VALUE clause:

```
77 COUNT-STUDENTS    PIC 99  VALUE IS 0.
77 MORE-DATA         PIC XXX VALUE IS 'YES'.
```

In the first line we have used the VALUE phrase to initialize a counter to 0. This is perhaps the most common use of VALUE. In the second line we have used the VALUE phrase to initialize the alphanumeric variable MORE-DATA to YES. This prevents our having to perform a MOVE statement in the PROCEDURE DIVISION to accomplish the same results. VALUE phrases are also used to insert constant values into print lines for display by your program.

Another useful entry is the OCCURS clause; it allows us to repeat individual pieces of data or even whole groups of data in a record. Consider this example:

```
01  GRADE-CARD.
    02  STUDENT-NO              PICTURE X(10).
    02  COURSE-GRADES OCCURS 6 TIMES.
        03  COURSE-NO           PICTURE X(6).
        03  UNITS               PICTURE 99.
        03  GRADE               PICTURE 9V99.
```

This record GRADE-CARD lets us describe a table for the student's grade information to the COBOL program. The group COURSE-GRADES is repeated six times by the OCCURS statement, and each of the six times can be thought of as corresponding to one of the lines in a six-line table.

If the table represents a student's grade information, then the card (or other record) for this table would have the format

585010987BA543203370BA983404250BA233103260CS543602350PE978701300MT450903330

Student Grade
Information
Student Number:
585010987

COURSE NUMBER	UNITS	GRADE
BA5432	03	3.7
BA9834	04	2.5
BA2331	03	2.6
CS5436	02	3.5
PE9787	01	3.0
MT4509	03	3.3

Notice that the fields are all run together but that the alignment of the fields in the GRADE-CARD record description tells where one leaves off and another begins.

The general format of the OCCURS **clause** is:

OCCURS clause

```
OCCURS [ integer-1 TO ] integer-2 TIMES

      [ DEPENDING ON data-name-1 ]
```

As we have seen, the OCCURS clause is used in a data description entry to set up tables or simply to cause a particular data item to be repeated a number of times. It cannot be used with a data item at level 01 or level 77. OCCURS clauses can also be nested up to three times. This means that each inner OCCURS is repeated the number of times specified by an outer OCCURS clause. Another restriction on the use of OCCURS clauses is that they cannot be used on the same level with a VALUE IS clause.

To gain access to a data item described by an OCCURS clause, it is necessary to use **subscripts**. A subscript is either an unsigned integer variable or an unsigned integer constant that represents the line in the table that we are talking about. In the PROCEDURE DIVISION of the program containing the GRADE-CARD definition, we could have executed this line:

subscripts

```
MOVE 'BA534203270' TO COURSE-GRADES (3).
```

This would have set the value of the COURSE-NO in level 3 to BA5342, UNITS to 03, and GRADE to 300. You must be careful in using subscripts with names that have to be qualified. If COURSE-GRADES was not a unique name in your program and you wanted to talk about the third line in the COURSE-GRADES table, you would have to write it as:

```
COURSE-GRADES OF GRADE-CARD (3)
```

giving the subscript at the end of the fully qualified name. This approach seems backwards to most students (and to the author), but this is the way COBOL handles it. You should also note that there is a space between the word GRADE-CARD and the parenthesis that starts the subscript. This is required, and COBOL will issue an error message if you leave it out.

    We use subscripts in a similar way when we are dealing with multiple OCCURS clauses in our data definitions. An OCCURS clause for a single variable defines a single line of data. If we use a double set of OCCURS clauses in a data definition, then we can consider ourselves to be defining a table. Consider this sample record definition:

```
01   GRADE-TABLE.
     02   CLASS OCCURS 4 TIMES.
          03   GRADE OCCURS 5 TIMES PICTURE 99.
```

This record could be used for building a grade summary table to give the number of grades in each category (A, B, C, D, and F) given to each of four classes (freshman, sophomore, junior, and senior) in the university. The table might look like this:

	A	B	C	D	F
Freshman					
Sophomore					
Junior					
Senior					

To gain access to a particular element in this table, we would have to use a double subscript. For instance, if we wanted to display the number of Bs given to sophomores, we could write a line in our COBOL program that said:

```
DISPLAY GRADE-TABLE (2, 2).
```

Be sure to leave a space after the word GRADE and one after the comma in the first subscript. The first subscript gives the row number, and the second gives the column number.

    A final useful feature in the data description entry is the REDE-   REDEFINES statement

FINES **statement.** It gives us a way of redefining an area of storage with a different PICTURE than was originally declared. Consider this example:

```
05  A                       PICTURE 99999.
05  B  REDEFINES A          PICTURE XXXXX.
05  C  REDEFINES A          PICTURE AAAAA.
```

The items being redefined must all be at the same level in the record. We cannot use REDEFINES at level 01 or level 77. The items A, B, and C above all occupy the same space in the computer, so the use of REDE-FINES saves storage. When we refer to the variable A, we are talking about a data item with a numeric picture. When we talk about the variable B, we are talking about an alphanumeric picture, and when we talk about C, we are talking about an item with an alphabetic picture. It is important to keep straight just what data we have stored in the area so that we do not cause errors in trying to compute with it or print it. We can redefine a data area as many times as we want, but all of the redefinitions should refer back to the original data area (some compilers, notably those of IBM, will let you refer back to any previous variable name in the chain of redefinitions). The first data item in the chain of REDEFINES should not contain an OCCURS clause, but the others may.

The REDEFINES statement does save space in the machine, but this is not really its purpose on larger machines. It can be used as a way to look at the same data area in different ways for different purposes. Suppose that in our student record system, we wanted to define the format of change cards for students that would allow them to change their address or change their college and major. A code appearing on the card would tell the computer what kind of change record the card represented. An example of the instructions for the card format is:

COLUMNS	CONTENT
Column 1–10	Student's identification number
Column 11–13	Special card code. These columns contain the characters ADR if the card is an address change card and the characters MAJ if the card is a major change card

FORMAT 1 ADDRESS CHANGE CARD

Column 14–33	Student's new street address
Column 34–53	Student's new city
Column 54–55	Student's new state
Column 56–60	Student's new zip code

FORMAT 2 MAJOR CHANGE CARD

Column 14–33   Student's new college

Column 34–53   Student's new major field of study

All of this data would not be present on a single card. Any given data card would either be an address change card or major change card. If a student wanted to change both address and major, he or she would have to file two cards. A possible data definition for these cards is:

```
01   CHANGE-CARD.
     02   STUDENT-NO        PICTURE X(10).
     02   CARD-TYPE         PICTURE X(3).
     02   ADDRESS.
          03   STREET       PICTURE X(20).
          03   CITY         PICTURE X(20).

          03   STATE            PICTURE XX.
          03   ZIP              PICTURE X(5).
     02   COLLEGE-INFO REDEFINES ADDRESS.
          03   COLLEGE          PICTURE X(20).
          03   MAJOR            PICTURE X(20).
          03   FILLER           PICTURE X(7).
```

In the CHANGE-CARD example, we would use the CARD-TYPE field as a flag to tell us whether we were dealing with an address change or with a major and college change. Using an IF statement, we could query this flag for each data card we read in to see if we should use the variables in the ADDRESS group or in the COLLEGE-INFO group.

Another handy way to use REDEFINES is in conjunction with the OCCURS clause. We can use it to redefine a data area so that we can use it either as a single block or as a group of individual items such as digits or alphabetic characters. Recall from Chapter 4 using the DIVIDE statement to check for errors in an account number. Suppose we had a five-digit account number and one check digit was added to test for mispunching and another check digit was added to check for transposition errors. We could set up the data areas to handle this checking as follows:

```
77   X                    PICTURE 99999.
77   Y                    PICTURE 99999.
77   Z                    PICTURE 99999.
01   TEST-NUMBER.
     02   NUMBR            PICTURE 9(7).
     02   D REDEFINES NUMBR  OCCURS 10 TIMES PICTURE 9.
```

Then in our PROCEDURE DIVISION we could execute this code:

```
MOVE STUDENT-NO TO NUMBR.
ADD D (1), D (2), D (3), D (4), D (5), D (6) GIVING X.
DIVIDE X BY 10 GIVING Y REMAINDER Z.
IF Z IS NOT EQUAL TO ZERO PERFORM DIGIT-ERROR.
ADD D (1), D (3), D (5), D (7) GIVING X.
DIVIDE X BY 10 GIVING Y REMAINDER Z.
IF Z IS NOT EQUAL TO ZERO PERFORM TRANSPOSITION-ERROR.
```

This code would perform the tests for both erroneous digit and a transposition error in the manner described in Chapter 4.

8.6 DATA EDITING

Editing data is an important consideration in the commercial use of COBOL. We want to be able to specify the exact format of different types of data. COBOL allows a great deal more flexibility in this area than other computer languages and offers editing capabilities specifically designed for commercial data processing applications.

As we have seen in Section 8.3, editing in COBOL is accomplished by moving the data in one variable to another variable with a different PICTURE. In the process of moving the data, COBOL also edits it. In this section, we will introduce a new type of MOVE statement that greatly simplifies the moving and editing of data. This statement is called MOVE CORRESPONDING **statement,** and its basic format is:

MOVE
CORRESPONDING
statement

$$\underline{\text{MOVE}} \left\{ \begin{array}{l} \underline{\text{CORRESPONDING}} \\ \text{CORR} \end{array} \right\} \text{identifier-1} \ \underline{\text{TO}} \ \text{identifier-2}$$

The MOVE CORRESPONDING option behaves just like the ordinary MOVE except that it is used for transferring data between groups and records rather than between simple data items.

To get an idea how the MOVE CORRESPONDING works, we shall take a simple example. Suppose we had two records, and we wanted to move certain data fields in one record to the other record. The two records are called STUDENT-CARD and PRINT-LINE, and their definitions are:

```
01  STUDENT-CARD.
    02  STUDENT-NO        PIC 999999.
    02  STUDENT-NAME      PIC X(20).
    02  ADDRESS1          PIC X(20).
    02  COLLEGE           PIC X(20).
    02  PHONE             PIC X(7).
    02  BIRTHDAY.
        03  MM            99.
        03  DD            99.
        03  YY            99.

01  PRINT-LINE.
    02  STUDENT-NO        PIC 999B999.
    02  FILLER            PIC X(3) VALUE IS SPACES.
    02  STUDENT-NAME      PIC X(20).
    02  FILLER            PIC X(3) VALUE IS SPACES.
    02  PHONE             PIC XXXBXXX.
    02  BIRTHDAY.
        03  FILLER        PIC X(3) VALUE IS SPACES.
        03  YY            PIC 99.
        03  FILLER        PIC X VALUE IS SPACES.
        03  MM            PIC 99.
```

The two records are not the same length, and they do not appear to contain the same information. We might use the STUDENT-CARD record for describing the information on a certain student data card, whereas the PRINT-LINE record might be used for printing the information derived from the card. Suppose we wanted to move data from the first record to the second. One approach might be to try the statement:

```
MOVE STUDENT-CARD TO PRINT-LINE.
```

But this would give us strange results. What would happen is that the data in STUDENT-CARD would simply be transferred from STUDENT-CARD to PRINT-LINE without regard to whether it was being moved to the proper place. The second approach would be to use the series of statements:

```
MOVE STUDENT-NO OF STUDENT-CARD TO STUDENT-NO OF
    PRINT-LINE.
MOVE STUDENT-NAME OF STUDENT-CARD TO STUDENT-NAME
    OF PRINT-LINE.
MOVE PHONE OF STUDENT-CARD TO PHONE OF PRINT-LINE.
MOVE YY OF STUDENT-CARD TO YY OF PRINT-LINE.
MOVE MM OF STUDENT-CARD TO MM OF PRINT-LINE.
```

This approach works, and the data will be moved and aligned properly. It is also rather tedious because it requires the use of five MOVE statements. However, these five MOVE statements can be replaced by a single MOVE CORRESPONDING statement:

```
MOVE CORRESPONDING STUDENT-CARD TO PRINT-LINE.
```

This single MOVE will have the same effect. A MOVE CORRESPONDING will move fields in the first record to those with the corresponding names in the second record. The fields do not have to be in the same order in both records; they do not have to have the same PICTURE; and all fields do not have to be present in both records. There are, however, some restrictions. The fields have to have the same level numbers to be considered corresponding, and fields that include an OCCURS statement and their subordinate fields are not considered to be corresponding. But aside from these exceptions, you will find the MOVE CORRESPONDING a very powerful tool in COBOL. Because we have the MOVE CORRESPONDING statement, we have used the same field names in the different records that we have applying to the MASTER-FILE.

We will now discuss some specific examples of editing and ways in which we can use COBOL to produce the kind of output we want. In alphanumeric editing, we have already mentioned that the PICTURE characters we can use are restricted to A, X, 9, B, and 0. Suppose, for example, we had a social security number with a picture:

```
02  SOC-SEC-NO          PICTURE 999999999.
```

and we wanted to print it out with spaces in the appropriate places. We could define another variable like:

```
77  SOC-SEC-NO1         PICTURE 999B99B9999.
```

Suppose that the social security number stored in the field was 585010795. To insert the spaces, all we have to do is perform:

```
MOVE SOC-SEC-NO TO SOC-SEC-NO1.
```

Then when we display SOC-SEC-NO1, we will get:

```
585 01 0795
```

We begin running into problems if we want to insert characters that do not appear as options in COBOL's alphanumeric editing. For instance, if we display the value stored in BIRTHDAY OF MASTER-RECORD in the MASTER-FILE, all the digits are run together. If the student's birthday is July 14, 1957, then the result printed will be 071457. Suppose we wanted to print this date out in a more standard form 07/14/ 57 with slashes inserted to separate the numbers for month, day, and year. One way to do this would be to set up a dummy record in WORKING-STORAGE like this:

```
01   RECORD1.
     02   BIRTHDAY.
          03   MM          PIC 99.
          03   FILLER      PIC X VALUE IS '/'.
          03   DD          PIC 99.
          03   FILLER      PIC X VALUE IS '/'.
          03   YY          PIC 99.
```

Then in our program we could execute the code

```
MOVE CORRESPONDING BIRTHDAY OF MASTER-RECORD TO
     BIRTHDAY OF RECORD1.
DISPLAY BIRTHDAY OF RECORD1.
```

If the value stored in BIRTHDAY OF MASTER-RECORD was 071457, then the result displayed by our program will be 07/14/57. This approach of using FILLER to contain characters we wish to insert in a data field can be very useful! for editing special characters into a character string.

Another problem arises when we want to insert characters into the middle of a field. In the MASTER-FILE we have a field for the telephone number that has an X(7) picture. Thus, a student's phone number might be displayed as 7443817. But the normal way of printing a phone number is with the first three digits separated from the last four by a hyphen, as in 744-3817. To accomplish this, we could use this type of a structure in WORKING-STORAGE:

```
01   PHONE-NUM.
     02   XCHANGE      PIC XXX.
     02   NUM          PIC XXXX.

01   PHONE-NUM-1.
     02   XCHANGE      PIC XXX.
     02   FILLER       PIC X VALUE IS '-'.
     02   NUM          PIC XXXX.
```

Then we could have these lines in our program:

```
MOVE PHONE OF MASTER-RECORD TO PHONE-NUM.
MOVE CORRESPONDING PHONE-NUM-1 TO PHONE-NUM-1.
DISPLAY PHONE-NUM-1.
```

If the PHONE OF MASTER-RECORD field contained 7443817, then these lines of code would cause a 744-3817 to be printed out. In this segment of code, we have extended the ideas of the previous example slightly. If you want to break up a data item and insert characters in the middle, you must perform two steps in COBOL: first, break the item up, and second, insert the characters.

Section 8.3 covered the possible options in numeric editing fairly completely. Generally, in numeric editing the possibilities provided by the COBOL compiler are sufficient for most applications. To do any type of editing in COBOL, you should be familiar with the rules and the results for performing any given action. For instance, it is not possible to move an alphabetic field into a numeric field and to be able to perform any computation with the results. Most COBOL compilers will flag any attempt to perform this type of action. Figure 8.3 gives a summary of the different types of moves possible and tells whether these are legal MOVE actions in COBOL. You must be careful when using the MOVE statement. For instance, it is legal to move a group item to any other type of item, but the results may be strange (at least to you) because no conversion takes place with such a move. Use the information in Figure 8.3 if you have any questions about what takes place during a MOVE.

FIGURE 8.3
Summary of Legal MOVE
Actions.

SENDING FIELD	RECEIVING FIELD					
	GROUP	ALPHA-BETIC	ALPHA-NUMERIC	NUMERIC	ALPHA-NUMERIC EDITED	NUMERIC EDITED
Group	Yes	Yes	Yes	Yes[1]	Yes[1]	Yes[1]
Alphabetic	Yes	Yes	Yes	No	Yes	No
Alphanumeric	Yes	Yes	Yes	Yes[2]	Yes	Yes[2]
Numeric	Yes	No	Yes[3]	Yes	Yes[3]	Yes
Alphanumeric Edited	Yes	Yes	Yes	No	Yes	No
Numeric Edited	Yes	No	Yes	No	Yes	No

[1] No conversion takes place in this move.
[2] Legal if all characters are numeric. No sign or decimal point can appear.
[3] Allowed only if the number is an unsigned integer.

8.7   THE FILE SECTION

The FILE SECTION is similar to the WORKING-STORAGE section in that it contains data description entries, but in the FILE SECTION the data description entries must all be records or subordinate to records, and each of these records must be linked with a particular file. The basic entries that describe the files our COBOL program will use are in this section. Here is an example of the FILE SECTION:

```
DATA DIVISION.
FILE SECTION.
FD ADDRESS-CHANGE BLOCK CONTAINS 800 CHARACTERS,
    RECORD CONTAINS 80 CHARACTERS, LABEL RECORDS
    ARE STANDARD, DATA RECORD IS ADDRESS-CARD.
01 ADDRESS-CARD.
    02  STUDENT-NO        PICTURE X(10).
    02  STREET            PICTURE X(20).
    02  CITY              PICTURE X(20).
    02  STATE             PICTURE XX.
    02  ZIP               PICTURE X(5).
    02  FILLER            PICTURE X(23).
```

The last part of this FILE SECTION has a familiar-looking record description entry. Only the header material after the letters FD looks unfamiliar. The FD introduces a file description entry that describes the file containing the records in the following data description entry. The FD entry is actually a little more complicated than those you are likely to use in your COBOL programs. The general format of an FD **entry** is:

FD entry

```
FD  file-name

        [ BLOCK CONTAINS clause ]

        [ RECORD CONTAINS clause ]

        LABEL RECORDS clause

        [ VALUE OF clause ]

        [ DATA RECORDS clause ]
```

As the definition above shows, only the LABEL RECORDS clause is always required. The others are optional under most circumstances.
    The general format of the LABEL RECORDS **clause** is:

LABEL RECORDS
clause

$$\text{LABEL} \begin{Bmatrix} \underline{\text{RECORD}} \text{ IS} \\ \underline{\text{RECORDS}} \text{ ARE} \end{Bmatrix} \begin{Bmatrix} \underline{\text{OMITTED}} \\ \underline{\text{STANDARD}} \\ \text{data-name-1} \ [\ \text{data-name-2} \ ] \ \dots \end{Bmatrix}$$

The LABEL RECORDS clause tells what type of labels (if any) your COBOL program should expect to find on the file. The use of machine readable labels on computer files prevents data errors that might occur because the operator of the machine mounted the wrong tape or disk file.

A LABEL RECORDS clause of the form

LABEL RECORDS ARE OMITTED

means either that no label records exist on the file or that the user does not want the label records processed. On unit record files such as punch card files, there are no label records, and this form would be used. If the programmer uses this to tell COBOL not to process the label record, then the program must handle the label that is read in as the first data record on the file.

The format you are most likely to use is:

LABEL RECORDS ARE STANDARD

This notifies COBOL that the labels exist and conform to the specifications for labels on the system you are using. The computer system itself will check the label for you.

For the third format for a LABEL RECORDS clause, you might write something like this:

LABEL RECORD IS USER-LABEL

where USER-LABEL is some user-defined data area. COBOL reads the data in the label into the variable USER-LABEL, and it is the responsibility of your COBOL program to scan this area to determine whether the label is valid. Ordinarily, this type of processing is not widely used.

The BLOCK CONTAINS and the RECORD CONTAINS clauses are used together. To explain them, however, we have to explain what **blocking** records means. Programmers normally speak of two types of records in a computer file, **logical** records and **physical** records. A physical record is the data that is read in by the machine when a READ statement is issued at the machine language level. An example would be the data on a magnetic tape between two interrecord gaps that is transferred into the machine when the tape is read. You are probably wondering whether or not this physical record on the tape is the same length as the record

blocking

logical   physical

definition for that record in your COBOL program. The answer to this question is *maybe*. It is a common practice to block several records together and write them as a single physical record. The records that are blocked together are called logical records. In practice, that might mean that on our student record MASTER-FILE, the records of several students would be written together on the tape to form a single physical record.

This may seem to complicate the picture unnecessarily, but there are good reasons for blocking several logical records together into a single physical record. Let's take our MASTER-FILE records as an example. If you have counted the number of characters in one of these records, you have noted that they are 387 bytes long (because 1 byte = 1 character). Suppose that we wrote each student's record as a single physical record on a magnetic tape. How many student records could we expect to get on a single tape?

To answer this, we have to know a little about magnetic tape. It comes in varying lengths and packing densities. Normally, a reel of magnetic tape is 2,400 feet long, and data on this tape can be packed at 1,600 BPI. But we cannot pack the whole tape solid with data. There must be interrecord gaps between the physical records on the tape. These gaps give the tape drive the space it needs to start and stop when reading data. Like a home tape recorder, a computer's tape drives must be moving at a certain speed before the data can be read meaningfully (about 120 inches per second compared to $1\frac{7}{8}$ inches per second for the home recorder). This interrecord gap is about ¾ inch.

This means, then, that the space required for each student record if we wrote it as a single physical record would be

$$387 \times (1/1600) + 3/4 = 0.99 \text{ inch}$$

This does not seem like very much space. Each student's record would take up a little less than an inch of magnetic tape, and that means that we could expect to get over 29,000 student records on a tape. But notice something else. The actual data would take up less than a quarter of an inch; the gap would take up the remaining ¾ inch of the space allocated to a single record. Our tape would be 75 percent empty.

But now suppose we packed twenty student records together and wrote all twenty as a single physical record on the tape. The space required for a physical record would be:

$$20 \times 387 \times (1/1600) + 3/4 = 5.59 \text{ inches}$$

At this density, we could store 5,154 physical records on the tape which is a lot fewer physical records than before. But each physical record would contain twenty logical records, which means that we could store the records of 103,080 students instead of 29,000. Instead of 75 percent of blank tape, we would have only 13 percent. We would be storing more data and making more efficient use of tapes by using a twenty-to-one blocking factor.

There are also disadvantages to blocking records. When we block records, we must provide a **buffer** or storage area in the core memory of the computer large enough to hold the whole block of data that composes a physical record. The larger the block size we choose, the larger the buffer area we must provide. Another disadvantage is that the records in the buffer must be deblocked one at a time and sent to our COBOL program when it executes a READ statement. This requires some time and planning in the computer's operating system, although this use of resource is usually not crucial.

COBOL is notified of the presence of blocked data records through the use of the BLOCK CONTAINS and the RECORD CONTAINS clauses. The general format of the BLOCK CONTAINS **clause** is:

BLOCK CONTAINS clause

$$\text{\underline{BLOCK} CONTAINS [integer-1 \underline{TO}] integer-2} \left\{ \begin{array}{l} \text{CHARACTERS} \\ \text{\underline{RECORDS}} \end{array} \right\}$$

If the BLOCK CONTAINS clause is omitted, it is assumed that each logical record is equivalent to a physical record and that the data is not blocked. If only integer-2 in the format above is shown, then it is assumed that the block of data is exactly that size in characters or records, depending on the options chosen. If integer-1 is also present, then there may be blocks of different size on the file. Normally, only integer-2 will be used in the specification.

The RECORD CONTAINS **clause** is similar and gives information about the records that comprise the block. Its general format is:

RECORD CONTAINS clause

RECORD CONTAINS [integer-1 TO] integer-2 CHARACTERS

As in BLOCK CONTAINS clauses, integer-1 and integer-2 give the sizes of the largest and smallest records in the file when there may be more than one type of record in the file. Only integer-2 is usually present.

Another type of clause used in the FD is the VALUE OF clause. An example of this clause might be:

VALUE OF LABEL-NAME IS 'STUDENT FILE 1978'

The VALUE OF clause specifies the contents that COBOL should expect to find in one of the data areas provided by the LABEL RECORDS clauses. It is used for label checking, although on most modern computers, this clause is treated as a comment. Label checking is handled by the operating system instead of the programming language.

The general format of the VALUE OF **clause** is

$$\text{\underline{VALUE} \underline{OF} data-name-1 IS} \quad \left\{ \begin{array}{l} \text{literal-1} \\ \text{data-name-2} \end{array} \right\}$$

$$\text{[data-name-3 IS} \quad \left\{ \begin{array}{l} \text{literal-2} \\ \text{data-name-4} \end{array} \right\} \quad \text{]} \quad \text{...}$$

This clause is not likely to be one that you will use a lot, but it can be handy in certain situations.

The final type of clause we will use in the FD is the DATA REC-ORDS clause. An example might be:

```
DATA RECORD IS STUDENTS
```

This clause points to the data record associated with the file. The general format of the DATA RECORDS **clause** is

$$\text{\underline{DATA}} \quad \left\{ \begin{array}{l} \text{\underline{RECORD} IS} \\ \text{\underline{RECORDS} ARE} \end{array} \right\} \quad \text{data-name-1 [data-name-2]} \quad \text{...}$$

When there is more than one record in the file occupying the same area, the DATA RECORDS clause points them out. This clause is never re-quired and is more of a comment.

This covers the header material on the file description entry. The next item is the file description entry for a sort file. This has a slightly different header than an ordinary FD entry; otherwise it is much the same. A sample sort file description might look like this:

```
SD  CHANGE-CARDS  DATA RECORD IS CHANGE-RECORD,
    RECORD CONTAINS 80 CHARACTERS.
01  CHANGE-RECORD.
    02  STUDENT-NO        PICTURE X(10).
    02  FILLER           PICTURE X(70).
```

In this example, the file header and its entries are followed by an ordi-nary record description entry. The file description is introduced by SD signifying sort file description rather than FD. This entry begins in area A. The entries required for an SD entry are simpler than those for an FD. Notice in this example that we have only described one field, the STUDENT-NO field, and that the rest of the record is FILLER. This does not mean that the rest of record is blank, only that it is being ignored. The

data in these fields will be passed along by the SORT routine without
being changed.

The general format for an SD **entry** is:

```
SD  sort-file-name

              ⎧ RECORD IS   ⎫
   [ DATA   ⎨ RECORDS ARE ⎬   data-name-1 [data-name-2 ] ... ]
              ⎩            ⎭

   [ RECORD CONTAINS [ integer-1 TO ] integer-2 CHARACTERS ]
```

As was the case with the FD, the DATA RECORDS clause points to the
records making up the file, and the RECORDS CONTAINS clause gives the
length of these characters. The other entries associated with the FD are
not needed for the SD because the sort file is only temporary and the other
declarations for this file are handled by the SORT routine provided with
your computer.

8.8 PROGRAM EXAMPLE

Now that we have completed the material on the DATA DIVISION,
we can write complete COBOL programs on our own rather than having
to rely on the predefined MASTER-FILE.

In this example, we have been given a set of data cards representing customer bills in an accounts receivable system. We would like to
print out these bills in order by date from the oldest to the newest. Such a
listing might be useful in helping an accounts manager track down de-
linquent accounts. The customer bill cards have the following format

COLUMNS	CONTENTS
1–10	Customer's account number
11–30	Customer's name
31–36	Date of the bill in mmddyy format
40–49	Bill amount, right-justified with two places after the decimal point

Figure 8.4 gives the hierarchy diagram and Figure 8.5 the flowcharts for each of the routines to perform this task. As usual, we have a
control routine that calls in the other procedures. The first initializes
the system by sorting the data in order by bill date, printing a header line
on our printout and reading in the first record from the account file. The
next routine edits the data by moving it from ACCOUNT to PRINT-LINE.

It prints out the data by displaying PRINT-LINE, which has reformatted the data. The final procedure cleans up our processing by closing the ACCOUNTS file and printing out a success message.

Figure 8.6 gives a structured COBOL program for accomplishing these tasks. Figure 8.6 is divided into three sections. The first section gives the IDENTIFICATION and ENVIRONMENT DIVISION material covered in Chapter 7. Notice that the remarks in the IDENTIFICATION DIVISION give a fairly complete statement of the program purpose and of the type of input that the program expects to find. This should help make the program self-documenting in case other documentation about it is destroyed or not prepared.

The ENVIRONMENT DIVISION describes the machine on which the job was implemented and the files that will be used. We will be using three files, a RAW-DATA file that contains the unsorted account cards, the SORT-FILE that is used as an intermediate file for sorting the account cards, and an ACCOUNTS file that is used to hold the sorted cards. The external names assigned to each of these files will be defined by the job control language cards that accompany the program when it is run.

The DATA DIVISION defines the three files needed for this job. Notice that the record area assigned to the unsorted RAW-DATA file is entirely composed of FILLER. This does not mean that the cards in the RAW-DATA file do not contain any information but only that we are not interested in what this information is. The definition for the SORT-FILE will tell us where to find the relevant field for sorting. Notice that this field is the BILL-DATE field and that it is surrounded by FILLER. Finally, we come to the ACCOUNTS file, and it gives a complete breakdown of the structure of the record card.

FIGURE 8.4
Hierarchy Chart for Bill Listing Program

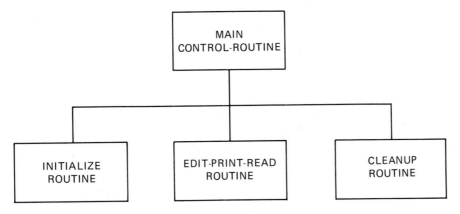

FIGURE 8.5
Flowchart for Bill Listing
Program

a. CONTROL-Routine

b. INITIALIZE Routine

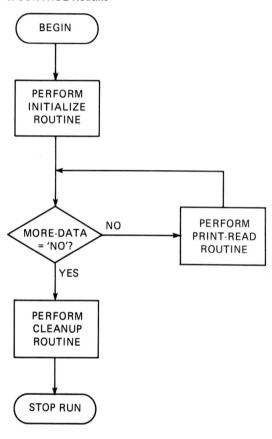
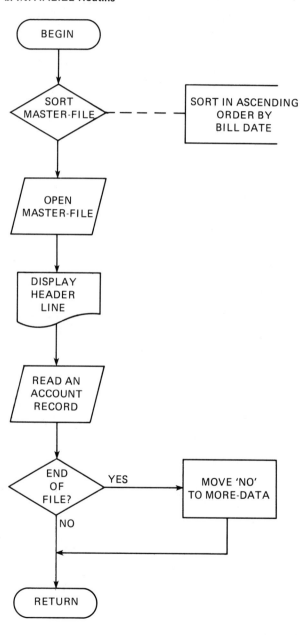

In the WORKING-STORAGE section of the DATA DIVISION, we have defined some more useful variables. We are using the variable MORE-DATA as a flag to tell us when we are out of data. We use the VALUE IS clause to initialize MORE-DATA to 'YES' so that we do not have to do this with a MOVE statement in the PROCEDURE DIVISION. We have also defined a record in WORKING-STORAGE called PRINT-LINE. We are going to use this record area to hold the data we have read in from the customer account file so that we can print it out in a reasonable format. We would

FIGURE 8.5
(Continued)

c. PRINT-READ Routine   **d. CLEANUP Routine**

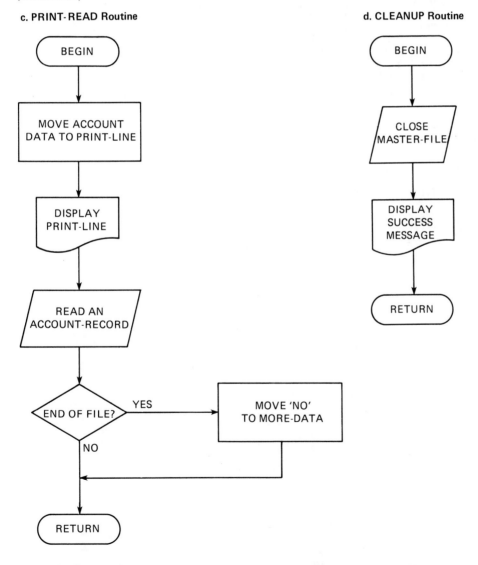

FIGURE 8.6
COBOL Program for Printing
Customer Bill List.

IDENTIFICATION and ENVIRONMENT DIVISIONS

```
000010 IDENTIFICATION DIVISION.
000020 PROGRAM-ID.  LISTER.
000030 AUTHOR.  NORMAN LYONS.
000040 DATE-WRITTEN.  JANUARY, 1980.
000050 DATE-COMPILED.  JANUARY,  1980.
000060*********VERSION  1.0 - LAST MODIFIED,  JANUARY,  1980*****
000070*       THE LISTER PROGRAM TAKES A SET OF BILLING        *
000080*       CARDS AND LISTS THEIR CONTENTS.  THE FORMAT OF   *
000090*       THE INPUT CARD IS AS FOLLOWS:                    *
000100*          COLUMNS           CONTENTS                    *
000110*          1 - 10    CUSTOMER ACCOUNT NUMBER             *
000120*          11 - 30   CUSTOMER NAME                       *
000130*          31 - 36   DATE IN MMDDYY FORMAT               *
000140*          40 - 49   BILL AMOUNT, RIGHT JUSTIFIED        *
000150*                    WITH 2 PLACES AFTER THE DECIMAL     *
000160*       THE LISTING IS ORDERED BY DATE FROM              *
000170*       EARLIEST TO LATEST.                              *
000180*************************************************************
000190 ENVIRONMENT DIVISION.
000200 CONFIGURATION SECTION.
000210 SOURCE-COMPUTER.  IBM-370-145.
000220 OBJECT-COMPUTER.  IBM-370-145.
000230 INPUT-OUTPUT SECTION.
000240 FILE-CONTROL.
000250     SELECT ACCOUNTS ASSIGN TO UT-S-ACCT.
000260     SELECT SORT-FILE ASSIGN TO UT-S-SORTIN.
000270     SELECT RAW-DATA ASSIGN TO UT-S-CARDS.
```

DATA DIVISION

```
000280 DATA DIVISION.
000290 FILE SECTION.
000300 FD  RAW-DATA LABEL RECORDS ARE OMITTED.
000310 01  DATA-CARD.
000320     02  FILLER          PICTURE X(30).
000330     02  BILL-DATE       PICTURE X(6).
000340     02  FILLER          PICTURE X(13).
000350 FD  ACCOUNTS LABEL RECORDS ARE OMITTED.
000360 01  ACCOUNT.
000370     02  ACCOUNT-NO      PICTURE X(10).
000380     02  CUSTOMER-NAME   PICTURE X(20).
000390     02  BILL-DATE.
000400       03  MM            PICTURE X(2).
000410       03  DD            PICTURE X(2).
000420       03  YY            PICTURE X(2).
000430     02  FILLER          PICTURE X(3).
000440     02  AMOUNT          PICTURE 99999999V99.
```

FIGURE 8.6
(Continued)

```
000450 SD  SORT-FILE DATA RECORDS ARE SORT-RECORDS.
000460 01  SORT-RECORDS.
000470     02  FILLER              PICTURE X(30).
000480     02  BILL-DATE.
000490        03  MM               PICTURE X(2).
000500        03  DD               PICTURE X(2).
000510        03  YY               PICTURE X(2).
000520     02  FILLER              PICTURE X(13).
000530 WORKING-STORAGE SECTION.
000540 77  MORE-DATA               PIC X(3)  VALUE IS 'YES'.
000550 01  PRINT-LINE.
000560     02  ACCOUNT-NO          PICTURE X(10).
000570     02  FILLER              PIC X(2)  VALUE IS SPACES.
000580     02  CUSTOMER-NAME       PICTURE X(20).
000590     02  FILLER              PIC X(2)  VALUE IS SPACES.
000600     02  BILL-DATE.
000610        03  MM               PICTURE X(2).
000620        03  FILLER           PIC X(1)  VALUE IS '/'.
000630        03  DD               PICTURE X(2).
000640        03  FILLER           PIC X(1)  VALUE IS '/'.
000650        03  YY               PICTURE X(2).
000660        03  FILLER           PIC X(2)  VALUE IS SPACES.
000670     02  AMOUNT              PICTURE $$$$$$$$9.99.


                    PROCEDURE DIVISION

000680 PROCEDURE DIVISION.
000690 CONTROL-ROUTINE.
000700     PERFORM INITIALIZE.
000710     PERFORM EDIT-PRINT-READ UNTIL MORE-DATA IS EQUAL TO 'NO'.
000720     PERFORM CLEANUP.
000730     STOP RUN.
000740 INITIALIZE.
000750     SORT SORT-FILE ON ASCENDING KEY YY OF SORT-RECORDS,
000760         ASCENDING KEY MM OF SORT-RECORDS,
000770         ASCENDING KEY DD OF SORT-RECORDS,
000780         USING RAW-DATA,
000790         GIVING ACCOUNTS.
000800     OPEN INPUT ACCOUNTS.
000810     DISPLAY 'NUMBER      CUSTOMER          DATE        AMO
000820-         'UNT'.
000830     DISPLAY ' '.
000840     READ ACCOUNTS AT END MOVE 'NO' TO MORE-DATA.
000850 EDIT-PRINT-READ.
000860     MOVE CORRESPONDING ACCOUNT TO PRINT-LINE.
000870     DISPLAY PRINT-LINE.
000880     READ ACCOUNTS AT END MOVE 'NO' TO MORE-DATA.
000890 CLEANUP.
000900     CLOSE ACCOUNTS.
000910     DISPLAY 'END OF PROGRAM'.
```

FIGURE 8.6
(Continued)

Sample Output

NUMBER	CUSTOMER	DATE	AMOUNT
0000608460	CARTER,BRUCE	03/10/73	$84.78
0000913819	CARTER,BRUCE	04/24/73	$99.92
0000410039	RICE,KNOX	05/09/73	$77.71
0000566826	EDWARDS,PATRICK	06/24/73	$89.92
0000579116	THOMAS,LOUIS	07/08/73	$69.72
0001049707	HURLEY,PAT	09/24/73	$142.41
0000503303	DUMAS,DONNA	11/02/73	$141.89
0000618843	WHITE,DIANNE	01/04/76	$118.19
0000839799	LANE,AMANDA	02/22/76	$90.21
0000692044	JACKSON,ROBERT	03/05/76	$121.43
0000199387	EDWARDS,PATRICK	03/18/76	$92.56
0000702476	GRIGGS,AMY	04/22/76	$103.97
0001007953	MARKS,STEPHEN	09/25/76	$84.93
0000670927	HURLEY,PAT	10/19/76	$90.49
0000482619	GRIMES,CYNTHIA	10/21/76	$119.77
0000378398	ANDERSON,WAYNE	11/03/76	$115.96
0000997857	JACKSON,ROBERT	11/16/76	$115.40

like to print slashes between the elements of the date; we want spaces between the fields; and we want the bill amount to be printed with a floating dollar sign editing symbol. We could not get this if we simply printed out the ACCOUNT record area. We have to edit the ACCOUNT record area by moving its contents to PRINT-LINE.

This program marks a real milestone in our experience with COBOL. It is the first time that we have written an entire COBOL program from start to finish without relying on somebody else's definitions. This means that we now no longer have to use COBOL just for information retrieval as we have up to this point, but we can now use it to design our own data processing applications systems. This is an important step in your work with COBOL, but there is still a greal deal to learn. You must gain experience with the different types of COBOL input–output and other statements.

STUDY EXERCISES

1. What three sections are found in the DATA DIVISION, and what is the purpose of each?

2. What level number is used for simple data items in WORKING-STORAGE?

3. What is level number 01 used for? What are level numbers 02 through 49 used for?

4. What characters can an alphabetic data item contain?

5. What characters can an alphanumeric data item contain?

6. Suppose we moved the data below into a variable with the given PIC-
   TURE. What result would be printed if we displayed the variable? (*Note:*
   Some of the moves may be illegal.)

DATA	PICTURE
'ABC'	A(3)
'ABCD'	AA
'ABCD'	XAXA
'ABCD'	XXBXBXBX
'ABCD'	XOXOXOXO
'123'	AAA
'123'	XOXOXO

7. Suppose that we moved the data below into a variable with the given
   PICTURE. What result would be printed if we displayed the variable?
   (*Note:* Some of the moves may be illegal.)

DATA	PICTURE
+123	S999
+123	999CR
−123	S999
−123	999CR
−123	999−
'$123'	$$$$$$$.$$
'ABC'	999
−123	$99999.99
−123	$$$,$$$,$$9.99
1.2345	99.99
1234	$***,***,***.99

8. How does the use of a VALUE IS clause in the DATA DIVISION differ from a
   MOVE statement in initialization of variables?

9. a. Write the COBOL record structure needed to store this data:

Automobile number	10 alphanumeric characters
Automobile description	30 alphanumeric characters
Date purchased	6 numeric characters
Purchase price	8 numeric characters with 2 after the decimal

REPAIR RECORD 30 LINES

Date of repair	6 numeric characters
Description of repair	50 alphanumeric characters
Cost of repair	8 numeric characters with 2 after the decimal

b. How long is the above record?

10. Write out the COBOL DISPLAY statement needed to print out the fifth line of your table in exercise 9.

11. A social security number in a certain COBOL program has the definition

```
02  SOCIAL-SECURITY          PIC 9(9).
```

Write the DATA DIVISION and PROCEDURE DIVISION statements needed to sum up the digits and print the sum.

12. Suppose one of the social security numbers in question 11 is 585010987. Write the necessary DATA DIVISION and PROCEDURE DIVISION code to print this out as 585-01-0987.

13. A card record has the format:

COLUMNS	CONTENTS
1–10	Customer account number
15–40	Customer name
51–60	Bill amount, right justified with two places after the implied decimal point
61–66	Bill date in mmddyy format
75–80	Department number—four digit numeric

Write a file definition for this file assuming that it is kept on data cards.

14. A magnetic tape is 1,600 feet long. It is written at 800 BPI, and the length of an interrecord gap is ¾ inch. How many records of 400 bytes can be stored on a single tape if the records are blocked at 5 to 1? 10 to 1? 20 to 1?

15. Write a sort file definition for sorting the card file in exercise 13 by department number (major key) and bill amount.

16. Suppose you have a set of data cards for your personal library. The card format is:

COLUMNS	CONTENTS
1–15	Call number
16–40	Author name
41–80	Book Title

Write a COBOL proram that will print a shelf list of your holdings in order by the author's name.

INPUT–OUTPUT IN COBOL

9.0 INTRODUCTION

In our work with COBOL so far, we have already done quite a bit with input–output statements. We have used the OPEN, CLOSE, READ, and DISPLAY statements for the programs we have had to work with. In this chapter we will continue our discussion of these statements to show the wider options possible, and we will introduce a few new statements. The difference between this chapter and earlier work is that we will be using these statements to build files rather than simply to print reports. File processing is the most important use of COBOL, and the printing of reports is only one type of file processing. We also want to be able to create new files, update old files, and perform all of these actions on a variety of different input–output devices.

At this point, you should go back over your understanding of the ENVIRONMENT and DATA divisions to make sure that you understand all of the entries necessary in a COBOL program to describe fully a file and use it. These relationships are:

ENVIRONMENT DIVISION	Contains the FILE SECTION that associates the internal name of a file with the external device name.
DATA DIVISION	Defines the structure of the file and refers back to the ENVIRONMENT DIVISION SELECT statements.
PROCEDURE DIVISION	Contains the processing statements that show how the file and its data are used.

When you are using a file, you must remember to provide the necessary entries for the file in each of the three divisions. In your previous work in COBOL, the descriptions that came with the MASTER-FILE provided these entries for you. Now you will be writing your own entries in these sections whether you are writing completely new programs or modifying existing programs to perform new tasks.

You should also remember that whatever machine you are using will have some sort of job control language (JCL), which will regulate your COBOL program's interaction with the computer's operating system. You will have to provide descriptions of the file for the computer's operating system in this job control language. Job control languages differ from machine to machine, and you should consult your instructor or the reference manual for your particular computer to see what job control language statements are necessary to set up the files for your COBOL programs.

9.1 THE OPEN AND CLOSE STATEMENTS

We have used the OPEN and CLOSE statements in our earlier COBOL programs, so they are not entirely new to you. These statements are housekeeping statements that announce to the computer that we intend to use a file and that it should be set up (the OPEN statement) or that we are finished with a file and that it can be disposed of (the CLOSE statement). There are additional options for the OPEN and CLOSE statements that we have not used so far, and we will discuss a few of them in this section.

The general format of the OPEN **statement** is: OPEN statement

```
OPEN   [ INPUT  {  file-name-1  [ REVERSED        ] } ... ]
                                [ WITH NO REWIND  ]
       [ OUTPUT {  file-name-2  [ WITH NO REWIND ]   } ... ]
       [ I-O       file-name-3     ...          ]
```

Some examples of particular OPEN statements are:

```
OPEN INPUT MASTER-FILE.
OPEN OUTPUT REPORT-FILE.
OPEN I-O DISK-FILE.
OPEN INPUT TAPE-FILE-1 WITH NO REWIND,
     OUTPUT TAPE-FILE-2 WITH NO REWIND,
     I-O DISK-FILE-1, DISK-FILE-2.
```

We can use separate OPEN statements for each file we use, or we can combine them all into a single OPEN statement as in the last example above. You must OPEN a file before you can use it in your program, and you must not OPEN it more than once without an intervening CLOSE statement. An exception to this rule is a SORT file. The opening and closing of SORT files is handled automatically by the SORT routine. The programmer does not have to do anything extra. The OPEN statement does not read any data into the file's record area. It is up to the programmer to issue a READ statement to do that.

The options REVERSED and WITH NO REWIND have the same effect when dealing with a tape file. They mean that the I/O activity will begin where the tape is currently positioned. In the REVERSED option, the tape file is opened for reading in reverse so that it may be read from last record to first. This can be useful since it saves the rewinding time. There may be special installation or system restrictions on the use of these statements, so if you are going to try them, check your system's manuals first.

The I-O option means that the file is opened for both input and output at the same time. This can only be done on a device like a disk or drum file that allows the machine access to individual records. It cannot be used on a device like a magnetic tape or card reader. Because this statement will allow you to do either input or output from the file, it implies that the file already exists. So, you cannot use the I-O option on a new file even if it is on the correct type of device.

When we are through processing the data on the file, we must CLOSE the file. The CLOSE statement handles the cleanup processing on the file. The general format of the CLOSE **statement** is:

CLOSE statement

```
                 ┌ REEL ┐              ┌ NO REWIND ┐
CLOSE file-name-1 │      │    [ WITH  {           }      ]
                 └ UNIT ┘              └ LOCK      ┘

                 ┌ REEL ┐              ┌ NO REWIND ┐
   [ file-name-2 │      │    [ WITH  {           }    ] ...
                 └ UNIT ┘              └ LOCK      ┘
```

Some examples of representative CLOSE statements are:

```
CLOSE TAPE1 WITH NO REWIND.
CLOSE TAPE2 WITH LOCK,
        TAPE3, DISK4.
CLOSE MASTER-FILE UNIT.
CLOSE ACCOUNT-RECORD REEL WITH LOCK.
```

The use of the term REEL implies that the unit is a magnetic tape, whereas the term UNIT implies that it is a mass storage device. Actually, this distinction means little on most machines since the actual type of device is assigned at program execution time by the operating system rather than by your program. The control over this assignment of devices is usually done by the job control language commands submitted with your program. The NO REWIND option prevents the file from rewinding at the end of I/O activity. This can be handy if you want to begin writing a second file on the same reel of tape (a multifile reel) or if you would like to back up and read the file again in reverse. The LOCK option causes the file to be dismounted (if it is a tape), although on many systems, this feature is also under the control of the operating system.

9.2 INPUT–OUTPUT STATEMENTS IN COBOL

The only COBOL input–output statements we have used so far are simplified versions of the READ and DISPLAY statements. We have been able to perform many tasks even though we have limited ourselves to these statements, but there are other, more sophisticated input–output statements available. With what we know so far, we would not be able to create a new tape or disk file from raw data or edit an old file to produce a new one. There are also a number of useful features that can be processed using certain types of COBOL input–output statements.

The first statements we will discuss are the low volume input–output ones, DISPLAY and ACCEPT. We have been using the DISPLAY statement to direct output to the printer in our work so far. It is also widely used on terminal-oriented systems to send data to a console to instruct the program user about the type of data the program requires. The general format of the DISPLAY statement is: DISPLAY statement

```
            ⎧ literal-1    ⎫  ⎡ literal-2    ⎤
 DISPLAY    ⎨ identifier-1 ⎬  ⎢ identifier-2 ⎥  ...  [ UPON mnemonic-name ]
            ⎩              ⎭  ⎣              ⎦
```

Some examples of the DISPLAY statement are:

```
DISPLAY 'SUCCESSFUL END OF PROGRAM'.
DISPLAY '********ERROR FINISH STUDENT-NO=', STUDENT-NO.
DISPLAY 'CALL JOHN SMITH AT X-3109' UPON CONSOLE-TYPEWRITER.
```

The DISPLAY statement can be used for the output of either literals or variables. It can be very useful for debugging programs. If you wish to know the value of a particular variable, simply insert a DISPLAY statement to print the desired values. The last example of the DISPLAY is used to print a message on the operator's console. The mnemonic name used for the console will vary from system to system. You can get around this variation by using the SPECIAL-NAMES section of the ENVIRONMENT

DIVISION. If the mnemonic name is omitted, the output from a DISPLAY goes to the normal system output device as we have already seen.

The DISPLAY has its corresponding input statement, ACCEPT. The ACCEPT **statement** is used to get input from low volume I/O devices (such as the console typewriter or a terminal), and it is also used for getting special values such as the date or time of day. The first format of the ACCEPT statement is:

```
ACCEPT identifier [ FROM mnemonic-name ]
```

Some examples are:

```
ACCEPT REPLY FROM CONSOLE-TYPEWRITER.
ACCEPT X.
```

The data values found on the I/O device are placed in the identifier associated with the ACCEPT statement. The PICTURE of the identifier is used to determine the length of the data item. No editing takes place on input.

It is frequently useful to have the time of day or the date. These values can be printed out to give a record of when a computer program was run, or they can be used in the header information of reports. The format of this version of the ACCEPT statement is:

$$\text{ACCEPT identifier} \quad \underline{\text{FROM}} \quad \left\{ \begin{array}{c} \text{DATE} \\ \text{DAY} \\ \text{TIME} \end{array} \right\}$$

The DATE, DAY, and TIME registers are special COBOL reserved words used to store the values of the current date and the current time. The formats used in this storage are:

```
DATE is PICTURE 999999 and is stored as yymmdd.
DAY  is PICTURE 99999 and is stored as yyddd.
TIME is PICTURE 99999999 and is stored as hhmmsscc.
```

The value returned by DATE is the normal date given as year, month, and day. The value returned by DAY gives the year first and then the day of the year (for example, January 20, 1978, would be 78020 and December 31, 1980, would be 80366). This is sometimes called the **Julian date.** The TIME register returns hours, minutes, seconds, and hundredths of a second.

Examples of the way in which these statements are used are:

```
ACCEPT TODAYS-DATE FROM DATE.
ACCEPT JULIAN-DATE FROM DAY.
ACCEPT CURRENT-HOUR FROM TIME.
```

The ACCEPT statement returns the desired value and places it in the variable given after the statement.

If we wish to do greater amounts of input–output activity, we can use the READ and WRITE statements. You are already familiar with the READ statement from your work in earlier chapters. Some examples of the READ statements are:

```
READ MASTER-FILE AT END MOVE 'NO' TO MORE-DATA.
READ ACCOUNT-RECORD AT END PERFORM ANALYSIS.
READ STUDENT-DATA INTO DATA-BUFFER AT END PERFORM CLEANUP.
```

The general format for the READ **statement** is: READ statement

```
READ file-name RECORD [ INTO identifier ]

    ⎧ AT END       ⎫
    ⎨              ⎬   imperative-statement
    ⎩ INVALID KEY  ⎭
```

Let us go over these examples and the definition. The INTO option in the definition and the third example are new. It has the effect of reading the data into the record area associated with the file STUDENT-DATA and then moving it to the record called DATA-BUFFER. In effect, it is a combination READ and MOVE. We have seen the AT END option in the READ before. This option tells the computer what to do when the file is out of data. In our programs to this point, we have been changing the value in a flag using a MOVE statement. This flag was then tested by a PERFORM to see if we had run out of data. We do not have to limit ourselves to MOVE statements. We could have used any imperative statement at this location. The INVALID KEY option is used in direct-access data processing. It will be discussed in the next section on direct-access files.

You should review all of the necessary statements before you set up a file for reading (or writing). It is not enough simply to use the name of the file in the READ statement. There must also be a file definition for the file in the DATA DIVISION, a SELECT sentence for the file in the ENVIRONMENT DIVISION, and some job control language with your program to tell the computer's operating system where to find the file.

The final input–output statement in this section is the WRITE statement. It is used for writing large amounts of data to a file. It can be used on any type of physical device, but it is usually used for large volume input–output. Some examples of WRITE statements are:

```
WRITE STUDENT.
WRITE PRINT-LINE FROM STUDENT BEFORE ADVANCING 2 LINES.
WRITE PRINT-LINE AFTER ADVANCING 5 LINES.
```

The general definition for a WRITE statement is: WRITE statement

```
WRITE record-name [ FROM identifier-1 ]

                          ┌ identifier-2 LINES ┐
      ┌ BEFORE ┐          │                    │
    [ │        │ ADVANCING │ integer LINES      │ ]
      └ AFTER  ┘          │                    │
                          └ mnemonic-name      ┘
```

You should note some points before you begin using the WRITE statement. First, notice that in the WRITE statement you are writing the record name and not the file name as you were in the READ statement. If the file is MASTER-FILE and the record associated with the file is MASTER-RECORD, then you would READ the MASTER-FILE, but you would WRITE MASTER-RECORD. It is a point that sometimes confuses beginners in COBOL.

The FROM option in the WRITE statement functions like the INTO option in the READ statement. It moves the data from the VARIABLE given after the FROM into the record area for the WRITE statement. It effectively combines a MOVE and a WRITE. The BEFORE and AFTER options are for use with printer files. BEFORE means that the WRITE is to be done before the printer vertical spacing. The AFTER phrase causes printing after the vertical spacing. It is a technique for controlling spacing on your printout.

To show how the input–output statements are used, we have prepared a sample program to update the MASTER-FILE. This program can handle changes to a student's address or major. The formats for the change cards are:

COLUMNS	CONTENTS
1–10	Student number
11–18	Card type—ADDRESS means address change MAJOR means major change

ADDRESS CHANGE CARD FORMAT

19–38	Street address
39–58	City
59–60	State
61–65	Zip code

MAJOR CHANGE CARD FORMAT

19–38	College name of new college
39–58	New major

As you can see from this format, the program will accept two types of input cards, an ADDRESS card to change the student's address and a MAJOR card to change the student's major. Both types of cards have the same information in columns 1–10. This matches the change card with the correct student record. The next eight columns give the type of card, and the remaining columns give the change data. In the program, a RE-DEFINES will be used to show the format of the data area. This set of card formats can be expanded easily to include other types of changes. For instance, it would be very easy to define change cards to change the

FIGURE 9.1
Hierarchy Diagram for
CHANGE Program

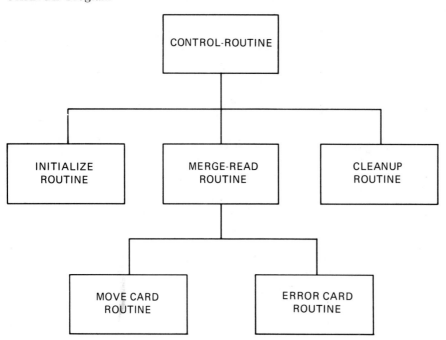

telephone number, name (to handle marriage or other name changes), and fields representing bills owed the university.

Figure 9.1 gives the hierarchy diagram for this program. As usual, there is a CONTROL ROUTINE to handle the calling of the other routines. The INITIALIZE routine sets up the data for processing, the MERGE-READ routine matches the change cards with the correct master file records, and the CLEANUP routine handles the terminal processing. The MERGE-READ routine must call on a MOVE-CARD routine to identify the type of change and an ERROR-CARD routine to handle processing in the event of an error on the input card.

This program will have to make use of six different files to handle the data processing. These files are:

MASTER-FILE	The MASTER-FILE contains all of the old student records that are to be updated.
RAW-DATA	Contains the unsorted change cards.
SORT-FILE	Used to sort the change cards in order by student number so that they can be matched with the corresponding student numbers on the MASTER-FILE.
CHANGE-CARDS	Contains the sorted change cards.
ERROR-FILE	A printer file used to print the images of erroneous cards so that clerks can correct the errors.
NEW-MASTER	Contains the student records after the changes have been made.

This may seem like a large number of files for a relatively simple task, but each of them is necessary. You may wonder why we have two master files, an old master file and a new master file. This is because we are using sequential files, and updates to a sequential file are not usually made directly on the old file. What we do is create a new master file that incorporates the changes. The old file will not be discarded. It is a good practice to save this file along with the change cards that were used to create it. This way, if something ever happened to the newly created master file, we could recreate it again by using the last old master file and the update cards used to create the new master. Data processing organizations usually save three generations of master files. This is called the grandfather-father-son scheme for data security. It is a good idea to take the grandfather and father versions of the master file and store them at a different location from your computer center. This way, if the center is physically destroyed (for example, by fire or flood), the files are not destroyed along with it.

Figure 9.2 gives the flowcharts for the program. The flowchart is fairly straightforward. The only routine that is likely to give you any trouble is the MERGE-READ routine. This routine consists of a set of nested IF statements that determine which record is to be changed. If the student number of the master record is less than the student number of the change card, the master record to be changed is somewhere further on down the master file. So we simply pass the old master record to the

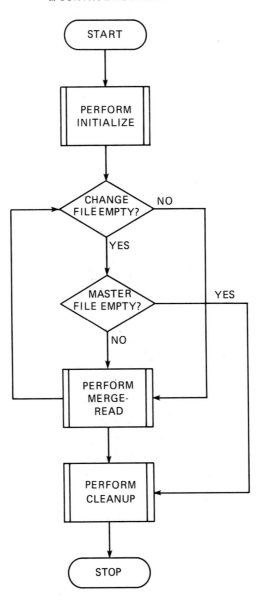

a. CONTROL-ROUTINE

FIGURE 9.2
Flowchart for *CHANGE*
Program

FIGURE 9.2
(Continued)

b. **INITIALIZE** Routine

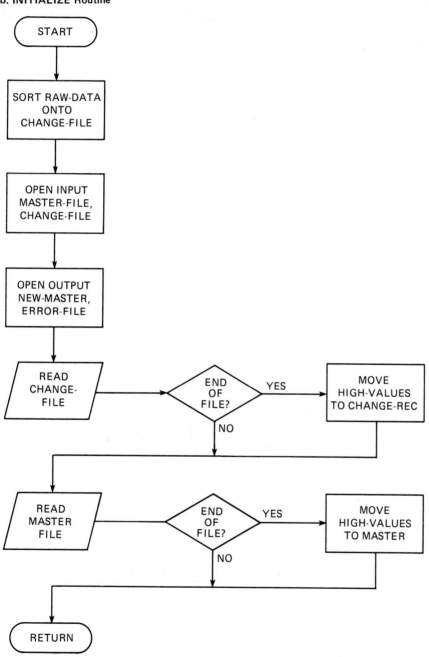

FIGURE 9.2
(Continued)

c. MERGE-READ Routine

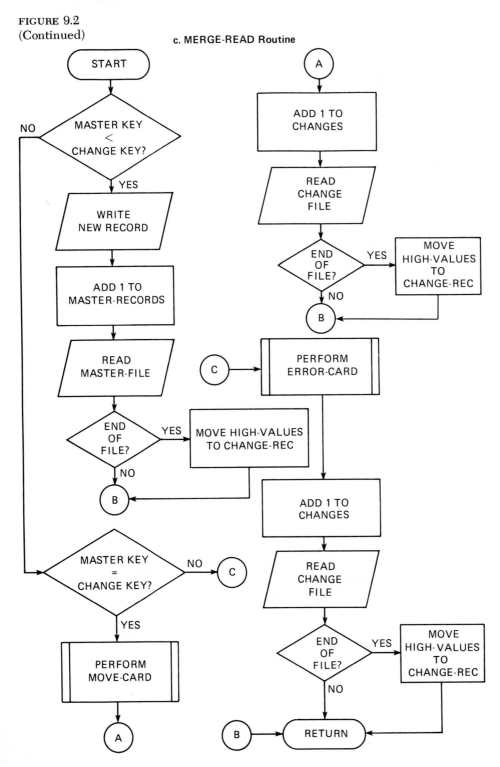

new master file. If the key of the master record equals the key of the student record, we have found a match, and the master record is changed. Finally, if we take the last ELSE condition, the student number of the change card is less than the student number of the master record. Since both the master file and the change file are in student number order, this means that we have a bad change card. The student number that appears on the card does not appear on the master file. The appropriate error fixup is taken.

Figure 9.3 gives a listing of the COBOL program to make the changes. The IDENTIFICATION DIVISION (Figure 9.3a) gives a series of comments that describes the format of the change cards and the purpose of the program. It is a good idea to document the program with comments in case other documentation is mislaid. The DATA DIVISION (Figure 9.3b) contains the necessary file descriptions. Notice that we have shortened the DATA DIVISION by not completely describing the structure of every file. For example, the FD for the NEW-MASTER does not lay out the field structure for the new master file even though it is the same as the old

FIGURE 9.2
(Continued)

d. MOVE-CARD Routine

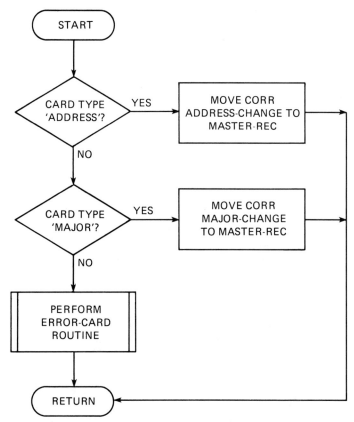

master file. We never make changes to the fields in the new master, so all we have to do is set aside a data area large enough to accommodate the records.

The PROCEDURE DIVISION (Figure 9.3c) contains the code to perform the update. Since the changes are being made to the file, this pro-

FIGURE 9.2
(Continued)

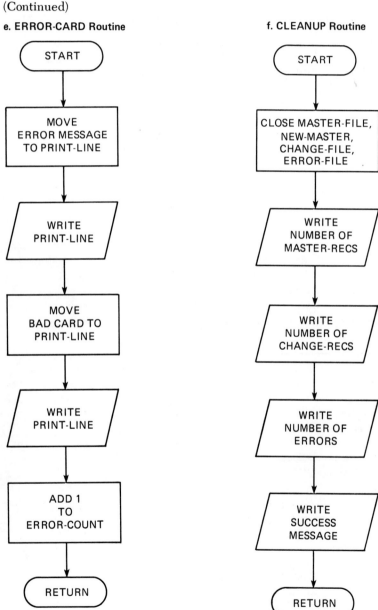

e. ERROR-CARD Routine

f. CLEANUP Routine

FIGURE 9.3
COBOL Program to Update
the MASTER-FILE

a. IDENTIFICATION and ENVIRONMENT DIVISIONS

```
000010 IDENTIFICATION DIVISION.
000020 PROGRAM-ID. CHANGE.
000030 AUTHOR.  NORMAN LYONS.
000040 DATE-WRITTEN.  JANUARY, 1980.
000050***************VERSION 1.0 - JANUARY, 1980***********************
000060*    THE CHANGE PROGRAM HANDLES CHANGES FOR EITHER ADDRESS OR  *
000070*    MAJOR.  THE BASIC FORMATS OF THE CHANGE CARDS ARE:        *
000080*       COL 1 - 10    STUDENT NUMBER.                          *
000090*       COL 11 - 18   CHANGE CARD TYPE.                        *
000100*                     ADDRESS - ADDRESS CHANGE CARD.           *
000110*                     MAJOR - MAJOR CHANGE CARD.               *
000120*            ADDRESS CHANGE CARD FORMAT                        *
000130*       COL 19 - 38   STREET ADDRESS.                          *
000140*       COL 39 - 58   CITY.                                    *
000150*       COL 59 - 60   STATE.                                   *
000160*       COL 61 - 65   ZIP CODE.                                *
000170*            MAJOR CHANGE CARD FORMAT                          *
000180*       COL 19 - 38   COLLEGE NAME.                            *
000190*       COL 39 - 58   MAJOR.                                   *
000200***************************************************************
000210 ENVIRONMENT DIVISION.
000220 CONFIGURATION SECTION.
000230 SOURCE-COMPUTER.  IBM-370-145.
000240 OBJECT-COMPUTER.  IBM-370-145.
000250 INPUT-OUTPUT SECTION.
000260 FILE-CONTROL.
000270     SELECT MASTER-FILE ASSIGN TO UT-S-OLDMAST.
000280     SELECT SORT-FILE ASSIGN TO UT-S-SORTIN.
000290     SELECT NEW-MASTER ASSIGN TO UT-S-NEWMAST.
000300     SELECT RAW-DATA ASSIGN TO UT-S-SYSIN.
000310     SELECT CHANGE-FILE ASSIGN TO UT-S-SORTOUT.
000320     SELECT ERROR-FILE ASSIGN TO UT-S-ERRFILE.
```

b. DATA DIVISION

```
000330 DATA DIVISION.
000340 FILE SECTION.
000350 FD  MASTER-FILE LABEL RECORDS ARE STANDARD.
000360 01  MASTER-RECORD.
000370     02  STUDENT-NO       PICTURE X(10).
000380     02  LAST-NAME        PICTURE X(20).
000390     02  FIRST-NAME       PICTURE X(20).
000400     02  INIT             PICTURE X.
000410     02  STREET           PICTURE X(20).
000420     02  CITY             PICTURE X(20).
000430     02  STATE            PICTURE XX.
000440     02  ZIP              PICTURE X(5).
000450     02  PHONE            PICTURE X(7).
```

FIGURE 9.3
(Continued)

```
000460      02   SEX              PICTURE X.
000470      02   AGE              PICTURE 99.
000480      02   BIRTHDAY.
000490       03   MM              PICTURE 99.
000500       03   DD              PICTURE 99.
000510       03   YY              PICTURE 99.
000520      02   COLLEGE          PICTURE X(20).
000530      02   MAJOR            PICTURE X(20).
000540      02   ADVISOR          PICTURE X(30).
000550      02   CREDITS          PICTURE 999.
000560      02   AVERAGE          PICTURE 99V999.
000570      02   COURSE OCCURS 5 TIMES.
000580       03   NUMBER          PICTURE X(6).
000590       03   NAME            PICTURE X(20).
000600       03   HOURS           PICTURE 99.
000610       03   P-F             PICTURE X.
000620       03   GRADE           PICTURE 9V99.
000630      02   ROOM-BAL         PICTURE 99999V99.
000640      02   TUITION-BAL      PICTURE 99999V99.
000650      02   FEE-BAL          PICTURE 99999V99.
000660      02   OTHER-BAL        PICTURE 99999V99.
000670      02   TOTAL-BAL        PICTURE 99999V99.
000680 FD   CHANGE-FILE LABEL RECORDS ARE STANDARD.
000690 01   CHANGE-RECORD.
000700      02   STUDENT-NO       PICTURE X(10).
000710      02   CARD-TYPE        PICTURE X(8).
000720      02   ADDRESS-CHANGE.
000730       03   STREET          PICTURE X(20).
000740       03   CITY            PICTURE X(20).
000750       03   STATE           PICTURE X(2).
000760       03   ZIP             PICTURE X(5).
000770      02   MAJOR-CHANGE REDEFINES ADDRESS-CHANGE.
000780       03   COLLEGE         PICTURE X(20).
000790       03   MAJOR           PICTURE X(20).
000800 FD   NEW-MASTER LABEL RECORDS ARE STANDARD.
000810 01   NEW-RECORD           PICTURE X(387).
000820 FD   RAW-DATA LABEL RECORDS ARE STANDARD.
000830 01   DATA-CARD            PICTURE X(80).
000840 FD   ERROR-FILE LABEL RECORDS ARE OMITTED.
000850 01   PRINT-LINE           PICTURE X(120).
000860 SD   SORT-FILE.
000870 01   SORT-RECORDS.
000880      02   STUDENT-NO       PICTURE X(10).
000890      02   FILLER           PICTURE X(70).
000900 WORKING-STORAGE SECTION.
000910 77  MASTER-RECORDS        PIC 99999 VALUE IS 0.
000920 77  CHANGES               PIC 99999 VALUE IS 0.
000930 77  ERRORS                PIC 99999 VALUE IS 0.
```

c. PROCEDURE DIVISION

```
000940 PROCEDURE DIVISION.
000950 CONTROL-ROUTINE.
```

FIGURE 9.3
(Continued)

```
000960     PERFORM INITIALIZE.
000970     PERFORM MERGE-READ UNTIL STUDENT-NO OF CHANGE-RECORD IS
000980         EQUAL TO HIGH-VALUES AND STUDENT-NO OF MASTER-RECORD IS
000990         EQUAL TO HIGH-VALUES.
001000     PERFORM CLEANUP.
001010     STOP RUN.
001020 INITIALIZE.
001030     SORT SORT-FILE ON ASCENDING KEY STUDENT-NO OF SORT-RECORDS,
001040         USING RAW-DATA,
001050         GIVING CHANGE-FILE.
001060     OPEN INPUT MASTER-FILE, CHANGE-FILE,
001070         OUTPUT NEW-MASTER, ERROR-FILE.
001080     READ CHANGE-FILE AT END MOVE HIGH-VALUES TO
001090         STUDENT-NO OF CHANGE-RECORD.
001100     READ MASTER-FILE AT END MOVE HIGH-VALUES TO
001110         STUDENT-NO OF MASTER-RECORD.
001120 MERGE-READ.
001130     IF STUDENT-NO OF MASTER-RECORD IS LESS THAN
001140         STUDENT-NO OF CHANGE-RECORD
001150         WRITE NEW-RECORD FROM MASTER-RECORD
001160         ADD 1 TO MASTER-RECORDS
001170         READ MASTER-FILE AT END MOVE HIGH-VALUES TO
001180             STUDENT-NO OF MASTER-RECORD
001190     ELSE
001200         IF STUDENT-NO OF MASTER-RECORD IS EQUAL TO
001210             STUDENT-NO OF CHANGE-RECORD
001220             PERFORM MOVE-CARD
001230             ADD 1 TO CHANGES
001240             READ CHANGE-FILE AT END MOVE HIGH-VALUES TO
001250                 STUDENT-NO OF CHANGE-RECORD
001260         ELSE
001270             PERFORM ERROR-CARD
001280             ADD 1 TO CHANGES
001290             READ CHANGE-FILE AT END MOVE HIGH-VALUES TO
001300                 STUDENT-NO OF CHANGE-RECORD.
001310 ERROR-CARD.
001320     MOVE '**********BAD CHANGE CARD' TO PRINT-LINE.
001330     WRITE PRINT-LINE.
001340     MOVE CHANGE-RECORD TO PRINT-LINE.
001350     WRITE PRINT-LINE.
001360     ADD 1 TO ERRORS.
001370 MOVE-CARD.
001380     IF CARD-TYPE IS EQUAL TO 'ADDRESS'
001390         MOVE CORRESPONDING ADDRESS-CHANGE TO MASTER-RECORD
001400     ELSE IF CARD-TYPE IS EQUAL TO 'MAJOR'
001410         MOVE CORRESPONDING MAJOR-CHANGE TO MASTER-RECORD
001420     ELSE PERFORM ERROR-CARD.
001430 CLEANUP.
001440     CLOSE MASTER-FILE, CHANGE-FILE, NEW-MASTER, ERROR-FILE.
001450     DISPLAY 'MASTER FILE RECORDS INPUT: ', MASTER-RECORDS.
001460     DISPLAY 'CHANGE RECORDS INPUT:      ', CHANGES.
001470     DISPLAY 'ERRORS ENCOUNTERED:        ', ERRORS.
001480     DISPLAY 'SUCCESSFUL END OF JOB.'.
```

FIGURE 9.3
(Continued)

Sample Output
Audit Output on Standard Output Device

```
MASTER FILE RECORDS INPUT:     00201
CHANGE RECORDS INPUT:          00005
ERRORS ENCOUNTERED:            00002
SUCCESSFUL END OF JOB.
```

Error File Output

```
**********BAD CHANGE CARD
0000000953ADDRESS 3287 CALIFORNIA ST. COVINA          CA94327
**********BAD CHANGE CARD
0000000971MAJUR    AGRICULTURE        WINE MAKING
```

gram produces very little printed output as we can see from Figure 9.3. The first printed output is generated by DISPLAY statements on the standard output device for the system. This gives the number of master file records input, the number of change records input, and the number of change records that were in error. This is a sort of standard audit report that should be produced at the end of a program. It provides a first check on the accuracy of the run. These audit reports should be dated and saved for future reference. The second type of printed output is on the error file. There is a line indicating that a bad change card was encountered and then the image of the card is printed. The first change card is incorrect because there is no student on the master file who has student number 0000000953. The second change card is incorrect because the field giving the change card type spells major as MAJUR. The program was designed to reject incorrect card types. This error printout could be given to control clerks who would pull the incorrect cards, change them, and then resubmit them with a later change run.

9.3 DIRECT FILE ORGANIZATIONS

In the file processing statements we have used so far, we have dealt entirely with sequential files, which are records stored so that they must be processed in order as they are encountered. If we want to read the Nth record on a file, we must also read or at least skip past the N-1 records that precede it. For some types of applications, it is very useful to be able to move directly to the record we want to access. An example of such an application might be an airlines reservation system. The computer that supports such a system has to be able to access directly information about a particular flight or customer without having to search through the records for all flights or customers (as it would have to do with a sequential file). If it could not provide such information quickly, airlines would have to look for a different approach for handling their ticket and reservation systems. There are several techniques for handling direct-access files (those stored on disks or drums) in COBOL. In this chapter, we will discuss two of the most useful.

One of the most useful types of file organization in COBOL is called the indexed file organization. Other terms applied to this technique for organizing the data on a file are **indexed sequential** or **ISAM** (Indexed Sequential Access Method). Indexed organization is a combination of the sequential access methods we have been using all along with the direct-access methods made possible by the use of mass storage devices such as disk files. In this technique the data is stored sequentially according to some key just like the data on our MASTER-FILE. But an index of the locations of the records on the mass storage device is also maintained, and if one wishes to retrieve records randomly scattered throughout the file, the index can be used to retrieve them.

The characteristics of the indexed organization are:

1. The data is stored sequentially on the storage device.

2. An index is maintained according to the key that was given when the file was created. This index allows access to any individual record.

The advantage of this more complicated technique of data storage can be easily seen. Suppose that we want to do a mass update to a file such as the student MASTER-FILE when it is time to enter the new grades at the end of a term. To do this, all we have to do is sort our grade change cards in order by the STUDENT-NO key and then read the indexed file sequentially and do the update as we would for any type of sequential file. But suppose we also have a terminal-oriented student record system, and we want to retrieve the records of individual students from the MASTER-FILE for display at our terminal. If the file is only a sequential file, that would mean reading through all the records that come before the one we want. If it is indexed, however, we can go to the index, look up the location of the record we want, retrieve it, and display it directly at our terminal. It is this ability to use a file in two different ways that accounts for the popularity of this type of file organization.

It may sound as if you will have to learn a lot of complicated new statements to use the indexed organization, but this is not the case. The computer will automatically handle the process of searching the index for you once you have given it a key. All you need supply in addition to the key is a statement telling whether you are using the file in sequential or in indexed mode.

The indexed organization means that a file can be opened for both input and output at the same time. With the indexed organization it is possible to add records to the file, delete records from the file, or to make changes to an existing record. The process of adding or deleting records can cause some problems. When records are deleted, gaps can occur in the file. The space where the deleted record was stored is no longer used and is wasted. When a record is added to the file, the opposite problem occurs. Since there is no room for it in the file (which is stored in physical sequential order), it must be added in an overflow area. Eventually, as an indexed file is used, gaps will begin to develop in the main file (as records are deleted) and the overflow area will begin to fill up (as records are added to the file). This may sound quite complicated, and it is, but you do not have to worry about the mechanism for handling these gaps and overflow areas. All of this will be handled automatically for you by COBOL and the operating system of your computer.

You might wonder what will happen when you run out of space in your overflow area or when too many gaps develop in your main file. This does not cause as much of a problem as you might think. On all computer systems, there are special programs called **utility programs**. A utility program is supplied by the manufacturer for handling common data processing chores. One of these chores is condensing an indexed file, closing the gaps in the main file, and emptying the overflow area. Check with your instructor or in the documentation of your computer system for information about the utility programs available on your machine.

utility programs

Generally, in setting up indexed files, you must supply three files or storage areas. These are:

1. An index area

2. A primary storage area

3. An overflow area

Check with your instructor or your computer's manuals for the job control language needed to set up an indexed file.

In setting up the indexed file, you must supply slightly different information in the ENVIRONMENT and DATA divisions than we have used so far. The SELECT statement in the FILE-CONTROL paragraph must supply additional information when using indexed files. Some examples of SELECT statements are:

```
SELECT STUDENT-FILE ASSIGN TO DA-I-OLDMAST,
     ACCESS IS SEQUENTIAL,
     RECORD KEY IS STUDENT-NO OF STUDENT-RECORD.
SELECT EMPLOYEE-FILE ASSIGN TO DA-I-MASTER1,
     ACCESS IS RANDOM,
     NOMINAL KEY IS EMPLOYEE,
     RECORD KEY IS EMPLOYEE-NO.
```

The format for the SELECT statement is: SELECT statement

SELECT file-name ASSIGN TO system-name

ORGANIZATION IS INDEXED

ACCESS MODE IS { SEQUENTIAL / RANDOM / DYNAMIC }

NOMINAL KEY IS data-name-1

RECORD KEY IS data-name-2

This is similar to the other SELECT examples we have used except for a couple of items. First of all, we must tell the system that the file organization is indexed. This is done by the ORGANIZATION phrase. Although the definition states that this phrase is necessary, it can be left out on many systems because the information about the file organization is carried along in the job control language statements. The ACCESS phrase tells how the file is to be accessed. SEQUENTIAL means that it is to be accessed sequentially, RANDOM means that it is to be accessed randomly (the records will not be chosen sequentially), and DYNAMIC means that it is possible to change from random to sequential access in the middle of the program. Be careful with DYNAMIC; this feature is not implemented on all systems.

The RECORD KEY phrase tells COBOL which field in the record area associated with the file contains the actual record key. The NOMINAL KEY phrase given the name of a data area that is used to hold a record key for file reading purposes. This data area holds the record key for which you are searching. The NOMINAL KEY feature is not part of standard ANSI COBOL but is part of the IBM OS/VS version.

Notice the examples before the definition. They offer another example of the naming conventions used for the system names for files on IBM systems. In the first case, we have a file referred to as DA-I-

OLDMASTER. The DA means that the file is a direct-access file, the I means that it is indexed, and the word OLDMASTER is the external file name. Your computer (if it is not IBM and using the OS/VS operating system) will probably have a slightly different naming convention.

The DATA DIVISION entries for direct-access files are conventional, although it is possible that your computer may require entries in the file description like BLOCK CONTAINS and RECORD CONTAINS clauses that are not required for sequential files. The information on this can be obtained from the language reference manual or programmer's guide for your machine. In the PROCEDURE DIVISION, the first statement you will use for dealing with your file is the OPEN statement. Recall that the general format is:

$$\underline{\text{OPEN}} \quad \begin{Bmatrix} \underline{\text{INPUT}} \\ \underline{\text{OUTPUT}} \\ \underline{\text{I-O}} \end{Bmatrix} \quad \text{file-name-1} \quad \dots$$

This is the same definition for the OPEN statement that we used earlier. Nothing changes for these indexed files except that it is now possible to open a file for I-O. If we open a file for INPUT or for I-O, it is assumed that the file we are using already exists. The I-O option means that we may do both reads and writes on the file in any order we choose (just how to do those reads and writes will be discussed shortly). When we open a file for OUTPUT, we are creating the file from scratch. In the case of an indexed file, then, the file will be given a SEQUENTIAL access mode in the SELECT sentence.

After we have opened the file, we may begin reading or writing. There are a number of new statements we can use with indexed files, and the old statements (like READ and WRITE) have slightly different versions. The first we will discuss is the READ statement. Some examples are:

```
READ STUDENT-FILE AT END MOVE 'NO' TO MORE-DATA.
READ ACCOUNT-FILE NEXT RECORD INTO ACCOUNT-BUFFER
     AT END PERFORM ANALYZE.
READ DATA-FILE INTO CARD-BLOCK INVALID KEY PERFORM
     ERROR-CHECK.
READ TRANSACTION-FILE RECORD KEY IS BILL-KEY
     INVALID KEY PERFORM ERROR-DUMP.
```

In the examples above, the first READ looks just like the sequential READ statements we have been using all along. There is no difference between an indexed sequential READ in SEQUENTIAL access mode and an ordinary sequential READ statement. The second READ statement looks a little less familiar. This one causes the next record in sequence to be read into the data area called ACCOUNT-BUFFER. This allows us the option of reading in direct-access mode and then switching over to sequential-access mode in reading our file. Check to be sure that this version of the READ is on your computer. It is not implemented on IBM machines probably because there is no real need for a separate READ statement of this type. The third READ statement is the one we would use for indexed access to the file DATA-FILE. The data will be read into the data area called CARD-BLOCK. If the key we have given for the READ statement is invalid, then the computer will do the imperative statement after the INVALID KEY phrase. There is no need for an AT END phrase when we are doing indexed access to the file. The concept of an end of file when we are accessing the file directly simply does not make sense. The record either exists or it does not, and there is no reason to check whether we are anywhere near an end of file marker. In the final example, we are also accessing the file directly using a KEY IS phrase to tell the computer where to find the key for the file. Again, check to see whether or not this particular ANSI COBOL feature is on your machine. It is not found on IBM machines.

There are two general formats for the READ **statement for indexed files.** They are:

READ statement for indexed files

FORMAT 1

```
READ  file-name  [ NEXT ] RECORD [ INTO  data-name ]

    [ AT END imperative-statement ]
```

FORMAT 2

```
READ  file-name  RECORD [ INTO  data-name ] [ KEY IS data-name ]

    [  INVALID KEY  imperative-statement ]
```

Format 1 is the sequential input format; Format 2 is the format used for indexed READ. The major difference between the two is that the AT END phrase has been replaced by the INVALID KEY phrase in the indexed READ statement. Again, be sure to check the documentation with your machine to see if the NEXT phrase and the KEY IS phrase are legal on your machine before you try to use these statements.

The output statement we will be using to create an indexed file or to create new records on the file will be the WRITE statement. The general format for the WRITE **statement for indexed files** is:

WRITE record-name [FROM data-name]

    [INVALID KEY imperative-statement]

Except for the INVALID KEY, this looks similar to the WRITE statement that we used earlier. You might be wondering how we can have an INVALID KEY if we are writing a completely new record on the file. There are two ways in which we can end up taking the INVALID KEY option. They are:

1. The key we have provided already exists in a record on the file.

2. The keys are out of order, and the key we have just tried to write is less than the last key written.

The WRITE statement is used only for the creation of new records on the file. It can be used either in the OUTPUT or the DYNAMIC mode.

You might be wondering how we would change an existing record in the file. When we were using ordinary sequential files, we would make a change to an existing record by producing a whole new copy of the file. We could do that as well with the indexed file if we wanted to change a record, but this would destroy the whole purpose of the indexed organization. Instead, if we want to make a change to an existing record in an indexed file, we use the REWRITE **statement.** The general format for this command is:

REWRITE record-name [FROM data-name]

    [INVALID KEY imperative-statement]

Some examples of WRITE and REWRITE statements are:

```
WRITE STUDENT-RECORD FROM DATA-BUFFER
      INVALID KEY PERFORM ERROR-CHECK.
REWRITE STUDENT-RECORD FROM UPDATE-BUFFER
      INVALID KEY PERFORM CHECK-DATA.
WRITE ACCOUNT-RECORD INVALID KEY PERFORM
      CHECK-ACCOUNT.
REWRITE TRANSACTION-RECORD INVALID KEY PERFORM
      ERROR-DUMP.
```

Margin notes: WRITE statement for indexed files

REWRITE statement

Notice that in both the WRITE and REWRITE statements, we use the record name and not the file name when we are writing data to a file. This is the same thing we did for the earlier sequential examples. In both the WRITE and REWRITE statements, the key to be used comes from the RECORD KEY phrase used in the SELECT statement in the ENVIRONMENT DIVISION (or from the NOMINAL KEY phrase if your computer uses that option). It is the responsibility of the programmer to see that the key is correctly set before trying to WRITE or REWRITE a record.

There are several other unique statements for accessing indexed files in addition to the ones we have discussed. Suppose we want to delete a record from the file. For this, we have the DELETE **statement,** the format of which is:

DELETE statement

```
DELETE  file-name  RECORD  [ INVALID KEY imperative-statement ]
```

Some examples of the DELETE statement are:

```
DELETE STUDENT-FILE.
DELETE MASTER-FILE RECORD.
DELETE ACCOUNT-FILE RECORD INVALID KEY PERFORM ERROR-CHECK.
```

The DELETE statement operates this way:

1. If the file is being accessed in the sequential mode, then the last record read is deleted.

2. If the file is being accessed in RANDOM or DYNAMIC mode, then the record specified by the RECORD KEY clause is deleted. If this key is invalid, then the imperative statement specified in the IN-VALID KEY phrase is performed.

There are instances in data processing when we would like to be able to delete records from a file. Suppose we have a payroll file and we want to delete the names of workers who have quit. The normal procedure then would be to produce any necessary last reports for them (such as a W-2 form and a final paycheck), dump out a copy of their records to the printer or to microfilm for long-term storage, and then use the DELETE statement to delete their records from the file.

The final thing we might want to do on an indexed file is to place it in a specific location so that we may begin sequential input–output activity. To do this, we can use the START **statement.** The general form is:

START statement

```
                     ┌                                              ┐
                     │          ┌                         ┐         │
                     │          │  IS EQUAL TO            │         │
                     │          │                         │         │
                     │          │  IS =                   │         │
                     │          │                         │         │
                     │          │  IS GREATER THAN        │         │
                     │          │                         │         │
                     │          │  IS >                   │         │
                     │          │                         │         │
                     │          │  IS NOT LESS THAN       │         │
                     │          │                         │         │
  START  file-name   │  KEY     │  IS NOT <               │ data-name│
                     └          └                         ┘         ┘
            [ INVALID KEY imperative-statement ]
```

Here is an example of a START statement:

```
MOVE '585010793' TO STUDENT-NO.
START MASTER-FILE KEY IS GREATER THAN STUDENT-NO.
```

In this example we are moving a literal into a field called STUDENT-NO. The START given in the next line positions the file so that the next record to be read will be the first one with a key larger than the one stored in STUDENT-NO. The key we are using to make the comparison is the one specified in the RECORD KEY clause for the file. If the computer is not able to position the file at this location (for instance, there are no records with keys larger) then the INVALID KEY option will be taken. If there is no INVALID KEY option as in the example above, the program will terminate with an error message.

These statements complete our formal discussion of the indexed file organization. There is also another file organization used by COBOL called **relative file organization**. Relative organization is similar to indexed organization except that instead of a file key, we use a counter to number the records in the file. We may access the file in order by the counters taking the first record, the second and so on, or we may access it directly by giving the counter number of the record that we want. Because of this ability to go directly to the record we want to retrieve, the data must be stored on a direct-access device, such as a disk or drum.

relative file organization

As with the indexed organization, the entires we will use in the FILE-CONTROL section are a little different from what we have been accustomed to. Some sample entries are:

```
SELECT STUDENT-FILE ASSIGN TO DA-R-STFILE,
    ORGANIZATION IS RELATIVE,
    ACCESS MODE IS SEQUENTIAL,
    NOMINAL KEY IS FILE-KEY.
SELECT ACCOUNT-FILE ASSIGN TO DA-R-ACCTS,
    ORGANIZATION IS RELATIVE,
    ACCESS MODE IS RANDOM,
    NOMINAL KEY IS ACCOUNT-KEY.
SELECT BILL-FILE ASSIGN TO TRANSACT,
    ORGANIZATION IS RELATIVE,
    ACCESS MODE IS RANDOM RELATIVE KEY IS
    TRAN-NUMBER.
```

In the three examples of the SELECT statements above, two are for IBM equipment, and the third is one that might be used on non-IBM ANSI COBOL. In our IBM-oriented statements, the system name conventions for our file are similar to those we have used earlier. The DA implies that the data is stored in a direct-access device; the letter R implies that the organization of the file is RELATIVE; and the system name follows these two qualifiers. As with indexed organization, there are lines giving the ORGANIZATION, the ACCESS MODE, and the NOMINAL KEY. The data name given in the NOMINAL KEY phrase contains the counter for the file.

The general format of the SELECT **statement for relative organiza-tion** is:

SELECT statement for relative organization

```
SELECT  file-name  ASSIGN TO system-name

    ORGANIZATION IS RELATIVE

  ┌                                                    ┐
  │ ACCESS MODE IS                                     │
  │                                                    │
  │     SEQUENTIAL [ RELATIVE KEY IS data-name-1 ]     │
  │   ⎧ RANDOM  ⎫                                      │
  │   ⎨         ⎬ [ RELATIVE KEY IS data-name-1 ]      │
  │   ⎩ DYNAMIC ⎭                                      │
  └                                                    ┘

    NOMINAL KEY IS data-name-2
```

This definition is not quite the one that would be found in the ANSI COBOL specifications. The NOMINAL KEY phrase is not used in ANSI COBOL, and instead, we use a RELATIVE KEY phrase after the reserved word that gives the access mode. The NOMINAL KEY phrase is strictly an IBM usage. For use of relative files, check the reference manual of your machine to see which of the forms is used in this statement. It may well be that if you are using non-IBM equipment, your SELECT statements for relative files will look like the third example above.

The SELECT statement gives the computer all the necessary data for access to relative files, and the input–output commands for this access mode are the same as those we discussed for the indexed organization. In general, we can think of the relative file organization as a specialized form of the indexed organization that restricts the keys used to numbers. This makes it somewhat less useful than the indexed organization, and it is less commonly found in data processing applications than the indexed organization.

As an example of the use of direct access file organizations, let us set up a simplified employee file application of the type that might be used by a company for its personnel or payroll files. In such applications, it is useful to be able to access the file sequentially for such things as payroll runs or company directory listings. It is also useful to be able to access the file directly to review the records of individual employees. We would want either an indexed or a relative file organization.

In the example we have prepared, we use two programs. The first reads in the raw data cards to create the employee records on an indexed file. The format of the data cards fed into the program is:

COLUMNS	CONTENTS
1–9	Employee identification number
10–19	Employee's last name
20–29	Employee's first name
30	Employee's middle initial
31–38	Employee's monthly salary, right justified with two places after the (implied) decimal point
39–48	Employee's department in the company
49–52	Employee's phone extension
53–58	Employee's office number
59–70	Employee's job title

Figure 9.4 gives the hierarchy diagram for the file creation program. It is divided into a control routine; an initialization routine, which sets up the files and variables; a read and write routine, which reads in the data cards and creates the indexed records; a cleanup routine, which finishes processing; and finally, an error routine, which handles erroneous records. Figure 9.5 shows the flowcharts of each of these routines.

Figure 9.6 lists the indexed file creation program. The file CARD-FILE contains the unsorted employee cards from which the indexed file will be created. After it is sorted, the cards will be stored on DATA-FILE and used as input to create MASTER-FILE, which is our indexed employee file. Notice that in our SELECT statement for MASTER-FILE we are declaring its access be sequential. In this run we must do this since we are creating a new file entirely.

The only thing different in the PROCEDURE DIVISION (Figure 9.6c) is that we are using the WRITE statement with an INVALID KEY option. If an invalid key is encountered in the data, we display an error message. The error message is set off on both sides by ten asterisks to make it more noticeable to the clerks who will be reading the output from the program. We also keep count of the total cards read in to create new records on the file and a count of the errors we have encountered. These are printed out at the end of the run as a sort of audit report to give the users of the programs some check on the accuracy of the data preparation for this program.

We give a sample of the input used for this program (Figure 9.6d). Notice that the first card and the second card in the input have the same key. The first card was obviously intended to have the same data on it as the second card, but because of a keypunch error, it was discarded, and later the clerk forgot to remove it from the input. This might be a common type of data processing error. Below this, we have some sample output

FIGURE 9.4
Hierarchy Diagram for Indexed File Create Program

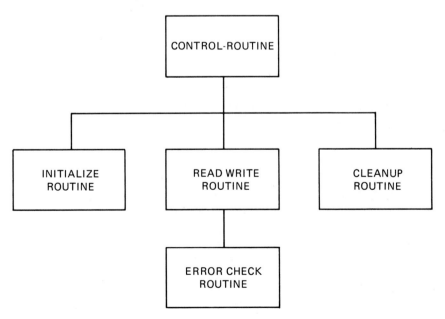

(Figure 9.6e) from the program. We get a line that tells us that the program ended normally, and then we are told that 101 cards were read in and that one of them (the one noted earlier) was an error card. In our error message reproduced in the figure we get a printout of the record that was in error. This will help the clerks when they go back and try to correct the problem. In this case, the bad record was rejected by the program, and the good one added to the file, so no further action on the part of the clerks is necessary.

After the file has been created, we want a routine to read data from it using the indexes rather than having to read it sequentially. Figure 9.7 gives the hierarchy diagram for such a program. Again, it has the same structure as our earlier program. The input to this program will be a series of employee numbers. We will read them in using an ACCEPT statement rather than our conventional READ statement, so we do not

a. CONTROL-ROUTINE

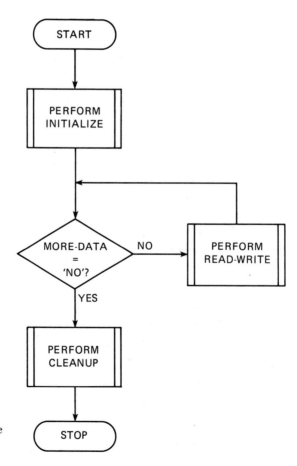

FIGURE 9.5
Flowchart for Indexed File
Create Program

have to set up any special lines in our FILE-CONTROL section for this input. There is another reason for doing this as well. One use for retrieving individual records from an indexed file might be to display them at some sort of remote console, and the ACCEPT and DISPLAY statements are frequently used for input–output activity to such devices (of course, it is also possible to use READ and WRITE on these devices with a proper choice of job control language). When we have input as many employee numbers as we care to, we input a line that says FINISH, and our program should terminate normally. Figure 9.8 shows the flowcharts of the indi-

FIGURE 9.5
(Continued)

b. INITIALIZE Routine

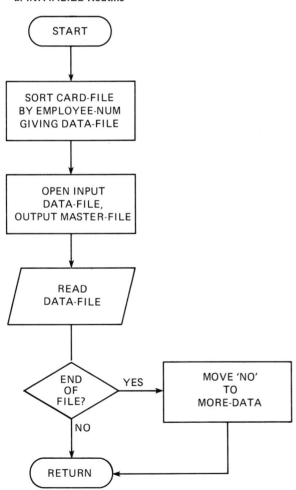

vidual routines that make up the program, and Figure 9.9 lists the COBOL program for doing direct access input from an indexed file.

The computer knows that the file is to be accessed directly rather than sequentially because in our SELECT statement for the MASTER-FILE, we have used a phrase that says that ACCESS IS RANDOM. We are also

FIGURE 9.5
(Continued)

c. READ-WRITE Routine

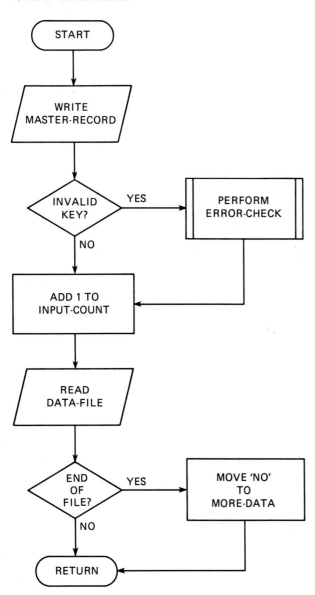

using the NOMINAL KEY phrase since this program was run on IBM equipment. The nominal key is a variable in the WORKING-STORAGE section that contains the key of the record we are looking for on the MASTER-FILE. In the CONTROL-ROUTINE, the DISPLAY-RECORD routine is performed to display the record we are going to retrieve and to read in the key of the next record. This routine is performed until we read in the characters FINISH. The INITIALIZE routine opens the MASTER-FILE for input and the ERROR-FILE and the PRINT-FILE for output. It then accepts the first employee number and returns control back to the CONTROL-ROUTINE.

FIGURE 9.5
(Continued)

d. CLEANUP Routine

e. ERROR-CHECK Routine

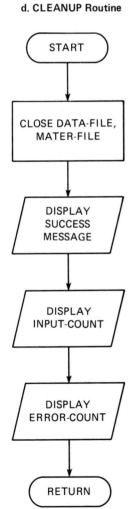

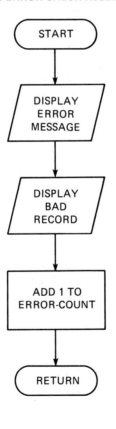

FIGURE 9.6
Listing of Indexed File
Create Program.

a. IDENTIFICATION and ENVIRONMENT DIVISIONS

```
000010 IDENTIFICATION DIVISION.
000020 PROGRAM-ID.  EMPLOY.
000030 DATE-WRITTEN.  JANUARY, 1980.
000040 DATE-COMPILED.  JANUARY, 1980.
000050**************VERSION 1.0 - LAST MODIFIED JANUARY, 1980*********
000060*     THE EMPLOY PROGRAM CREATES AN INDEXED SEQUENTIAL EMPLOYEE*
000070*     FILE FROM A CARD DECK.  THE FORMAT OF THE INPUT CARDS    *
000080*     IS GIVEN BELOW:                                          *
000090*          COL 1 - 9    THE EMPLOYEE NUMBER.                   *
000100*          COL 10 - 19  THE EMPLOYEE'S LAST NAME.              *
000110*          COL 20 - 29  THE EMPLOYEE'S FIRST NAME.             *
000120*          COL 30       THE EMPLOYEE'S MIDDLE INITIAL.         *
000130*          COL 31 - 38  THE EMPLOYEE'S SALARY, RIGHT           *
000140*                       JUSTIFIED WITH TWO PLACES AFTER        *
000150*                       THE DECIMAL.                           *
000160*          COL 39 - 48  THE EMPLOYEE'S DEPARTMENT.             *
000170*          COL 49 - 52  THE EMPLOYEE'S PHONE EXTENSION.        *
000180*          COL 53 - 58  THE EMPLOYEE'S OFFICE NUMBER.          *
000190*          COL 59 - 70  THE EMPLOYEE'S JOB TITLE.              *
000200************************************************************
000210 ENVIRONMENT DIVISION.
000220 CONFIGURATION SECTION.
000230 SOURCE-COMPUTER.  IBM-370-145.
000240 OBJECT-COMPUTER.   IBM-370-145.
000250 INPUT-OUTPUT SECTION.
000260 FILE-CONTROL.
000270     SELECT CARD-FILE ASSIGN TO UT-S-CARDS.
000280     SELECT DATA-FILE ASSIGN TO UT-S-INPUT.
000290     SELECT SORT-FILE ASSIGN TO UT-S-SORTIN.
000300     SELECT MASTER-FILE ASSIGN TO DA-I-OLDMAST
000310        ACCESS IS SEQUENTIAL,
000320        RECORD KEY IS EMPLOYEE-NO OF MASTER-RECORD.
```

b. DATA DIVISION

```
000330 DATA DIVISION.
000340 FILE SECTION.
000350 FD  CARD-FILE LABEL RECORDS ARE OMITTED.
000360 01  CARD-RECORD.
000370     02  EMPLOYEE-NO       PIC X(9).
000380     02  FILLER            PIC X(100).
000390 FD  DATA-FILE LABEL RECORDS ARE STANDARD.
000400 01  DATA-RECORD           PIC X(70).
000410 FD  MASTER-FILE
000420     LABEL RECORDS ARE STANDARD,
000430     BLOCK CONTAINS 10 RECORDS,
000440     RECORD CONTAINS 100 CHARACTERS.
```

FIGURE 9.6
(Continued)

```
000450 01  MASTER-RECORD.
000460     02  EMPLOYEE-NO        PICTURE X(9).
000470     02  LAST-NAME          PICTURE X(10).
000480     02  FIRST-NAME         PICTURE X(10).
000490     02  INIT               PICTURE X.
000500     02  SALARY             PICTURE 999999V99.
000510     02  DEPARTMENT         PICTURE X(10).
000520     02  EXTENSION          PICTURE X(4).
000530     02  OFFICE             PICTURE X(6).
000540     02  JOB-TITLE          PICTURE X(12).
000550     02  FILLER             PICTURE X(30).
000560 SD  SORT-FILE.
000570 01  SORT-RECORD.
000580     02  EMPLOYEE-NO        PIC X(9).
000590     02  FILLER             PIC X(100).
000600 WORKING-STORAGE SECTION.
000610 77  INPUT-COUNT            PIC 999999 VALUE IS ZERO.
000620 77  ERROR-COUNT            PIC 999999 VALUE IS ZERO.
000630 77  MORE-DATA              PIC XXX VALUE IS 'YES'.
```

c. PROCEDURE DIVISION

```
000640 PROCEDURE DIVISION.
000650 CONTROL-ROUTINE.
000660     PERFORM INITIALIZE.
000670     PERFORM READ-WRITE UNTIL MORE-DATA IS EQUAL TO 'NO'.
000680     PERFORM CLEANUP.
000690     STOP RUN.
000700 INITIALIZE.
000710     SORT SORT-FILE ON ASCENDING KEY EMPLOYEE-NO OF
000720         SORT-RECORD,
000730     USING CARD-FILE,
000740     GIVING DATA-FILE.
000750     OPEN INPUT DATA-FILE, OUTPUT MASTER-FILE.
000760     READ DATA-FILE INTO MASTER-RECORD.
000770         AT END MOVE 'NO' TO MORE-DATA.
000780 READ-WRITE.
000790     WRITE MASTER-RECORD INVALID KEY PERFORM ERROR-CHECK.
000800     ADD 1 TO INPUT-COUNT.
000810     READ DATA-FILE INTO MASTER-RECORD
000820         AT END MOVE 'NO' TO MORE-DATA.
000830 ERROR-CHECK.
000840     DISPLAY '**********DUPLICATE KEY OR SEQUENCE ERROR**********'
000850     DISPLAY '    RECORD IS ', DATA-RECORD.
000860     ADD 1 TO ERROR-COUNT.
000870 CLEANUP.
000880     CLOSE DATA-FILE, MASTER-FILE.
000890     DISPLAY '*END OF INDEXED SEQUENTIAL FILE CREATE*'.
000900     DISPLAY '    INPUT CARDS READ:', INPUT-COUNT.
000910     DISPLAY '        ERRORS FOUND:' ERROR-COUNT.
```

FIGURE 9.6
(Continued)

d. SAMPLE INPUT

```
000000971NEMANX
000000971NEWMAN    LOIS        D00381200MARKETING 5107F-5858PROGRAMMER
000002143POST      BERL        B00228600SHIPPING  3262F-6679SUPERVISOR
000003847MARTIN    DELTON      N00421800SHIPPING  4941E-9501STAFF
000005775PIMM      MARIE       G00150600SYSTEMS   3298E-7464SUPERVISOR
000007271MICHOLS   ALLEN       G00118300PRODUCTION2260A-1993STAFF
000008743RESON     DWAYNE      L00289900ACCOUNTING6402A-2315STAFF
000010047ADAMS     DELTON      D00589300SHIPPING  0104F-2740STAFF
000011175MARTIN    DELTON      P00937300SHIPPING  0556B-4369MANAGER
000013071RESON     ALAN        C02950700PRODUCTION1080A-7855STAFF
000014343CARTER    HARRY       A02489000ACCOUNTING2635B-1058SUPERVISOR
000016247NEWELL    RUTH        I00596000PRODUCTION2489D-5066PROGRAMMER
000017575LYONS     LAWRENCE    K00052600MARKETING 9380E-6369STAFF
```

e. SAMPLE OUTPUT

```
*END OF INDEXED SEQUENTIAL FILE CREATE*
     INPUT CARDS READ:000101
        ERRORS FOUND:000001
```

f. SAMPLE ERROR MESSAGE OUTPUT

```
**********DUPLICATE KEY OR SEQUENCE ERROR**********
     RECORD IS 000000971NEMANX
```

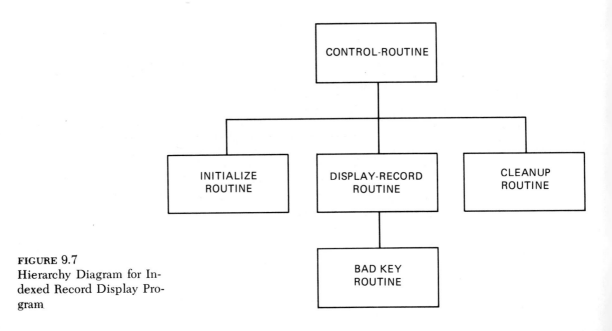

FIGURE 9.7
Hierarchy Diagram for Indexed Record Display Program

The DISPLAY-RECORD routine is a little more complicated. The first thing we do is read the MASTER-FILE using the last key that was read into the EMPLOYEE variable by an ACCEPT statement. If this represents an invalid key (one that does not exist in the MASTER-FILE), then control is transferred to the BAD-KEY routine. In this routine, we first move a 1 to the variable BAD-KEY-FLAG (a variable we have declared in WORKING-STORAGE). This flag is used to tell the program that we have just read in a bad key and that we should not try to print out the record in the MASTER-FILE data area. We then add one to the ERR-COUNT variable we are using to keep track of the number of bad keys, and then we write out an image of the bad key on the ERROR-FILE. This can be used to check

FIGURE 9.8
Flowchart for Indexed Record Display Program

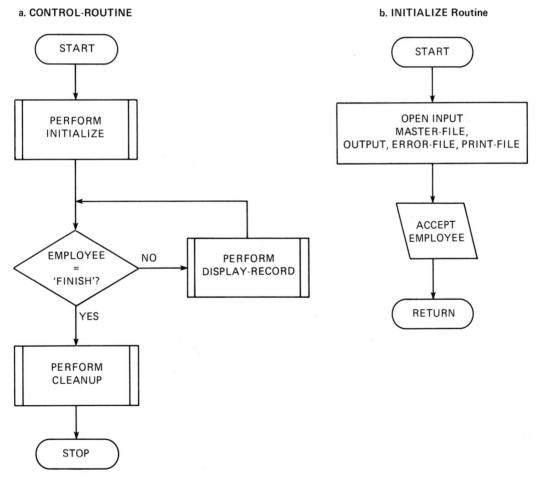

a. CONTROL-ROUTINE

b. INITIALIZE Routine

FIGURE 9.8
(Continued)

c. DISPLAY-RECORD Routine

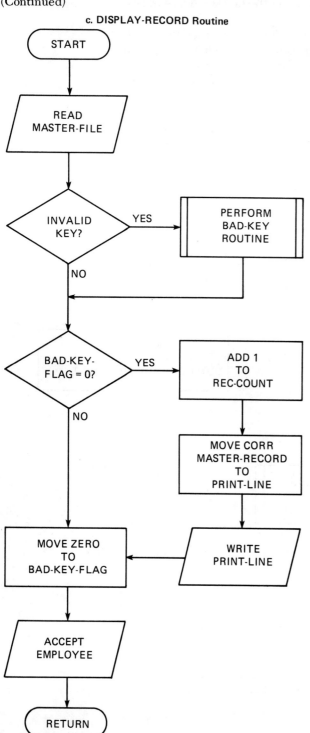

our input later on if we desire. Control is then transferred back to the DISPLAY-RECORD routine at the line immediately following the READ statement.

The next statement is an IF statement that checks the BAD-KEY-FLAG. If it is equal to zero, the READ must have been successful, and we can print out the record. We add one to the count of the number of records printed, move the MASTER-RECORD to the PRINT-RECORD, which edits the data into a more readable format, and then we print the record we retrieved. If the key was bad, we will skip this entire section of code. The next thing we do is move a zero to the BAD-KEY-FLAG. This means that

FIGURE 9.8
(Continued)

d. BAD-KEY Routine

e. CLEANUP Routine

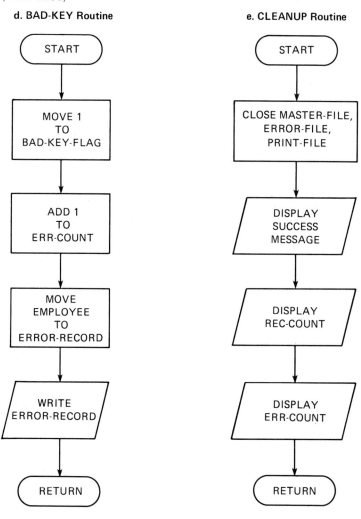

FIGURE 9.9
Listing of Indexed Record
Display Program.

a. IDENTIFICATION and ENVIRONMENT DIVISIONS

```
000010 IDENTIFICATION DIVISION.
000020 PROGRAM-ID.  SHOWREC.
000030 DATE-WRITTEN.  JANUARY, 1980.
000040 DATE-COMPILED.  JANUARY, 1980.
000050**************VERSION 1.0 - LAST MODIFIED JANUARY, 1980*********
000060*    THE SHOWREC PROGRAM ACCESSES THE INDEXED SEQUENTIAL   *
000070*    FILE CREATED BY THE EMPLOY PROGRAM.  IT USES THE      *
000080*    ACCEPT COMMAND TO READ IN EMPLOYEE NUMBERS. THESE     *
000090*    EMPLOYEES RECORDS ARE PRINTED OUT.  IF THERE IS NO    *
000100*    EMPLOYEE WITH THAT NUMBER, AN ERROR MESSAGE IS PRINTED. *
000110*    AN EMPLOYEE NUMBER OF 'FINISH' ENDS THE JOB.          *
000120************************************************************
000130 ENVIRONMENT DIVISION.
000140 CONFIGURATION SECTION.
000150 SOURCE-COMPUTER.  IBM-370-145.
000160 OBJECT-COMPUTER.   IBM-370-145.
000170 INPUT-OUTPUT SECTION.
000180 FILE-CONTROL.
000190     SELECT MASTER-FILE ASSIGN TO DA-I-OLDMAST
000200         ACCESS IS RANDOM,
000210         NOMINAL KEY IS EMPLOYEE,
000220         RECORD KEY IS EMPLOYEE-NO OF MASTER-RECORD.
000230     SELECT ERROR-FILE ASSIGN TO UT-S-ERR.
000240     SELECT PRINT-FILE ASSIGN TO UT-S-PRINTER.
```

b. DATA DIVISION

```
000250 DATA DIVISION.
000260 FILE SECTION.
000270 FD  MASTER-FILE LABEL RECORDS ARE STANDARD,
000280     BLOCK CONTAINS 10 RECORDS,
000290     RECORD CONTAINS 100 CHARACTERS,
000300     RECORDING MODE IS F.
000310 01  MASTER-RECORD.
000320     02  EMPLOYEE-NO      PICTURE X(9).
000330     02  LAST-NAME        PICTURE X(10).
000340     02  FIRST-NAME       PICTURE X(10).
000350     02  INIT             PICTURE X.
000360     02  SALARY           PICTURE 999999V99.
000370     02  DEPARTMENT       PICTURE X(10).
000380     02  EXTENSION        PICTURE X(4).
000390     02  OFFICE           PICTURE X(6).
000400     02  JOB-TITLE        PICTURE X(12).
000410     02  FILLER           PICTURE X(30).
000420 FD  ERROR-FILE LABEL RECORDS ARE OMITTED.
000430 01  ERROR-RECORD         PICTURE X(120).
000440 FD  PRINT-FILE LABEL RECORDS ARE OMITTED.
```

FIGURE 9.9
(Continued)

```
000450 01  PRINT-RECORD            PICTURE X(71).
000460 WORKING-STORAGE SECTION.
000470 77  BAD-KEY-FLAG            PICTURE 9 VALUE IS ZERO.
000480 77  REC-COUNT              PICTURE 9999 VALUE IS ZERO.
000490 77  ERR-COUNT              PICTURE 9999 VALUE IS ZERO.
000500 77  EMPLOYEE               PICTURE X(9).
000510 01  PRINT-LINE.
000520     02  LAST-NAME          PICTURE X(10).
000530     02  FILLER             PICTURE X(2) VALUE IS ','.
000540     02  FIRST-NAME         PICTURE X(10).
000550     02  FILLER             PICTURE X VALUE IS ' '.
000560     02  INIT               PICTURE X.
000570     02  FILLER             PICTURE XX VALUE IS ','.
000580     02  JOB-TITLE          PICTURE X(12).
000590     02  FILLER             PICTURE X VALUE IS ' '.
000600     02  DEPARTMENT         PICTURE X(10).
000610     02  FILLER             PICTURE X(10) VALUE IS ' SALARY: '.
000620     02  SALARY             PICTURE $$$$$$9.99.
000630 01  ERROR-LINE.
000640     02  FILLER             PICTURE X(10) VALUE IS 'BAD KEY = '.
000650     02  ERR-KEY            PICTURE X(9).
```

c. PROCEDURE DIVISION

```
000660 PROCEDURE DIVISION.
000670 CONTROL- ROUTINE.
000680     PERFORM INITIALIZE.
000690     PERFORM DISPLAY-RECORD UNTIL EMPLOYEE = 'FINISH'.
000700     PERFORM CLEANUP.
000710     STOP RUN.
000720 INITIALIZE.
000730     OPEN INPUT MASTER-FILE, OUTPUT ERROR-FILE,
000740         PRINT-FILE.
000750     ACCEPT EMPLOYEE.
000760 DISPLAY-RECORD.
000770     READ MASTER-FILE INVALID KEY PERFORM BAD-KEY.
000780     IF BAD-KEY-FLAG = 0
000790         ADD 1 TO REC-COUNT
000800         MOVE CORR MASTER-RECORD TO PRINT LINE.
000810         WRITE PRINT-RECORD FROM PRINT-LINE.
000820     MOVE 0 TO BAD-KEY-FLAG.
000830     ACCEPT EMPLOYEE.
000840 BAD-KEY.
000850     MOVE 1 TO BAD-KEY-FLAG.
000860     ADD 1 TO ERR-COUNT.
000870     MOVE EMPLOYEE TO ERR-KEY.
000880     WRITE ERROR-RECORD FROM ERROR-LINE.
000890 CLEANUP.
000900     CLOSE MASTER-FILE, ERROR-FILE.
000910     DISPLAY 'END OF EMPLOYEE RECORD DISPLAY PROGRAM'.
000920     DISPLAY 'RECORDS RETRIEVED: ', REC-COUNT.
000930     DISPLAY 'BAD KEYS:        ', ERR-COUNT.
```

FIGURE 9.9
(Continued)

d. Sample Input

```
000000971
000003847
000029375
000044343
999999999
888888888
000047575
000002143
FINISH
```

e. Sample Output

```
NEWMAN     , LOIS       D. PROGRAMMER   MARKETING  SALARY:  $3812.00
MARTIN     , DELTON     N. STAFF        SHIPPING   SALARY:  $4218.00
SCOTT      , EMMA       F. STAFF        MARKETING  SALARY:  $6421.00
GELDMAN    , PATRICIA   H. STAFF        ACCOUNTING SALARY:  $6957.00
SEGRIST    , DWAYNE     K. SUPERVISOR   SYSTEMS    SALARY:  $2774.00
POST       , BERL       B. SUPERVISOR   SHIPPING   SALARY:  $2286.00
SEGRIST    , DWAYNE     K. SUPERVISOR   SYSTEMS    SALARY:  $2774.00
```

f. Sample Error Output

```
BAD KEY = 999999999
BAD KEY = 888888888
```

g. Sample Audit Output

```
END OF EMPLOYEE RECORD DISPLAY PROGRAM
RECORDS RETRIEVED:  0006
BAD KEYS:           0002
```

whatever happened on the last read, it will have no effect on the next reading of a key, and then finally, we accept a new employee number.

The CLEANUP routine is conventional. It prints out a success message and then displays an audit report giving the number of records input and the number of bad keys encountered. If you will examine the data in the sample input (Figure 9.9), you will notice that there are two bad keys, 999999999 and 88888888. These were included to give you an idea how the program will work. The sample output shows the records that were retrieved. Notice that the order in which they were printed has nothing to do with the order in which they were stored in the MASTER-FILE. The only thing determining their order is the order in which we present the keys. The sample error output shows how we have displayed the erroneous keys, and the final audit output shows the summary of the results of the run.

The examples in this section show that the indexed file creation and access is really no more formidable than dealing with sequential files. The job control language required is generally more complicated, but you can find out how to set this up by consulting your instructor or by going to the programmer's guide for the computer you are using. Indexed files are very useful because of their great flexibility, and increasingly businesses are using indexed files, particularly as they establish distributed data processing systems with input terminals in many different places in their organizations. The use of indexed files allows individual records (or parts of records) to be retrieved and displayed at these remote terminals. The sample retrieval program given here might be used for just such an application.

STUDY EXERCISES

1. Write the ENVIRONMENT and DATA DIVISION entries needed to read in a file of eighty column cards with alphanumeric data printed on them.

2. Write a COBOL program that will produce a listing of a deck of cards. The program should produce one line for each card showing exactly what is on the card. Document your program well, including structure diagrams, flowcharts, and comments in the program itself to tell how the program is put together.

3. Modify the program in exercise 2 to produce line numbers to the left of each card image printed, such as:

```
1.  THIS IS CARD 1
2.  THIS IS CARD 2
```

Do not do this modification to your own program. Exchange decks with another student and modify his or her deck to produce the desired output.

4. Write a computer program that will delete student records from the MASTER-FILE. Your program should take as input cards that look like this:

Col 1–6	DELETE
Col 11–19	Student number
Col 21–40	Student's last name

Your program should be set up so that it will delete a student's MASTER-FILE record only if both the student number and the last name on the DELETE card agree with that found on the record. Your program should produce the following output:

   a. A listing of the names and student numbers of those students whose records were deleted

   b. A listing of the erroneous DELETE cards encountered

   c. A count of the records deleted from the file and of the errors encountered

5. A gasoline credit card company has bill cards made up for customer purchases at its stations in the following format:

COLUMNS	CONTENTS
1–10	Customer account number
11–30	Customer name
31–40	Station account number
41–60	Station name
61–70	Bill amount in 9999999V99 format

Make up some sample data for this problem, and then write a computer program that will read in the bills (they are in no particular order) and print out each customer's bill in this form:

```
CUSTOMER ACCOUNT:  XXXXXXXXX
CUSTOMER NAME:     XXXXXXXXXXXXXX

           PURCHASES

   STATION                 AMOUNT

1  XXXXXXXX                XXXXX
2  XXXXXXXX                XXXXX

   TOTAL                   XXXXX
```

Do a report like this for each customer on the file.

6. Using the data from exercise 5, produce a similar report that will produce a listing for each service station of the names of customers who purchased products at its location. The format of the report should be similar to that in exercise 5.

7. Write a single program that will produce the same reports as the ones generated in exercises 5 and 6.

8. Write a computer program to change the bill amounts in the MASTER-FILE records. The input to your program should look like this:

COLUMNS	CONTENTS
1–10	Card Type. The following codes should be used: TUITION means change the tuition amount. ROOM means change the amount for room and board. FEE means change the fee amount. OTHER means change the miscellaneous fees in OTHER-BAL.
11–19	Student number.
20–40	Student last name.
41–46	The bill amount in 9999V99 format.

Your program should read in the bill cards (they are in no particular order) and match them with the proper record in the MASTER-FILE. The match must be on both the student number and the last name. When a match occurs, add the bill to the total already in the appropriate field, and change the TOTAL-BAL field to reflect the new activity. If there is no student with the given number and name, then print out an error message and the image of the erroneous card. At the end of the run, your program should print out the total number of changes read in and the number of erroneous changes encountered.

9. Write a computer program to print bills from the updated MASTER-FILE records in exercise 8. The bill should contain the name and address of the student owing the bill, the amount owed in each category and the total amount owed. Print the bills in order by zip code.

10. Write a computer program to change the student data on the MASTER-FILE to an indexed file.

11. Using the indexed file in exercise 10, write a COBOL program that will read in a student number and retrieve the record represented by that student number.

10 1
0 10
10
10 1
0 10
10
10 1
0 10
10
10 1
0 10
10

THE PERFORM STATEMENT

10.0 INTRODUCTION

In this chapter we are going to present the different options available with the PERFORM statement. The PERFORM statement is not new to you. We have already used some versions of it extensively to segment our programs and give them a readable structure. But, in our work so far, we have only used a small part of the options possible in PERFORM. There are a number of other ways in which this statement can be used.

Basically, the PERFORM statement caused control in your program to be transferred to some other block of code. Control is returned to the normal flow of control when this block of code has been executed. The PERFORM statement can be used to execute some specific block of code:

1. Once and only once

2. A specified number of times

3. A number of times specified by a counter

4. Until some specific condition occurs

In our work so far, we have used only the first and fourth of these possibilities.

It is also possible to nest PERFORM statements so that the block of code to be performed also contains a PERFORM statement. This can be very useful, but you must also be careful not to complicate your program needlessly.

10.1 SIMPLE PERFORM STATEMENTS

We have already covered the simplest version of the PERFORM in our programs. A typical COBOL program's control routine might look like this:

```
PERFORM INITIALIZE.
PERFORM EDIT-DATA.
PERFORM CLEANUP.
```

The rules for this version of the PERFORM statement are simple. Control is transferred to the paragraph named after the PERFORM statement. The statements in this paragraph are executed until a new paragraph heading is reached. At this point, control is transferred back to the statement *after* the PERFORM.

The general format for this type of PERFORM **statement** is: PERFORM statement

FORMAT 1

$$\underline{\text{PERFORM}} \text{ procedure-name-1 } \left[\left\{ \begin{array}{l} \underline{\text{THROUGH}} \\ \underline{\text{THRU}} \end{array} \right\} \text{ procedure-name-2 } \right]$$

The format allows a slightly different version of the PERFORM than we have used so far. We could do a PERFORM like:

```
PERFORM INITIALIZE THRU CLEANUP.
```

This version of the PERFORM would transfer control to the procedure INITIALIZE, and it would keep executing statements after the end of the INITIALIZE paragraph until it came to the CLEANUP paragraph. When it had completed the CLEANUP paragraph, control would be transferred back to the statement after the PERFORM. All statements between the beginning of the INITIALIZE paragraph and the end of the CLEANUP paragraph would be performed. We will not use this format of the PERFORM in this book because it detracts from the simple structure that we are trying to maintain in our programs.

In any of these comments about the PERFORM statement, we are assuming that the procedure being performed does not contain any statement (such as a STOP RUN) that would cause the program to halt or transfer control someplace else without the possibility of returning to the main control routine. If you write your programs so that control is not transferred back to the main routine, then the structure of your programs is much more complicated, and your code becomes much more difficult to understand (even for you).

The second format of the PERFORM is also quite easy to understand and use. Some examples are:

```
PERFORM TEST-GRADES 5 TIMES.
PERFORM GET-ACCOUNTS THRU TEST-ACCOUNTS 10 TIMES.
PERFORM CHECK-GRADES N TIMES.
```

This version of the PERFORM statement is used for repeating blocks of code a specified number of times. The number of times that the code is repeated can be specified by a constant or variable. The general format of this type of PERFORM is:

FORMAT 2
_____

PERFORM procedure-name-1 [$\left\{ \begin{array}{l} \text{THROUGH} \\ \text{THRU} \end{array} \right\}$ procedure-name-2]

$\left\{ \begin{array}{l} \text{identifier-1} \\ \text{integer-1} \end{array} \right\}$ TIMES

    This version allows us the same THRU option as did Format 1, and we will not use it in this book for the same reasons. The number of times the block of code given by procedure-name-1 is performed is specified by the integer or variable given before the word TIMES. If this value is negative or zero, then the block of code is not performed at all.
    The final format of the PERFORM statement that we will present in this section is also one we have been using for some time. Some examples of this format are:

```
PERFORM READ-PRINT UNTIL MORE-DATA IS EQUAL TO 'NO'.
PERFORM TEST-ACCOUNT UNTIL BALANCE = 0.
PERFORM CHECKER UNTIL X + 1 = 0.
```

In this format, the procedure is performed until some specified condition is true. You must make sure that this condition can become true in the course of executing your program, or you will have an infinite loop. We have used this format extensively in our programs to this point in order to control the reading of data. The general format of this PERFORM is:

FORMAT 3
_____

PERFORM procedure-name-1 [$\left\{ \begin{array}{l} \text{THROUGH} \\ \text{THRU} \end{array} \right\}$ procedure-name-2]

    UNTIL condition-1

The condition in format 3 can be any condition that you would be able to use in an IF statement. The same advice applies here as it did in the IF statements. Keep the conditions as simple as possible, or you may have difficulty in understanding your code.

There are many possible uses for the different versions of the PERFORM statement we have presented here. One possible use is the manipulation of tables in data records. For example, suppose we wished to print out the grade tables in the student records we have used. We could first declare a variable in WORKING-STORAGE:

```
77  I      PICTURE 9999.
```

Then, in the PROCEDURE DIVISION, we might have this code:

```
DISPLAY 'COURSE        COURSE-NAME        GRADE'.
MOVE 1 TO I.
PERFORM PRINT-GRADE 5 TIMES.
```

The code for the PRINT-GRADE procedure might look like this:

```
PRINT-GRADE.
    DISPLAY COURSE-NO OF MASTER-RECORD (I),
            COURSE-NAME OF MASTER-RECORD (I),
            GRADE OF MASTER-RECORD (I).
    ADD 1 TO I.
CLEANUP.
```

Notice how we have used the variable I in this example. Before you perform PRINT-GRADE, it is necessary to set I to the correct value. Each time we reenter PRINT-GRADE, the value of I is updated.

If we had wished to use a different format of the PERFORM, we could have substituted:

```
PERFORM PRINT-GRADE UNTIL I = 6.
```

To make sure you understand what is going on, you should be able to explain why we perform PRINT-GRADE until I is equal to 6 and not 5. The answer to this lies in the sequence of operations we are performing. The variable I is initially set to 1, and it is not updated until after we have printed out the grades. On the last pass through the PRINT-GRADE routine, the variable I will have the value 5 and the fifth line of grades will be printed. When we have printed the line, we add 1 to the variable I, making it 6. When it becomes 6, we do not want to perform PRINT-GRADE again.

The sequence of operations we execute is very important. If we had written PRINT-GRADE like this:

```
PRINT-GRADE.
    ADD 1 TO I.
    DISPLAY COURSE-NO OF MASTER-RECORD (I),
        COURSE-NAME OF MASTER-RECORD (I),
        GRADE OF MASTER-RECORD (I).
```

we would have problems. The first line of grades would not be printed, and the computer would attempt to print out a sixth (nonexistent) line of grades. When you are writing this type of PERFORM, make sure you consider these points carefully in constructing your code.

10.2 ADVANCED PERFORM STATEMENTS AND TABLE HANDLING

So far, we have been using the PERFORM statement to segment our programs and give us structured, modular code. This is only one of the reasons for using the PERFORM statement, and indeed, it was not the first reason for including PERFORM in the COBOL language. Generally, programmers think of the PERFORM statement as one to be used to repeat blocks of code a specified number of times. This is a very handy thing to be able to do when we are searching tables (recall from Section 8.2 how to use an OCCURS clause in the DATA DIVISION to build tables). We have already had a hint of how we might do this in the earlier sections of this chapter. It is possible to search tables using the PERFORM option to perform a block a specified number of times and then update our index within the block. The next version of the PERFORM, which has the VARYING option, will let us do this explicitly.

Suppose we want to print out the class lines in the table COURSE in the MASTER-FILE records. We can do this using this code:

```
        PERFORM DISPLAY-CLASS VARYING I FROM 1 BY 1
            UNTIL I IS GREATER THAN 5.
                .
                .
                .

    DISPLAY-CLASS.
        DISPLAY COURSE OF MASTER-RECORD (I).
                .
                .
                .
```

In this PERFORM example we are using the variable I (presumably it has

been declared in WORKING-STORAGE with an appropriate numeric picture) as both a counter in the PERFORM statement and as a subscript for
accessing levels in the COURSE table. The variable I is initially set to 1,
and the specified block of code is performed. The variable I is then
incremented by 1, and its value is compared with 5. If it is greater, then
the DISPLAY-CLASS block is not performed. If it is less, then the block is
performed again. This process is continued until I becomes greater than
5. Figure 10.1 gives a flowchart of this process. Notice that we do the
comparison of the variable I with 5 first. This means that if we had written
our PERFORM statement as:

```
PERFORM DISPLAY-CLASS VARYING I FROM 10 BY 1
      UNTIL I IS GREATER THAN 5.
```

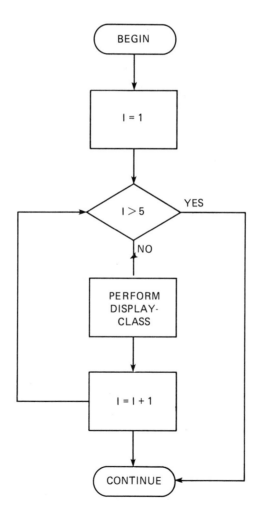

FIGURE 10.1
Flowchart of a *PERFORM*
Statement with *VARYING*
Option

we would have not reached the DISPLAY-CLASS routine at all since the initial value of I was greater than 5.

Caution is required in using PERFORM statements. You should be very careful about changing the value of the index variable down in one of the routines being performed. Suppose, for instance, in the example above the DISPLAY-CLASS routine that we were performing contained a statement like:

```
MOVE 1 TO I.
```

This would automatically set the value of I back to 1, and I would never meet the condition "I IS GREATER THAN 5." This would result in an infinite loop. This may seem like a silly thing to do, but you will probably find that you do the equivalent in your code someday. It is possible to modify index values without causing infinite loops, but it is a bad practice to modify them at all down inside the routine that is being performed. It makes your logic difficult to follow, and this is to be avoided in structured programming. It is a better idea just to make it a rule never to modify an index value of a PERFORM down in one of the routines being performed.

The general format of the PERFORM **with the** VARYING **option** is more complicated than our simple example shows. The general format is:

PERFORM with the VARYING option

FORMAT 4

```
                                      ┌ THROUGH ┐
PERFORM  procedure-name-1  [  ⎨ THRU   ⎬   procedure-name-2 ]

                                   ⎧ data-name-2 ⎫
    VARYING data-name-1   FROM  ⎨ literal-1    ⎬

         ⎧ data-name-3 ⎫
    BY   ⎨ literal-2    ⎬      UNTIL   condition-1

                                      ⎧ data-name-5 ⎫
    [ AFTER data-name-4   FROM  ⎨ literal-3    ⎬

             ⎧ data-name-6 ⎫
        BY   ⎨ literal-4    ⎬   UNTIL   condition-2 ]

                                      ⎧ data-name-8 ⎫
    [ AFTER data-name-7   FROM  ⎨ literal-5    ⎬

             ⎧ data-name-9 ⎫
        BY   ⎨ literal-6    ⎬   UNTIL   condition-2 ]
```

The definition seems quite complicated, but it will be easier to understand if you look at a few examples first. Generally, you will not be using the PERFORM statement in its most complicated forms. If you look carefully at the definition above, you will notice that it allows you to vary only three sets of indices. This corresponds to the three levels that COBOL allows in a table defined by the use of the OCCURS phrases. To see how we might use a more complicated version of the PERFORM, suppose we had a set of data on the sales of our products in different districts. We have ten different districts and a variable number of products. The information on the number of products our firm has at any point is in the variable called PRODUCT-NUM. Then we might write a PERFORM statement like this to do the analysis:

```
PERFORM SALES-ANALYSIS VARYING DISTRICT FROM 1 BY 1
    UNTIL DISTRICT IS GREATER THAN 10
    AFTER PRODUCT FROM 1 BY 1
    UNTIL PRODUCT IS GREATER THAN PRODUCT-NUM.
```

In this example we are using the variables DISTRICT and PRODUCT as our counters for the PERFORM statement. DISTRICT is varied up to a constant 10, and the upper limit taken on by PRODUCT depends on the value in the variable PRODUCT-NUM.

You should be sure you understand how this statement operates. The variable PRODUCT is varied most rapidly when the statement is executed. The value of DISTRICT is set to 1, and then PRODUCT is varied from 1 to PRODUCT-NUM. Then the value of DISTRICT is incremented by 1 to 2, and PRODUCT is again varied from 1 to PRODUCT-NUM. This continues until we have run through all possible combinations of values for DISTRICT and PRODUCT. When setting up PERFORM statements, you should realize that it is possible to cause the computer to do a great deal of work with this very compact statement. In this example the routine SALES-ANALYSIS will be performed:

```
10 x PRODUCT-NUM
```

times. For a large number of products, this might be a costly routine.

As an example of an even more complicated PERFORM, suppose we had a set of data on the sales of our products where the country was divided up into various sales regions; each region could be handled by any number of salesmen; and each sales representative could handle a number of products. A PERFORM statement to analyze this type of situation might look like this:

```
PERFORM SALES-CHECK VARYING SALES-REGION FROM 1 BY 1
        UNTIL SALES-REGION IS GREATER THAN
        TOTAL-REGIONS,
    AFTER SALES-REP FROM 1 BY 1
        UNTIL SALES-REP IS GREATER THAN TOTAL-
        SALES-REPS,
    AFTER PRODUCT FROM 1 BY 1
        UNTIL PRODUCT IS GREATER THAN TOTAL-
        PRODUCTS.
```

In this example, we have three indexes, SALES-REGION, SALES-REP, and PRODUCT. The variable PRODUCT is varied first, followed by SALES-REP, and finally, SALES-REGION. The total number of times that the SALES-CHECK routine is performed is:

```
TOTAL-REGIONS x TOTAL-SALES-REPS x TOTAL-PRODUCTS
```

This means that the amount of work performed by this routine can become quite large.

The PERFORM statement with the VARYING option is most useful in accessing tables, and to get an idea how this is done, go to the example given in the next section.

10.3 PROGRAMMING EXAMPLE USING PERFORM

To show you how you can use the various options of the PERFORM statement, we will do a program that will build a summary table. The building of summary tables is one of the commonest types of activities for programs in management information systems, and the PERFORM statement is very handy for accessing such tables. In Chapter 12 we will learn another technique for setting up summary reports—namely, the REPORT writer. However, the REPORT writer is not available on all COBOL systems (particularly the ones implemented on smaller computers), so you may well find yourself using the PERFORM to build summary tables.

In this particular summary report, we would like to find out what the average GPA is for students in the different colleges and classes represented on the MASTER-FILE. We would like to generate a table that looks like this:

```
                      GRADE AVERAGE SUMMARY

                   FRESHMAN  SOPHOMORE  JUNIOR  SENIOR  COLLEGE AVERAGE
ARTS AND SCIENCES    x.xx      x.xx      x.xx    x.xx       x.xx
BUSINESS             x.xx      x.xx      x.xx    x.xx       x.xx
EDUCATION            x.xx      x.xx      x.xx    x.xx       x.xx
AGRICULTURE          x.xx      x.xx      x.xx    x.xx       x.xx
ENGINEERING          x.xx      x.xx      x.xx    x.xx       x.xx
CLASS AVERAGE        x.xx      x.xx      x.xx    x.xx       x.xx
```

By reading down the columns, you can get the averages for a given class in each college. The last entry in any column is the overall class average. By reading across any row, you can get the class averages for all the students in any particular college, and the last entry in any row gives the overall college average. The entry in the last row and column gives the overall university GPA.

This report is typical of many types of reports required by management in different organizations. For instance, a sales manager might like to have a report listing the dollar amount of sales for each sales representative on each of several different products. Or a bank manager might like to have a report listing the total checking account deposits at each of several branches of the bank. Any of these reports would be prepared in much the same way that we will prepare this grade summary report.

To prepare this report, we will have to set up three tables in the WORKING-STORAGE SECTION of our program. The first table will be the one we call SUMMARY-TABLE, and it will contain the sums of the GPAs in each of the categories. This table will have six rows and five columns. The second table we will call COUNT-TABLE, and it will also have six rows and five columns. It will contain a count of the number of students in each category. Each of these tables will be initialized to zero. The third table we are calling PRINT-TABLE, and it is used to hold the edited result of the GPA computations. This will be the table that we print to generate the results above. We will also have to generate other tables to hold the headings for the rows and the columns.

This program is going to be somewhat more complicated than the others we have written so far. A hierarchy diagram for the program is given in Figure 10.2. As usual, the CONTROL routine calls in the other routines to perform their functions. The INITIALIZE routine zeros out all the tables we will use, opens the MASTER-FILE for input, and reads in the first record. The FILL-TABLE routine sums up the GPAs in the SUMMARY-TABLE and counts the number of students in each category.

To do this, it must be able to look at a student record and determine to which category the student belongs. First, it finds the college using the FIND-COLLEGE routine to match the college recorded on the MASTER-FILE record with one of the ones given as a summary table title. If there is no match, then an error message is printed and no entry is made for that student. If the match on the college is successful, then the FIND-CLASS routine is called to determine the class of the student. This is done by examining the number of credits that the student has completed. This would be used to determine the student's class as follows:

CREDITS VALUE	CLASS
Less than 30	Freshman
30–59	Sophomore
60–89	Junior
90 or more	Senior

There is no need for an error check routine for the student's class since all students will fall into one of the categories above.

FIGURE 10.2
Hierarchy Diagram for
Grade Summary Program

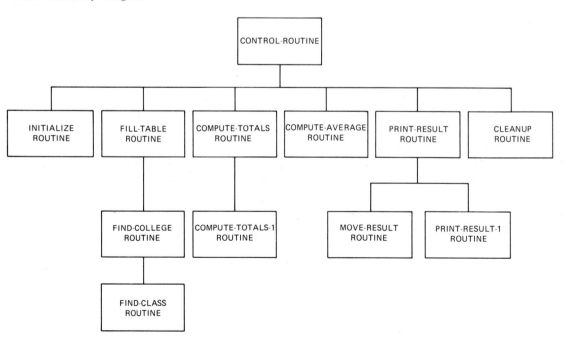

The FILL-TABLE routine is performed until we run out of data on the MASTER-FILE. At that point, the COMPUTE-TOTALS routine is called in. This routine computes the column totals and the row totals for our summary table. We could have computed these totals as we went along and saved ourselves the trouble of writing the COMPUTE-TOTALS and the COMPUTE-TOTALS-1 routines, but this would not have been as efficient with the computer's time. If we had used that approach, we would have had to do three additions for each student record. As it is, we only have to do one, and then at the end, we must do $4 \times 5 + 1$ more. For a large number of students, our approach will be more efficient even though it causes us to have to add a few extra lines of code.

After we have computed the row and column totals, we are ready to compute the averages. This is done by the COMPUTE-AVERAGE routine, which simply divides each element in the SUMMARY-TABLE by its corresponding element in the COUNT-TABLE (provided that the corresponding element is not zero).

After that, we print out the summary table using the PRINT-RESULT routine. This routine closes the MASTER-FILE and opens the PRINT-FILE for output. The PRINT-FILE has both a line title and a line content. We first move the header to the line content and then print that out. Then we move the column headings to the line content and print them out. We transfer control to the MOVE-RESULT routine, which moves each line of our SUMMARY-TABLE to the PRINT-TABLE and returns control to the PRINT-RESULT routine where the PRINT-RESULT-1 routine moves the line title to the line and prints it out, once for each line.

The listing of the program and sample output is given in Figure 10.3. Pay special attention to the WORKING-STORAGE section where the tables are located. The way in which we have handled the ROW-NAME table may look a little strange at first. We define a group of COLLEGE-NAMES. The field names for these colleges are all FILLER, and we use the VALUE IS phrase to initialize them to the different college names. After that, we use the REDEFINE option to redefine the whole data area as a table. We have to do this because we want to be able to use the PERFORM to access each of the row names individually, and we cannot use the VALUE IS phrase to define the different levels in a table. So, we use this approach instead. The REDEFINE statement must be given after the original data area has been initialized. There is no particular reason for any of this. It is merely the way COBOL does things, and you may as well accept it.

Notice that with the example in this chapter, we have not done a flowchart. This is because you would not normally produce the kind of detailed flowcharts that we have done for earlier chapters to document real-world computer programs, and you now know enough about computing that we can stop doing it for the examples in this book. The

FIGURE 10.3
Listing and Sample Output
for Grade Summary Program.

a. IDENTIFICATION and ENVIRONMENT DIVISIONS

```
000010 IDENTIFICATION DIVISION.
000020 PROGRAM-ID. SUMMARY.
000030 AUTHOR.  NORMAN LYONS.
000040 DATE-WRITTEN.  JANUARY, 1980.
000050 DATE-COMPILED.  JANUARY, 1980.
000060 SECURITY.  NONE.
000070***************VERSION 1.0 - LAST MODIFIED JANUARY, 1980**********
000080*    THE GRADES PROGRAM PRODUCES A GRADE SUMMARY TABLE FROM THE   *
000090*    STUDENT MASTER FILE.  THE SUMMARY TABLE GIVES THE GRADE      *
000100*    POINT AVERAGES ON A COLLEGE BY COLLEGE AND CLASS BY          *
000110*    CLASS BASIS.                                                 *
000120*******************************************************************
000130 ENVIRONMENT DIVISION.
000140 CONFIGURATION SECTION.
000150 SOURCE-COMPUTER.  IBM-370-145.
000160 OBJECT-COMPUTER.  IBM-370-145.
000170 INPUT-OUTPUT SECTION.
000180 FILE-CONTROL.
000190    SELECT MASTER-FILE ASSIGN TO UT-S-OLDMAST.
000200    SELECT PRINT-FILE ASSIGN TO UT-S-PRINTER.
```

b. DATA DIVISION-FILE Section

```
000210 DATA DIVISION.
000220 FILE SECTION.
000230 FD  MASTER-FILE LABEL RECORDS ARE STANDARD.
000240 01  MASTER-RECORD.
000250     02  STUDENT-NO        PICTURE X(10).
000260     02  LAST-NAME         PICTURE X(20).
000270     02  FIRST-NAME        PICTURE X(20).
000280     02  INIT              PICTURE X.
000290     02  STREET            PICTURE X(20).
000300     02  CITY              PICTURE X(20).
000310     02  STATE             PICTURE XX.
000320     02  ZIP               PICTURE X(5).
000330     02  PHONE             PICTURE X(7).
000340     02  SEX               PICTURE X.
000350     02  AGE               PICTURE 99.
000360     02  BIRTHDAY.
000370        03  MM             PICTURE 99.
000380        03  DD             PICTURE 99.
000390        03  YY             PICTURE 99.
000400     02  COLLEGE           PICTURE X(20).
000410     02  MAJOR             PICTURE X(20).
000420     02  ADVISOR           PICTURE X(30).
000430     02  CREDITS           PICTURE 999.
000440     02  AVERAGE           PICTURE 99V999.
000450     02  COURSE OCCURS 5 TIMES.
000460        03  NUMBR          PICTURE X(6).
000470        03  NAME           PICTURE X(20).
```

FIGURE 10.3
(Continued)

```
000480      03  HOURS              PICTURE 99.
000490      03  P-F                PICTURE X.
000500      03  GRADE              PICTURE 9V99.
000510   02  ROOM-BAL              PICTURE 99999V99.
000520   02  TUITION-BAL           PICTURE 99999V99.
000530   02  FEE-BAL               PICTURE 99999V99.
000540   02  OTHER-BAL             PICTURE 99999V99.
000550   02  TOTAL-BAL             PICTURE 99999V99.
000560 FD  PRINT-FILE LABEL RECORDS ARE OMITTED.
000570 01  PRINT-RECORD.
000580   02  LINE-TITLE            PICTURE X(20).
000590   02  LINE-CONTENT          PICTURE X(115).
```

c. DATA DIVISION-WORKING-STORAGE Section

```
000600 WORKING-STORAGE SECTION.
000610 77  I                       PICTURE 999.
000620 77  J                       PICTURE 999.
000630 77  MORE-DATA               PICTURE X(3) VALUE IS 'YES'.
000640 77  COL-IDX                 PICTURE 99.
000650 77  ROW-IDX                 PICTURE 99.
000660 77  FLAG                    PICTURE 9.
000670 01  SUMMARY-TABLE.
000680   02  COLLS OCCURS 6 TIMES.
000690     03  CLASSES OCCURS 5 TIMES PICTURE 999999V99.
000700 01  COUNT-TABLE.
000710   02  COLL-COUNT OCCURS 6 TIMES.
00720      03  CLASS-COUNT OCCURS 5 TIMES PICTURE 99999.
000730 01  ROW-NAME.
000740   02  COLL-NAMES.
000750     03  FILLER              PICTURE X(20).
000760        VALUE IS 'ARTS AND SCIENCES'.
000770     03  FILLER              PICTURE X(20)
000780        VALUE IS 'BUSINESS'.
000790     03  FILLER              PICTURE X(20).
000800        VALUE IS 'EDUCATION'.
000810     03  FILLER              PICTURE X(20).
000820        VALUE IS 'AGRICULTURE'.
000830     03  FILLER              PICTURE X(20).
000840        VALUE IS 'ENGINEERING'.
000850     03  FILLER              PICTURE X(20).
000860        VALUE IS 'CLASS AVERAGE'.
000870   02  COLL REDEFINES COLL-NAMES OCCURS 6 TIMES PICTURE X(20).
000880 01  COL-NAME.
000890   02  CLASS-NAMES.
000900     03  FILLER              PICTURE X(15).
000910        VALUE IS 'FRESHMAN'.
000920     03  FILLER              PICTURE X(15).
000930        VALUE IS 'SOPHOMORE'.
000940     03  FILLER              PICTURE X(15).
000950        VALUE IS 'JUNIOR'.
000960     03  FILLER              PICTURE X(15).
000970        VALUE IS 'SENIOR'.
000980     03  FILLER              PICTURE X(15).
```

FIGURE 10.3
(Continued)

```
000990          VALUE IS 'COLLEGE AVERAGE'.
001000 01  PRINT-TABLE.
001010     02  COLLEGES OCCURS 6 TIMES.
001020        03  CLASSES OCCURS 5 TIMES PICTURE Z(3)9.99B(8)
001030           BLANK WHEN ZERO.
```

d. PROCEDURE DIVISION

```
001040 PROCEDURE DIVISION.
001050 CONTROL-ROUTINE.
001060     PERFORM INITIALIZE.
001070     PERFORM FILL-TABLE UNTIL MORE-DATA IS EQUAL TO 'NO'.
001080     PERFORM COMPUTE-TOTALS VARYING I FROM 1 BY 1
001090         UNTIL I IS GREATER THAN 5.
001100     PERFORM COMPUTE-AVERAGE VARYING I FROM 1
001110         BY 1 UNTIL I IS GREATER THAN 6
001120         AFTER J FROM 1 BY 1
001130         UNTIL J IS GREATER THAN 5.
001140     PERFORM PRINT-RESULT.
001150     PERFORM CLEANUP.
001160     STOP RUN.
001170 INITIALIZE.
001180     OPEN INPUT MASTER-FILE.
001190     READ MASTER-FILE AT END MOVE 'NO' TO MORE-DATA.
001200     MOVE ZEROS TO SUMMARY-TABLE, COUNT-TABLE.
001210 FILL-TABLE.
001220     MOVE ZERO TO FLAG.
001230     PERFORM FIND-COLLEGE VARYING I FROM 1 BY 1 UNTIL
001240         I IS GREATER THAN 5.
001250     IF FLAG IS EQUAL TO ZERO
001260         DISPLAY '**********BAD COLLEGE CODE FOR'
001270         DISPLAY 'STUDENT NUMBER=', STUDENT-NO
001280     ELSE
001290         ADD 1 TO CLASS-COUNT (ROW-IDX, COL-IDX)
001300         ADD AVERAGE TO CLASSES OF
001310           SUMMARY-TABLE (ROW-IDX, COL-IDX).
001320     READ MASTER-FILE AT END MOVE 'NO' TO MORE-DATA.
001330 FIND-COLLEGE.
001340     IF COLLEGE IS EQUAL TO COLL (I)
001350         MOVE I TO ROW-IDX
001360         MOVE 1 TO FLAG
001370         PERFORM FIND-CLASS.
001380 FIND-CLASS.
001390     IF CREDITS IS LESS THAN 30
001400         MOVE 1 TO COL-IDX
001410     ELSE IF CREDITS IS LESS THAN 60
001420         MOVE 2 TO COL-IDX
001430     ELSE IF CREDITS IS LESS THAN 90
001440         MOVE 3 TO COL-IDX
001450     ELSE MOVE 4 TO COL-IDX.
001460 COMPUTE-TOTALS.
001470     PERFORM COMPUTE-TOTALS-1 VARYING J FROM 1
001480         BY 1 UNTIL J IS GREATER THAN 4.
001490 COMPUTE-TOTALS-1.
```

FIGURE 10.3
(Continued)

```
001500      ADD CLASS-COUNT (I, J) TO CLASS-COUNT (I, 5),
001510          CLASS-COUNT (6, J), TO CLASS-COUNT (6, 5).
001520      ADD CLASSES OF SUMMARY-TABLE (I, J) TO CLASSES OF
001530          SUMMARY-TABLE (I, 5), CLASSES OF SUMMARY-TABLE (6, J),
001540          CLASSES OF SUMMARY-TABLE (6, 5).
001550 COMPUTE-AVERAGE.
001560      IF CLASS-COUNT (I, J) IS GREATER THAN ZERO
001570          DIVIDE CLASS-COUNT (I, J) INTO
001580          CLASSES OF SUMMARY-TABLE (I, J).
001590 PRINT-RESULT.
001600      CLOSE MASTER-FILE.
001610      OPEN OUTPUT PRINT-FILE.
001620      MOVE SPACES TO LINE-TITLE.
001630      MOVE '            GRADE AVERAGE SUMMARY'TO
001640          LINE-CONTENT.
001650      WRITE PRINT-RECORD.
001660      MOVE COL-NAME TO LINE-CONTENT.
001670      MOVE SPACES TO LINE-TITLE.
001680      WRITE PRINT-RECORD.
001690      PERFORM MOVE-RESULT VARYING I FROM 1 BY 1
001700          UNTIL I IS GREATER THAN 6
001710          AFTER J FROM 1 BY 1 UNTIL J IS GREATER THAN 5.
001720      PERFORM PRINT-RESULT-1 VARYING I FROM 1
001730          BY 1 UNTIL I IS GREATER THAN 6.
001740 MOVE-RESULT.
001750      MOVE CLASSES OF SUMMARY-TABLE (I, J) TO
001760          CLASSES OF PRINT-TABLE (I, J).
001770 PRINT-RESULT-1.
001780      MOVE COLL (I) TO LINE-TITLE.
001790      MOVE COLLEGES (I) TO LINE-CONTENT.
001800      WRITE PRINT-RECORD.
001810 CLEANUP.
001820      CLOSE PRINT-FILE.
001830      DISPLAY 'SUCCESSFUL END OF JOB'.
```

e. Success Message on Standard Print File

```
SUCCESSFUL END OF JOB
```

f. Grade Summary Printed on PRINT-FILE

```
                    GRADE AVERAGE SUMMARY
```

	FRESHMAN	SOPHOMORE	JUNIOR	SENIOR	COLLEGE AVERAGE
ARTS AND SCIENCES	2.66	2.88	2.61	2.57	2.67
BUSINESS	2.48	2.83	2.64	2.34	2.58
EDUCATION	3.08	2.99	2.67	2.75	2.86
AGRICULTURE	3.01	2.47	2.56	2.92	2.73
ENGINEERING	2.89	2.66	2.94	2.85	2.83
CLASS AVERAGE	2.77	2.81	2.67	2.62	2.71

flowcharts we have been producing were intended to help you understand the programming examples given. They do not add any information not available from reading the program itself. They gave you an alternate representation of the program so that you could understand it more easily. Instead of flowcharting the whole program, you might simply flowchart the CONTROL-ROUTINE and give a hierarchy diagram of the whole process. It would also be useful to have a page listing the routine names and briefly explaining the purpose of each one. This, along with a listing of the program (with appropriate comments imbedded in the code) and samples of the input and output, should constitute all of the required documentation.

If you find flowcharts helpful in getting yourself started on a program (and many people do), then by all means, continue to use them. But remember that they are not a cure for all possible ailments in programming. It is just as easy to make a mistake in a flowchart as it is in a COBOL program.

STUDY EXERCISES

1. Write a COBOL program that will print the numbers from 1 to 10 using a PERFORM statement. Do not use the VARYING option.

2. Repeat exercise 1, using the VARYING option.

3. Write a program using PERFORM that will read the first five records from the MASTER-FILE and display them.

4. Modify the program in exercise 3 to read in the first N records, where the value of N is read in from a data card using the ACCEPT statement.

5. Write a COBOL program that will read in a first name, middle initial, and last name formatted like this:

```
FIRST-NAME          PICTURE X(20)
INIT                PICTURE X
LAST-NAME           PICTURE X(20)
```

You may use an ACCEPT to initialize these fields and declare them in WORKING-STORAGE if you wish. Use a PERFORM to compress the names in these fields into a field:

```
FULL-NAME           PICTURE X(45)
```

If you read in the following data:

```
FIRST-NAME           CHARLES
INIT                 R
LAST-NAME            MAXWELL
```

Then the FULL-NAME field should contain CHARLES R. MAXWELL.
Hint: You can define FULL-NAME this way:

```
01  BUFFER.
    02  FULL-NAME            PICTURE X(40).
    02  CHRS REDEFINES FULL-NAME OCCURS 40 TIMES PICTURE X.
```

Then, you can manipulate the individual characters in the FULL-NAME
field by using CHRS to handle them character by character.
Note: In Chapter 11 we will have some additional commands for string
handling that could solve this problem much more simply. But not all
computers have these string-handling statements in their versions of
COBOL, and you may have to use the approach in this problem for complicated string-handling work.

6. Write a COBOL program that will produce a summary of the totals for
   male and female students at the school whose students are listed on the
   MASTER-FILE. The summary table should look like this:

```
COLLEGE        MEN     WOMEN     TOTAL
AGRICULTURE    xxxx    xxxx      xxxx
                        .
                        .
                        .
TOTAL          xxxx    xxxx      xxxx
```

7. Write a COBOL program that will produce a list of all students taking the
   course HIS431. The students should be listed in alphabetical order like
   this:

```
            STUDENTS IN HIS431
         NAME          COLLEGE        MAJOR
1.  xxxxxxx            xxxxxx         xxxxxx
2.  xxxxxxx            xxxxxx         xxxxxx

            .
            .
            .
```

8. Take the program you wrote in exercise 4 and modify it to produce mailing
   labels. A label should look like this:

```
CHARLES R. MAXWELL
9721 OAK CANYON RD.
LOS ANGELES, CA 94687
```

Produce your labels sorted by zip code.

9. Write a COBOL program that will produce total registration by major. The output should look like this:

```
MAJOR       TOTAL
ART         xxxx
      .
      .
      .
TOTAL       xxxx
```

11 1
1 11
11
11 1
1 11
11
11 1
1 11
11
11 1
1 11
11

ADVANCED COBOL FEATURES

11.0 INTRODUCTION

The previous ten chapters of this book have covered enough COBOL features to allow you to do very nearly anything that can be done with the language. Most of what you require beyond this is a great deal of practice with computing, for this is the only way that you will ever really grasp the concepts and become proficient at data processing. In addition to the features we covered in the first ten chapters, there are a number of advanced COBOL features that can be very useful. You will find the features discussed in this chapter to be mostly extensions of the things that we did in earlier chapters. Very little will be presented in this chapter that could not have been done (although perhaps less conveniently) by using methods from earlier chapters.

The features will include:

1. Advanced data declaration features that will give you more control over the internal structure of your data.

2. Special table-handling statements that will allow more power and flexibility than were possible using the PERFORM statements we covered earlier.

3. String manipulation statements that will let you break fields apart, combine fields into new fields, and examine the characters that make up fields.

4. Debugging statements that will help you isolate your program errors more quickly.

5. Statements that will allow you to build up a library of record definitions and other data items that will give a collection of programs some degree of data independence.

6. Two new control statements—GO TO and ALTER, which are widely used in COBOL and more often widely abused.

The statements presented in this chapter are not unified in type as were the presentations in earlier chapters. But by now you have enough sophistication in computing to be able to find places in your work where these statements would have been useful.

11.1 ADVANCED DATA DECLARATIONS

In Chapter 5 we dealt with a wide range of data declaration options that we could use in the DATA DIVISION of our COBOL programs. There are a few options that we did not cover there that we will go over in this section. The material covered in this section deals with ways of controlling the internal storage of our data and with ways of declaring special conditionals and regroupings of data in our programs. The material presented here is not essential to COBOL programming, but there are a number of instances in which use of this material can result in more efficient code.

The first item we will cover is the USAGE clause. The general format of the USAGE clause is:

$$\left[\; \underline{\text{USAGE}}\; \text{IS}\; \right] \quad \left\{ \begin{array}{l} \underline{\text{COMPUTATIONAL}} \\ \underline{\text{COMP}} \\ \underline{\text{DISPLAY}} \\ \underline{\text{INDEX}} \end{array} \right\}$$

The USAGE clause is included with the other clauses in the definition of a field (clauses like PICTURE, VALUE IS, etc.). Some examples of the use of this option are:

```
02   SALARY      PICTURE S99999V99      USAGE IS COMPUTATIONAL.
02   TOTAL-BAL   PICTURE S9999          USAGE IS COMP.
02   AVG-PURCH   PICTURE 9999           USAGE IS DISPLAY.
```

The phrase COMPUTATIONAL or its abbreviation COMP implies that the data item is stored in an internal form suitable for the representation of numbers. This will vary from machine to machine. It might mean that the data item is stored as a pure binary number (this is the case on IBM 360 and 370 systems). Check your machine's manual for the exact form of storage. DISPLAY means that the data is stored in character form. The INDEX option means that the data item is a special index used with the table-handling features to be discussed in Section 11.2.

On IBM equipment the possible options in the USAGE clause have been expanded to include these items:

OPTION	ABBREVIATION	MEANING
COMPUTATIONAL-1	COMP-1	Single precision floating point
COMPUTATIONAL-2	COMP-2	Double precision floating point
COMPUTATIONAL-3	COMP-3	Packed decimal
COMPUTATIONAL-4	COMP-4	Binary, equivalent to COMPUTATIONAL

Items used as COMPUTATIONAL of any type must have a numeric picture. There may be certain length restrictions, so check with the COBOL manual for your computer.

You might wonder why anybody would want to control the internal format of data. There are several reasons. First, if you have a program that must do a lot of computation (which is somewhat unusual in COBOL), then it is more efficient to do the computation using variables that have been declared USAGE IS COMPUTATIONAL. In this way the computer does not have to convert back and forth between the external and internal representations of the numbers while it is doing the arithmetic. It can deal with the internal representations from start to finish. A second reason for the USAGE options would be to let you read data created by other languages. Suppose that you had to use COBOL to read a data tape created by a FORTRAN program. FORTRAN uses binary and floating point exclusively for its variables, and the values on the tape might be one of those types as well. The USAGE IS COMPUTATIONAL phrase would allow you to set up internal data storage in COBOL that was compatible with the representations on your tape.

We also might like to align data stored in the machine on certain storage boundaries. For instance, on IBM 360/370 equipment, it is more efficient to align data on full-word and half-word boundaries. It is not necessarily true that this will happen for USAGE IS COMPUTATIONAL. To handle this, we can use the SYNCHRONIZED phrase. An example is:

```
05  X    PICTURE S9999  USAGE IS COMPUTATIONAL
                        SYNCHRONIZED LEFT.
```

This states that the storage assigned for the variable X is to be aligned to the left on the next storage boundary. The general format for the SYNCHRONIZED **phrase** is:

$$\left\{ \begin{array}{l} \underline{\text{SYNCHRONIZED}} \\ \underline{\text{SYNC}} \end{array} \right\} \quad \left[\begin{array}{l} \underline{\text{LEFT}} \\ \underline{\text{RIGHT}} \end{array} \right]$$

On IBM 360/370 equipment, the LEFT and RIGHT phrases are treated as comments and may be omitted. The computer will control the direction of the storage alignment.

A similar option exists for alphanumeric data items. Recall that when we move an alphanumeric item from one field to another, the data is left-justified. If the receiving field is shorter than the sending field, then the extra places on the right are truncated. It is possible to alter these rules in COBOL if we want to justify alphanumeric items on the right. Suppose that we had these field definitions:

```
77  FIELD1    PICTURE A(5)    VALUE IS 'HELLO'.
77  FIELD2    PICTURE A(3)    JUSTIFIED RIGHT.
77  FIELD3    PICTURE A(10)   JUST.
```

The phrase JUSTIFIED or its abbreviation JUST may be used to denote that the usual rules of justification are being suspended. The phrase RIGHT is merely a comment and may be omitted. In the example above, if we execute the line:

```
MOVE FIELD1 TO FIELD2.
```

then FIELD2 will contain the value 'LLO'. The two characters 'HE' on the left will be truncated because the receiving field is not large enough for them. If we execute the code:

```
MOVE FIELD1 TO FIELD3.
```

then FIELD3 will contain the value 'bbbbbHELLO'. The data will be right-justified, and the spaces on the left will be filled with blanks. Note that the receiving field is the one that contains the JUSTIFIED phrase and not the sending field.

Occasionally, we would like to manipulate the position of the sign in a data item. We can do this using the SIGN **clause.** The general format of this option is:

SIGN clause

$$
\text{SIGN IS}
\left\{
\begin{array}{l}
\underline{\text{LEADING}} \\
\text{TRAILING}
\end{array}
\right\}
\quad
[\ \underline{\text{SEPARATE}} \ \text{CHARACTER} \ ]
$$

You would use this option in a data definition as in this example:

```
02  ACCT-TOTAL   PICTURE S999V99
        SIGN IS LEADING.
02  ACCT-BALANCE PICTURE S999V99
        SIGN IS TRAILING.
02  SALES-TOTAL PICTURE S999V99
        SIGN IS TRAILING SEPARATE CHARACTER.
```

The SIGN clause may be used once and only once in the definition of a data item. It specifies the position of the operational sign of the item. If the sign is specified as LEADING, then the operational sign is associated with the leading digit of the data item. If it is specified as trailing, then the operational sign is associated with the last digit of the item (as is normal in zoned decimal notation). Unless the sign is specified as a separate character, it is not used in figuring the length of the data item. If it is a separate character, then it is figured in the length. For example, the length of the variable ACCT-BALANCE above is 5, but the length of SALES-TOTAL is 6.

The next idea we will discuss in data declarations is some new ways of using level numbers. Suppose we have an accounting system set up that provides account numbers for different units in a company. Some examples of an account number system might look like this:

DIVISION	ACCOUNT NUMBER
Corporate headquarters	1175
Advertising department	1179
Shipping department	1185
Manufacturing department	1189

Suppose we wanted to set up tests in our COBOL program to perform certain blocks of code depending on the department that generated the transaction. We might have to write code looking like this:

```
IF DEPT-NO IS EQUAL TO '1175'
    PERFORM AUDIT-HEADQUARTERS.
```

We would have similar IF statements for other blocks of code for the other departments, and we would have huge problems if we ever decided to change our account numbers (which happens occasionally). We would have to search our COBOL programs for examples of tests like the one above and substitute the new account number for the old one. We would probably not find all the tests, and the programs in our accounting system would be in a hopeless mess for a period of time.

COBOL's level 88 data items offer us a way out. For instance, in our data definitions for DEPT-NO, we could set things up this way:

```
02  DEPT-NO  PICTURE X(4).
    88  HEADQUARTERS  VALUE IS '1175'.
    88  ADVERTISING  VALUE IS '1179'.
    88  SHIPPING     VALUE IS '1185'.
```

Then, we could write our IF statements this way:

```
IF HEADQUARTERS PERFORM AUDIT-HEADQUARTERS.
```

The computer checks to see if the field DEPT-NO contains the value assigned to the condition HEADQUARTERS. If it does, the condition is true, and the routine AUDIT-HEADQUARTERS is performed.

Now, if we change account numbers, all we have to do is change the table of level 88 entries associated with the field DEPT-NO. The computer program entries in the PROCEDURE DIVISION can remain unchanged, and all relevant entries will be changed automatically to reflect the new account numbers. The use of the level 88 conditional entries can save a great deal of trouble in the event that we make changes to our accounting system. It can also be used to provide conditions in IF statements that are somewhat clearer-looking than entries that use all the relational operators and field names.

The general format for a **level 88 entry** is

level 88 entry

```
                              ( VALUE IS  )
   88   condition-name        { VALUES ARE }     literal-1
                              (           )

      [ ( THROUGH )                    ]
      [ {         }  literal-2         ]
      [ ( THRU    )                    ]

   [                 [ ( THROUGH )                  ] ]
   [  literal-3      [ {         }  literal-4  ...  ] ]
   [                 [ ( THRU    )                  ] ]
```

As you can see from this definition, it is possible to assign a range of values to a condition. If this option is used, then literal-1 must be less than literal-2 and so on. The test performed using the conditional will check to see if the data item is in the desired range.

A final type of data entry is one that allows us to regroup our data. This is the level 66 data entry. You are already familiar with the idea of treating a set of fields as a unit by making them subordinate to a group data name. By using the level 66 entry, we can regroup data items to a limited extent. Suppose, for instance, we wanted to know the month and year in which a student was born, but that we were not interested in the day. We could make the following change to our MASTER-FILE record definition:

```
   02   BIRTHDAY.
            03   DD   PICTURE 99.
            03   MM   PICTURE 99.
            03   YY   PICTURE 99.
   66 MONTH-YEAR RENAMES MM THRU YY.
```

This change would allow us to refer to the fields MM and YY together by the single group name MONTH-YEAR. The general format of the **level 66 data item** is: level 66 data item

$$66 \quad \text{data-name-1} \quad \underline{\text{RENAMES}} \quad \text{data-name-2} \left[\left\{ \begin{array}{l} \underline{\text{THROUGH}} \\ \underline{\text{THRU}} \end{array} \right\} \text{data-name-3} \right]$$

The use of a level 66 entry provides a minor convenience in reformatting the way in which we look at a set of data. Any items with a level 66 must begin in area A.

11.2   TABLE-HANDLING FEATURES AND TABLES

We have already introduced tables in Chapter 10, using them with the PERFORM statement with the VARYING option. We will introduce nothing in this section that could not also be done using the PERFORM statement, but some of the options presented in this section would be cumbersome to program if we could use only PERFORM. The features presented in this section will enable you to work with tables in a very convenient fashion.

To work with tables, we will introduce a new type of data item. This is the index data item, and it is used only for indexing tables. Recall that we discussed it briefly in Section 11.1 in terms of the USAGE clause. We can declare a data item to be an index as in this example:

```
05  X           USAGE IS INDEX.
```

We cannot use the USAGE IS INDEX clause with SYNCHRONIZED, VALUE, JUSTIFIED, BLANK, or PICTURE phrases. But we would not usually use a data declaration like the one above to define an index at all. We would normally declare the index in the OCCURS phrase that sets up the table. This might be done as in this example:

```
05  COURSE-TABLE OCCURS 10 TIMES INDEXED BY COURSE.
```

This would automatically set up an index variable called COURSE that could be used with some special index-handling commands (to be introduced shortly) to access entries down in the table called COURSE-TABLE.

The general format of the OCCURS **phrase**, including the use of the INDEXED and other options, is   OCCURS phrase

$$\text{OCCURS} \begin{Bmatrix} \text{integer-1 } \underline{\text{TO}} \text{ integer-2 } \text{TIMES } [\underline{\text{DEPENDING ON}} \text{ data-name-1 }] \\ \text{integer-2 TIMES} \end{Bmatrix}$$

$$\begin{bmatrix} \begin{Bmatrix} \underline{\text{ASCENDING}} \\ \underline{\text{DESCENDING}} \end{Bmatrix} \text{KEY IS data-name-2 } [\text{ data-name-3 }] \dots \end{bmatrix}$$

[<u>INDEXED</u> BY index-name-1 [index-name-2] ...]

Some examples of these expanded versions of the OCCURS phrase are:

```
05   GRADE-TABLE PICTURE 999V99
     OCCURS 1 TO 10 TIMES DEPENDING ON TOTAL-GRADES
     INDEXED BY GRADE.
02   SALES-TABLE PICTURE 999V99 OCCURS 100 TIMES
     INDEXED BY SALE.
02   COURSE-TABLE OCCURS 1 TO 20 TIMES DEPENDING ON TOTAL-COURSES,
     ASCENDING KEY IS COURSE-NO,
     INDEXED BY COURSE.
```

The definition and the examples introduce several new facilities of the OCCURS phrase that we have not used before. First, we use the DEPEND-ING ON phrase in the first example defining the GRADE-TABLE. This phrase allows us to vary the size of a table. The GRADE-TABLE can have a minimum of 1 and a maximum of 10 entries. The exact number of entries in the table for any given record will depend on the value stored in the variable TOTAL-GRADES. This means, then, that on the external storage medium used for the record, we will have a variable number of charac-ters in the record. This is very convenient, because it allows us to save the space we would have had to otherwise waste for unused storage in some records of the GRADE-TABLE.

The INDEXED BY phrase in all of the examples is used to name the variable that will be used solely for indexing the table. The index vari-able does not appear as a part of the record containing the OCCURS, nor can it be manipulated or printed using the ordinary COBOL arithmetic commands we have had up to this point. The final new option, the KEY phrase, allows us to establish one field of the table as a key. We are telling the computer that the data in the table will be stored in order by one of the field or fields in the table.

In the last example for the declaration of COURSE-TABLE, we make use of the KEY option. We are telling COBOL in this example that the entries in the COURSE-TABLE will be sorted in ascending order by the field COURSE-NO. The programmer has the responsibility of seeing that the fields are actually in order. By using an ordered table, we can perform various searching options on the table much more efficiently than we could with an unordered table.

The last example might have been used in the MASTER-FILE record definition in place of the rather unrealistic assumption that all students took exactly five courses. This declaration would have allowed a student's record to have from one to twenty courses. The actual size of the table would be determined by the field TOTAL-COURSES, which we would have to add to the record definition. We would also have to see that the courses were kept in course number order when we originally built the table. This would not have been difficult to do. The only requirement would have been to sort the cards that created the COURSE-TABLE into order, first by student number and then within any given student number in order by course number. Then we could build our ordered table by a simple sequential read and write.

To be able to use the index feature to manipulate data in a table, we must have some way of manipulating the index values. But we cannot use the ordinary COBOL arithmetic statements on an index (statements like MOVE, ADD, SUBTRACT, etc.). The index variables have their own set of commands for data manipulation. Some examples are:

```
SET ROW-IDX TO 1.
SET STATE-IDX TO COUNTER.
SET COL-IDX UP BY 1.
SET ROW-IDX, COL-IDX TO 1.
SET ROW-IDX, COL-IDX UP BY COUNTER-VALUE.
```

This type of statement is called the SET **statement,** and it is used for manipulating index values. Its general format is: SET statement

FORMAT 1

$$\underline{\text{SET}} \quad \left\{ \begin{array}{l} \text{index-name-1 [index-name-2] ...} \\ \text{identifier-1 [identifier-2] ...} \end{array} \right\} \quad \underline{\text{TO}} \left\{ \begin{array}{l} \text{index-name-3} \\ \text{identifier-3} \\ \text{literal-1} \end{array} \right\}$$

Format 2

$$\underline{\text{SET}} \text{ index-name-1 [index-name-2] ...} \left\{ \begin{array}{l} \underline{\text{UP BY}} \\ \underline{\text{DOWN BY}} \end{array} \right\} \left\{ \begin{array}{l} \text{identifier-1} \\ \text{literal-1} \end{array} \right\}$$

The SET statement can be used either to initialize or to manipulate the values in index variables. In the first example, we have used it to set the value in ROW-IDX (we are assuming that ROW-IDX is an index variable) to the value 1. In the second example, we set the value in the index STATE-IDX to the value in the identifier COUNTER. The third example shows how to do arithmetic on an index value. The UP BY phrase in the SET statement allows us to increase the value in the index by 1. The last examples show how we can change the values in several index variables at once.

The SET statement is used primarily to initialize index values so that we can use them in SEARCH statements. To introduce the SEARCH statements, suppose that we have the table:

```
01  STATE-NAMES.
    02  STATE-ID.
        03  FILLER    PICTURE XX VALUE IS 'AL'.
        03  FILLER    PICTURE X(15) VALUE IS 'ALABAMA'.
        03  FILLER    PICTURE XX VALUE IS 'AK'.
        03  FILLER    PICTURE X(15) VALUE IS 'ALASKA'.
                          .
                          .
                          .
        03  FILLER    PICTURE XX VALUE IS 'WY'.
        03  FILLER    PICTURE X(15) VALUE IS 'WYOMING'.
    02  STATES OCCURS 50 TIMES ASCENDING KEY IS POSTAL-CODE,
        INDEXED BY STATE-IDX.
        03  POSTAL-CODE    PICTURE XX.
        03  STATE-NAME     PICTURE X(15).
```

We might use this STATE-NAMES table for translating the two-letter post office abbreviation for the states into the full state name. This would allow us to store the shorter code on the individual records (as we do for the STATE field in the MASTER-FILE, for example) and still allow us to translate the two-letter codes easily to the full name. Note that in the definition of the table, we have used our familiar trick of defining the area first to initialize the data items, and then redefining the data area using an OCCURS clause so that we may index the predefined table easily.

We could use the SET and SEARCH statements to find the home state of a record on our MASTER-FILE by using the code:

```
        SET STATE-IDX TO 1.
        SEARCH STATES
            AT END PERFORM BAD-STATE-CODE
            WHEN STATES (STATE-IDX) IS EQUAL TO STATE OF MASTER-RECORD
            PERFORM DISPLAY-STATE.
DISPLAY-STATE.
        DISPLAY FIRST-NAME OF MASTER-RECORD, LAST-NAME OF MASTER-RECORD,
            STATES (STATE-IDX).
```

In this code the SET statement sets the index, STATE-IDX to 1. The SEARCH statement searches the STATE-NAMES table beginning at 1 until the condition following the WHEN phrase is satisfied. In this case that condition is satisfied when the code for the state in the MASTER-RECORD is equal to one of the two-character codes in the STATE-NAMES table. If the code in the MASTER-RECORD is never equal to one in the table, then we take the AT END exit from the SEARCH and perform the BAD-STATE-CODE routine. The SEARCH routine searches by increasing the index value for the table by 1 each time until it runs out the bottom of the table. At that point, the AT END exit is taken.

The general format of this SEARCH **statement** is: SEARCH statement

FORMAT 1

SEARCH table-name [<u>VARYING</u> $\left\{ \begin{array}{c} \text{index-name-1} \\ \text{identifier-1} \end{array} \right\}$]

   [AT <u>END</u> imperative-statement-1]

   <u>WHEN</u> condition-1 $\left\{ \begin{array}{l} \text{imperative-statement-2} \\ \underline{\text{NEXT}}\ \underline{\text{SENTENCE}} \end{array} \right\}$

   [<u>WHEN</u> condition-2 $\left\{ \begin{array}{l} \text{imperative-statement-3} \\ \underline{\text{NEXT}}\ \underline{\text{SENTENCE}} \end{array} \right\}$] ...

In the general form of the SEARCH, we can have more than one WHEN condition to terminate the SEARCH process. In this event, the WHEN conditions are evaluated, one at a time until one is found that is true. If none are found, then we increment the index by 1 and continue the search. If we do not use the VARYING option with SEARCH, then it is automatically assumed that we are varying the index associated with the table. Otherwise, we will vary the index or identifier given with VARYING. A flowchart of the SEARCH routine is given in Figure 11.1.

This approach to searching out the state names from our STATE-NAMES table is actually quite inefficient. As you will notice from our table, the states are in order alphabetically, and the field POSTAL-CODE is used as a key. This means that we can use search techniques much more efficient than one-at-a-time search to search the table. The technique we will use is called **binary search** because it searches the whole   binary search table by successively splitting it in half. You do not have to worry about the details of programming. Binary search works this way: Let us suppose we are looking for a particular state (say, South Dakota with postal code SD). We divide the state table in half and look at the middle postal code (it will be Missouri with code MO). South Dakota's postal code is greater than that of the middle entry, so we throw away the bottom half of the list and concentrate on searching the top half. The table below outlines the search process for our table of fifty states trying to come up with South Dakota:

Binary Search Table

ENTRIES REMAINING	ITEM INDEX	POSTAL CODE	STATE
25	50/2 = 25	MO	Missouri
12	25 + 25/2 = 38	PA	Pennsylvania
6	38 + 12/2 = 44	UT	Utah
3	44 − 6/2 = 41	SD	South Dakota

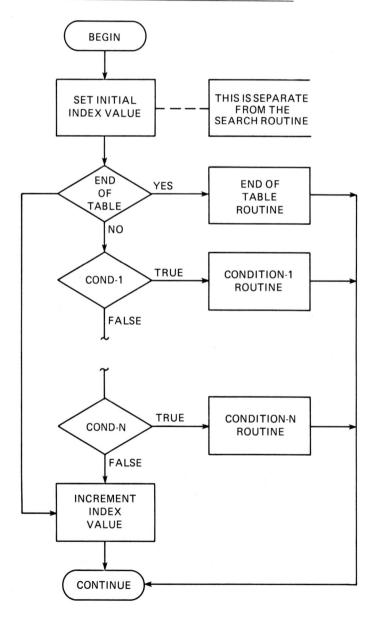

FIGURE 11.1
Flowchart of a *SEARCH*
Statement

In the table it took four comparisons to isolate the full state name for South Dakota. If we had had to search the full table one item at a time, it would have taken us forty-one comparisons to isolate South Dakota. It would have taken on the average twenty-five comparisons before we found a match. As it was, we got lucky on the fourth comparison, but we would have had to do, at most, six comparisons using binary search. In a sequential search, we would have had, at most, fifty comparisons.

The use of binary search can substantially cut down on the effort that the computer has to make in searching a table. In fact, the number of comparisons that must be made is on the order of $\log_2 N$, where N is the number of items in the table. This means that for our example using the fifty states, it would take us $\log_2 50 = 5.644$ or six comparisons at most.

COBOL offers us a SEARCH option with the binary search built in so that we do not have to write the code for a binary search (although writing the code is not too difficult). In the case of searching the STATE-NAMES table, we could have written our SEARCH statement this way:

```
SEARCH ALL STATES
    AT END PERFORM BAD-STATE-CODE,
    WHEN STATES (STATE-IDX) IS EQUAL TO STATE OF MASTER-RECORD,
    PERFORM DISPLAY-STATE.
```

This form of the SEARCH statement is the SEARCH ALL **form,** and it will automatically perform a binary search on the table names. If it gets to the end of the search without a match, then it will perform the code in the AT END option. Only one WHEN condition is allowed in this format. The general format is:

SEARCH ALL form

FORMAT 2

SEARCH ALL identifier-1   [AT END imperative-statement-1]

WHEN condition-1 $\left\{ \begin{array}{l} \text{imperative-statement-2} \\ \text{NEXT SENTENCE} \end{array} \right\}$

The SEARCH ALL form of the SEARCH statement should be used only when the data in the table has been keyed. A little reflection on the way a binary search works should serve to convince you that it would not make any sense to try to perform a SEARCH ALL on a table that was not already in order.

Judicious use of tables and the SEARCH statement allows us to translate codes into expanded fields. We have used it to translate postal codes into full state names, but it could also be used to translate department numbers into department names, job codes into job titles, and so on. The advantage of using translation tables and SEARCH statements is that we do not have to store the full data title out on the external storage device. For some storage devices, such as disk files, this can result in a considerable monetary savings.

The disadvantage of using tables and SEARCH statements is that they require both active core memory to store the table and time to perform the search. In the case of SEARCH ALL, the time would probably not be prohibitive. We could search a 1,000-item table in, at most, ten comparisons, but the process of reading in a program with a 1,000-item table might be beyond the memory size of many machines. (It would depend on the size of the machine and how the table entries were structured.) Trade-offs of this type are typical in computing, and you will have to provide answers that fit your particular machine and application.

11.3   STRING MANIPULATION FEATURES

It may seem odd to have a special section on the manipulation of character strings. After all, every COBOL program we have written has done some manipulation of character string data. But you have probably felt somewhat confined by the character string techniques we have used so far. We have dealt only with whole fields rather than with individual characters within a field. At times, this can prove cumbersome. Suppose we wanted to print out a student's full name from the MASTER-FILE. We could use this command to perform the printout:

```
DISPLAY FIRST-NAME OF MASTER-RECORD, ' ',
        INIT OF MASTER-RECORD, '. ',
        LAST-NAME OF MASTER-RECORD.
```

Suppose our student's name were John R. Smith. Then the printout generated by the code above would look like this (the character ƀ represents a blank):

```
JOHNƀƀƀƀƀƀƀƀƀƀƀƀƀR.ƀSMITHƀƀƀƀƀƀƀƀƀƀƀƀƀ
```

There would be large numbers of blanks (depending on how long the first and last names were) between the different words making up the name. This can look pretty silly in a telephone directory or in the address of a letter. We would really like the printout to look like this:

```
JOHN R. SMITH
```

so that a normal number of spaces was left between the names.

With what we learned in Chapter 10 on the PERFORM statement, it is possible to do this. We could define a full-name field and a source field as alphanumeric strings of adequate length and then REDEFINE them with fields of individual characters using the OCCURS. Once we did that, we could use PERFORM and IF to manipulate the individual characters in any way we liked. But this procedure can be tedious, especially when you consider that we are likely to want to perform certain actions on character strings over and over. These actions are:

1. Count certain characters in a field.

2. Replace selected individual characters in a field.

3. String two fields together into a single field (with some controls on the number of characters we want to string together).

4. Break a field into two fields.

As a first example, suppose we wanted to count the number of words in a block of text. For our purposes, we will define a word to be a string of nonblank characters separated by blanks. We will assume that the text has no extra imbedded blanks, although it does follow the usual typist's convention of leaving two blanks after a period or colon. The code to count words would be:

```
MOVE ZEROS TO COUNT1, COUNT2, COUNT3.
INSPECT TEXT-AREA,
      TALLYING COUNT1 FOR ALL 'b',
              COUNT2 FOR ALL '.bb',
              COUNT3 FOR ALL ':bb'.
SUBTRACT COUNT2, COUNT3 FROM COUNT1.
```

The statement we are using above is the INSPECT statement with the TALLYING option. This statement scans the TEXT-AREA character by character, performing the actions that are listed as options. In the case of the example above, it adds 1 to COUNT1 each time it finds a blank. This means that the variable COUNT1 contains a count of all the blanks in the TEXT-AREA. The variable COUNT2 contains a count of all character strings with a period followed by two blanks, and COUNT3 contains a count of all character strings with a colon followed by two blanks. At the end of the INSPECT statement, we subtract COUNT2 and COUNT3 from COUNT1 (since the two blanks a typist would insert after a period or a colon would also be counted as single blanks), and the result is the number of words in the text. The general format of the INSPECT statement with TALLYING option is:

INSPECT statement with TALLYING option

FORMAT 1

```
INSPECT identifier-1 TALLYING
```

$$\left\{ \begin{array}{l} \{ \text{identifier-2 } \underline{FOR} \end{array} \right. \left\{ \left\{ \left\{ \begin{array}{l} \underline{ALL} \\ \underline{LEADING} \end{array} \right\} \left\{ \begin{array}{l} \text{identifier-3} \\ \text{literal-1} \end{array} \right\} \right. \right.$$

$$\left. \left. \left[\left\{ \begin{array}{l} \underline{BEFORE} \\ \underline{AFTER} \end{array} \right\} \text{INITIAL} \left\{ \begin{array}{l} \text{identifier-4} \\ \text{literal-2} \end{array} \right\} \right] \right\} \ldots \right\} \ldots$$

Other possible examples of the INSPECT statement might be:

```
INSPECT TEXT-BUFFER TALLYING
    SIGN-COUNT FOR LEADING '$' AFTER INITIAL 'b'.
INSPECT TEXT LINES TALLYING
    COUNTER (1) FOR ALL 'A',
    COUNTER (2) FOR ALL 'B',
            .
            .
            .
    COUNTER (26) FOR ALL 'Z'.
INSPECT TEXT-LINES TALLYING
    COUNT-PUNCTUATION FOR ALL '.', ALL ',',
        ALL ';', ALL ':'.
```

In the examples above, we use some of the different options of the INSPECT. In the first one, we count only the first dollar sign that occurs after an initial blank. This would allow us to use the INSPECT statement to determine if this string were present in a field. The second INSPECT is used to count up the occurrences of each of the characters of the alphabet in a text area. The final INSPECT counts all the punctuation in the text area.

In addition to counting the occurrences of certain strings, we would also like to be able to replace characters within a string with something else. Suppose we wanted to pull all punctuation out of string of text. We have a version of the INSPECT statement that will allow us to do this as well. An example would be:

```
INSPECT TEXT-BUFFER REPLACING
    ALL '.' BY 'b',
    ALL ',' BY 'b',
    ALL ':' BY 'b',
    ALL ';' BY 'b'.
```

The computer would scan the identifier called TEXT-BUFFER and replace all punctuation (or at least that listed above) with blanks. The general format of the INSPECT **statement with** REPLACING **option** is:

INSPECT statement
with REPLACING
option

FORMAT 2

```
INSPECT identifier-1 REPLACING

                     ┌ identifier-6 ┐  ┌ ┌ BEFORE ┐          ┌ identifier-7 ┐ ┐
CHARACTERS BY        {              }  | {        } INITIAL  {              } |
                     └ literal-4    ┘  └ └ AFTER  ┘          └ literal-5    ┘ ┘

┌ ┌ ALL     ┐                                                                      ┐
| {         |                                                                      |
| { LEADING }   ┌ ┌ identifier-5 ┐      ┌ identifier-6 ┐                            |
| {         |   | {              }  BY  {              }                           |
| └ FIRST   ┘   └ └ literal-3    ┘      └ literal-4    ┘                            |
|                                                                                  |
|    ┌ ┌ BEFORE ┐          ┌ identifier-7 ┐ ┐                                       | ...
|    | {        } INITIAL  {              } |                                      |
|    └ └ AFTER  ┘          └ literal-5    ┘ ┘ ...                                   |
└                                                                                  ┘ ...
```

The definitions for both the first and second format of the INSPECT statement look quite formidable, but they are really not very difficult to use. The identifier given after the reserved word INSPECT tells us which variable we are inspecting. After that, we have a series of keys telling which characters are being either counted or replaced, depending on which format we have chosen. The ALL implies that all identifiers in the field that match the identifier after the ALL will be counted or replaced. The keyword LEADING implies that only the first left-most occurrence in the field will be counted. The CHARACTERS keyword implies that all characters in the field will be counted or replaced. No special criteria need be met. The BEFORE and AFTER phrases establish boundaries for the counting and replacement. The INSPECT actions will take place only before or after the given criteria have been met.

    The INSPECT statement is useful for only fairly limited kinds of editing in COBOL. It does not occur in older versions of COBOL. Instead, you will use the EXAMINE statement, which is similar in its effect, although slightly more limited in scope than INSPECT. If you are using an older version of COBOL, check your reference manual for the definition of the EXAMINE statement. This statement was phased out in the 1974 ANSI version of COBOL.

    A much more useful set of string-processing statements are those used for joining two fields together or for breaking two fields apart. Using these types of statements allows us to join two fields together and edit them in some surprisingly powerful and useful ways. For example, suppose that we have three fields:

```
FIRST-NAME
INITL
LAST-NAME
```

These fields contain the first name, middle initial, and last name of the person whose name is on the file. In our MASTER-FILE, these fields were twenty characters long for the first and last names and one character for the initial. Suppose we wanted to string these fields together into a single FULL-NAME field (declared in WORKING-STORAGE), and that this FULL-NAME field should contain the name in the usual format (e.g., John R. Smith with only single blanks between the names). We could use this statement to fill the FULL-NAME field:

```
STRING FIRST-NAME DELIMITED BY 'b',
      'b', INITL, '.b' DELIMITED BY SIZE,
      LAST-NAME DELIMITED BY 'b',
      INTO FULL-NAME,
      ON OVERFLOW PERFORM DUMP-NAMES.
```

In the example above, the character b represents a blank. If the fields had the following contents:

```
FIRST-NAME     JOHNbbbbbbbbbbbbbbbb
INITL          R
LAST-NAME      SMITHbbbbbbbbbbbbbbb
```

then the field FULL-NAME would contain JOHNbR.bSMITH. We would not include all of the characters in the FIRST-NAME and LAST-NAME fields in FULL-NAME (remember that blanks are counted as characters and that character string fields are blank-filled on the right). We would only move characters from FIRST-NAME until we hit a blank because we asked for the blank to be the delimiter. The literals 'b' and '.b' and the variable INITL are moved as they are because they are delimited by the actual size of the field. The LAST-NAME field is again delimited by a blank. All these items are moved one at a time into the field FULL-NAME. If the data that we are moving overflows the FULL-NAME variable, then we will perform the routine called DUMP-NAMES. This could be used to print out an error message and perhaps take some sort of corrective action. If we choose our field lengths carefully, there is no reason why we should have any problem with overflows.

The STRING statement is a sort of extended version of the MOVE statement, and it can be extremely useful in a variety of text-editing activities. For example, we might use it in preparing mailing labels to see that the address lines (for city, state, and zip code) did not contain unnecessary blanks. It could also be used for providing neat formats for bills

and reports by centering titles and headings. As you begin to use
COBOL for a wider variety of reports, you will encounter many places
where it would be useful to use the STRING statement.

The general format of the STRING statement is:

```
STRING {identifier-1}  [identifier-2]  ... DELIMITED BY {identifier-3}
       {literal-1   }  [literal-2  ]                   {literal-3    }
                                                        {SIZE         }

       [{identifier-4}  [identifier-5]  ... DELIMITED BY  {identifier-6}] ...
        {literal-4   }  [literal-5  ]                     {literal-6   }
                                                          {SIZE        }
       INTO identifier-7  [ WITH POINTER identifier-8]

       [ ON OVERFLOW imperative-statement ]
```

There are some things to remember in using the STRING statement. First,
we can string as many data items together as we need. The data items are
simply concatenated (the next one begins where the last one ended), and
the length of the data items is controlled by the DELIMITED phrase. Second, it is possible to have a single DELIMITED phrase apply to several
data items, or we can supply a new DELIMITED phrase for each individual
data item.

The data we are stringing together is placed in the variable denoted by identifier-7. We can control the placement of the data by using
the POINTER option. The value set in identifier-8 gives the character
position in identifier-7 where data entry will start. This means that we
can use the INSPECT and STRING statements together to control the
placement of data in a variable.

Some additional examples of the STRING statement are:

```
STRING CITY OF MASTER-RECORD DELIMITED BY 'b',
    ',b', STATE OF MASTER-RECORD, 'b',
    ZIP OF MASTER-RECORD DELIMITED BY SIZE
    INTO STATE-LINE.
MOVE 10 TO LINE-POSITION.
MOVE SPACES TO PRINT-LINE.
STRING MAJOR OF MASTER-RECORD, COLLEGE OF
    MASTER-RECORD,DELIMITED BY SIZE INTO
    PRINT-LINE, WITH POINTER LINE-POSITION.
```

In the first example above, we are building an address line for the city,
state, and zip code from the MASTER-RECORD. These fields are joined
together with appropriate blanks to separate the words. We might use this
version of the STRING to build a final line on a mailing label or other
address entry. In the second example we are using the POINTER option to

control the placement of the data in the PRINT-LINE field. We move the number 10 to the variable LINE-POSITION (declared in WORKING-STORAGE) and fill the variable PRINT-LINE with spaces. Then we string the MAJOR and COLLEGE fields together into the PRINT-LINE using the variable LINE-POSITION as a pointer. This has the effect of indenting the data over to the tenth column. In this second example we are not compressing the MAJOR and COLLEGE fields, so they will contain the trailing blanks at the end.

Finally, we may sometimes want to break up fields into even smaller data items. This can be useful in text editing where we might like to isolate individual words in a piece of text. We might also use it to write our own free-field input routines rather than having to use the rigid data field positions that would be specified by a COBOL input file. As an example, suppose we had a field called FULL-NAME that contained:

```
SMITH, JOHN R.
```

Suppose the contents of the field are left-justified and the field is called FULL-NAME. If we wanted to break the field into the words making up the full name, we could do it with the following sequence of statements:

```
UNSTRING FULL-NAME DELIMITED BY 'b'
     INTO LAST-NAME, FIRST-NAME, INIT.
INSPECT LAST-NAME REPLACING ALL ',' BY 'b'.
```

The statement we are using here is the UNSTRING one. It will take the character strings in FULL-NAME delimited by the blank and place them in the variables that follow the keyword INTO. We use the INSPECT statement to strip the comma off the last name. We are assuming that the INIT field is one character long, so there is no need to strip off the period that follows the initial (if this were not true, we could use another INSPECT statement).

The general format of the UNSTRING statement is: UNSTRING statement

```
UNSTRING identifier-1

[ DELIMITED BY [ ALL ]  { identifier-2 }   [ OR [ ALL ]
                        { literal-1    }

    { identifier-3 }
    { literal-2    }   ] ...   ]

INTO identifier-4 [ DELIMITER IN identifier-5 ] [ COUNT IN identifier-6 ]

[ identifier-7 [ DELIMITER IN identifier-8 ] [ COUNT IN identifier-9]] ...

[ WITH POINTER identifier-10 ] [ TALLYING IN identifier-11 ]

[ ON OVERFLOW imperative-statement ]
```

The UNSTRING statement is fairly straightforward, although it does allow a wide variety of options. The ALL option treats all occurrences of the delimiter as a single occurrence so that multiple blanks (if blanks were the delimiter, for example) would be treated as a single blank. It is also possible to save the delimiters (this might prove useful if the delimiters were also some sort of text identifier) and to count the length of the data items we are unstringing. If used, the pointer variable, identifier-10, tells us where to begin the unstringing process. The TALLYING identifier tells us how many of the receiving identifiers were used in the UNSTRING operation. Again, we could use this result with the INSPECT statement.

The techniques we have learned in this section for processing string data can be very powerful. They transform COBOL from a mere text storage language to a real text processor and make it possible to edit our stored data in a wide variety of ways. You will find it very useful to master these statements in your professional work with COBOL. Unfortunately, the string-processing statements are not always available on smaller computers. If you are working on one of these machines, you can still do string processing using the PERFORM statement and the REDEFINES in the DATA DIVISION of your programs. It will not be as convenient, but the type of string manipulation presented in this section can still be done.

11.4 DEBUGGING FEATURES

By now, you have done enough computer programming to realize that you do not write perfect code on your first attempt. Even after your program is free of syntactical errors, it usually takes some time before you have found all the logical errors and have a program that does what you intend. You should also have learned a few tricks for debugging your programs. One important technique is to use the DISPLAY statement to print out messages to trace the flow of control in your program and to print out the actual value of variables at some point in the execution of your code. After your program runs, these extra DISPLAY statements can be removed.

Beyond this, most COBOL compilers have some sort of debugging statements built in to make things easier when you are trying to get your program to work. The statements presented in this section are IBM's, but those on other machines are likely to be similar. Check your particular reference manual for the details of debugging statements on your machine.

The first of the debugging statements is:

```
READY TRACE.
```

This statement causes the name of each paragraph or section head to be printed when the flow of control reaches it. The statement is given once, and then the tracing mode remains active until you turn it off. You turn it off by executing the statement:

```
RESET TRACE.
```

You can use these statements to trace the flow of control through your program. You could accomplish the same function by placing a DISPLAY statement after each paragraph or section entry point with an appropriate message, but the READY TRACE is simpler to use.

The next debugging statement is called EXHIBIT and is a sort of sophisticated version of the DISPLAY statement. Its general format is:

$$\text{EXHIBIT} \begin{Bmatrix} \underline{\text{NAMED}} \\ \underline{\text{CHANGED}} \ \underline{\text{NAMED}} \\ \underline{\text{CHANGED}} \end{Bmatrix} \begin{Bmatrix} \text{identifier-1} \\ \text{literal-1} \end{Bmatrix} \begin{bmatrix} \text{identifier-2} \\ \text{literal-2} \end{bmatrix} \dots$$

The EXHIBIT statement causes the identifiers or literals in the list following the statement to be printed out each time the EXHIBIT is executed. If we use the EXHIBIT NAMED option, then the name of the identifier as well as its current value is printed. For example, if the LAST-NAME field contains the value SMITH and we execute:

```
EXHIBIT NAMED LAST-NAME
```

the result will be:

```
LAST-NAME = 'SMITH'
```

If we use the CHANGED option, then the data value is printed only if it has changed from the last time the EXHIBIT statement was executed. The first time that an EXHIBIT CHANGED is executed, the values are all printed. The EXHIBIT CHANGED statement causes the data to be printed in fixed columns rather than printing out the identifier with its value. If we want to print the identifier name as well, then we use the EXHIBIT CHANGED NAMED statement.

These statements can be useful, but they should be used carefully. It is much better to design you programs with a clean structure and to examine your code carefully when errors occur. Too much reliance on the debugging statements found on any machine can be a little like using an elephant gun to kill mice. It is really much more than the job demands. If you try to let the computer do your debugging for you, you will probably end up doing more work than you would if you simply examined the program thoughtfully to find the errors in it.

11.5 THE COPY STATEMENT

In the first work we did in this book, everybody used the same data definitions for the MASTER-FILE and other files used by our programs. Later, as we gained confidence in COBOL and learned the basic file-processing statements, we could define our own individual files. Now we are back to a point in our experience with COBOL where it could be extremely convenient to have everybody accessing the same files. In a real-world data processing situation, it is very useful to have one set of record definitions for the master files and let all programmers use this set. The advantages of this approach are easy to see. If the data base administrator wants to make changes to the files, all he or she has to do is change the master copy of the file or record definition. The other programmers can copy these changes into their programs, recompile them, and continue running as usual. It is very common to want to make changes to master file definitions, usually to add new fields.

In COBOL there is a special statement for performing this copying operation. It is called the COPY **statement,** and its definition is:

COPY statement

```
                      ┌  OF  ┐
COPY text-name       {        }  library-name
                      └  IN  ┘

                    ┌ identifier-1 ┐      ┌ identifier-2 ┐
  REPLACING         { literal-1    }  BY  { literal-2    }
                    └ word-1       ┘      └ word-2       ┘
```

In the IBM 370 OS/VS version of the COPY statement, the phrase IN library-name is not used. Instead, the system uses special types of files called partitioned data sets that are defined using the job control language of the machine. The text name given is one of the partitions in the data set, and the library is defined with a JCL card. There may be similar differences on the version of COBOL you are using, so check the reference manual for your machine.

An example of the use of the COPY statement is:

```
FILE-CONTROL.  COPY PAYFILE.
FD PAYROLL FILE COPY EMPL.
RD PAYCHECKS COPY PAYRPT.
```

The data on the files copied is inserted in the program at the point at which the COPY statement appears. Check the restrictions on this statement on your machine. For example, it is usually not possible to include COPY statements in the file that is being copied.

The COPY statement can be one of the most useful COBOL statements available in an operating data processing environment. It enables the managers of the computer center to set up standard code, and it allows the programmers to access large data files without having to bother rewriting the file definitions each time. The COPY statement is one that will serve you well in your professional career in computing.

11.6 TRANSFER OF CONTROL

We have not yet covered several statements in COBOL for transfer of control within a program. In our programs we have always used the PERFORM statement to transfer control within the program. There is a good reason for this. After we are through performing the routine to which we have transferred, we automatically return to the statement following the PERFORM that called the routine. This allows us to segment our programs into nice readable structures that are easy to follow. If we did not return control back to our calling point, it would be a lot more difficult to follow what was happening. The flowcharts of the programs we have been writing would cease to be well-structured charts that could be contained on a single page and instead become something resembling a Rube Goldberg plumbing diagram.

The statements for transfer of control we will cover in this section have the disadvantage that they do not return control back to their calling point. Once you execute one of them, you have altered the flow of control in your program. The first of these is the simple GO TO **statement.** Its general format is:

GO TO statement

```
GO TO procedure-name
```

Some examples of the GO TO statement are:

```
GO TO CONTROL-ROUTINE.
GO TO END-OF-PROGRAM.
GO TO CLEANUP.
```

When we encounter one of these statements, control is transferred immediately to the procedure named in the statement. As an example of how we might use one of these statements in a program, consider the piece of a COBOL program below. It prints out the numbers from 1 to 10 using a DISPLAY statement. We are assuming that the variable X has been declared in WORKING-STORAGE.

```
        MOVE 1 TO X.
PRINT-LOOP.
        DISPLAY X.
        ADD 1 TO X.
        IF X IS LESS THAN OR EQUAL TO 10 GO TO PRINT-LOOP.
```

In the program above, control is transfered back up to the procedure name, PRINT-LOOP, as long as the value in the variable X is less than or equal to 10. When X exceeds that value, the statement after the IF is executed.

The example above looks simple enough, but programs that make extensive use of the GO TO option to control loops have a tendency to grow out of control. They tend to grow without any particular pattern, and after a while, it is almost impossible to find all the tests and transfers of control that are buried within them. This is particularly noticeable in the code written by beginning programmers, but it is a problem that is encountered at all levels. In your professional work with COBOL, you will no doubt encounter programs that you will have to maintain that make extensive use of the GO TO. The disadvantage of writing poorly structured programs will be much clearer to you.

We have a second form of the GO TO statement that is a kind of combination IF statement and GO TO statement. Its format looks like this:

```
GO TO procedure-name-1  [ procedure-name-2 ]  ...

    DEPENDING ON identifier
```

In this form of the GO TO, the value in the identifier is tested. If it is equal to 1, then control is transferred to the first procedure name. If it is 2, control is transferred to the second procedure, and so on. If the identifier contains a number larger than the number of procedures, then the GO TO statement is simply bypassed.

As an example of the way in which this form of the GO TO might be used, suppose we had a program that processed income taxes, and it would execute different blocks of code depending on whether the taxpayer was single, married, or had some other tax status. We could set up a tax code associated with each record that might be set as follows:

```
1 = Single
2 = Married
3 = Married filing separately
4 = Unmarried head of household
```

Then we could use this piece of COBOL code to process the test:

```
TOP.
    ACCEPT TAX-CODE.
    GO TO SINGLE, MARRIED-JOINT, MARRIED-SEPARATE,
        HEAD-OF-HOUSEHOLD
        DEPENDING ON TAX-CODE.
    DISPLAY 'BAD TAX CODE = ', TAX-CODE
    DISPLAY ' INPUT A NEW TAX CODE.'.
    GO TO TOP.
```

The value we read in for the variable TAX-CODE determines the transfer. If it is a 1, we go to the procedure SINGLE, if it is a 2, we go to MARRIED-JOINT, and so on. If the value in TAX-CODE is outside the 1 to 4 range, then the GO TO is ignored and we drop down to the DISPLAY statements, which print out an error message and then transfer back to TOP to input a new TAX-CODE.

The final form of the GO TO statement is both simple and strange. Its format is:

```
GO TO
```

As you may have noticed, there is no procedure name given to tell where the program should transfer, because this form of the GO TO will be changed at the time the program is executed and the transfer location will be inserted then. To do this, we use another statement called the ALTER statement. Its format is: **ALTER statement**

ALTER procedure-name-1 <u>TO</u> [<u>PROCEED</u> <u>TO</u>] procedure-name-2

      [procedure-name-3 <u>TO</u> [<u>PROCEED</u> <u>TO</u>] procedure-name-4] ...

An example of this statement is:

```
ALTER TRANSFER-1 TO CLEANUP.
```

The code at the location TRANSFER-1 should look like this

```
TRANSFER-1.
    GO TO.
```

The TRANSFER-1 paragraph should contain a single GO TO. It may be of the type that has a procedure name after the GO TO, or it may be of the type with no specified procedure name. It makes no difference. When the ALTER statement is executed, the GO TO will be modified so that when it is executed, it will transfer control to the procedure called CLEANUP. The ALTER statement is probably a leftover from the very early days of computing. On early computers, it was common to write programs that would modify themselves at execution time. This practice has been dropped in other languages because it means that programs can be written that are very nearly impossible to debug. You should *never* use the ALTER statement because it will make your programs too hard to maintain. It is always possible to achieve the same effect as an ALTER by other means.

The material in this section was presented largely to complete your knowledge of COBOL. It is not recommended that you use the GO TO statement in any of its forms in your programs. There are always simpler and better ways to accomplish the same thing. You should know how the GO TO works because you will probably have to maintain and modify programs that have been written by progammers who make extensive use of the GO TO.

STUDY EXERCISES

1. What is the value of being able to control the internal format of data in COBOL?

2. Write a program that will print out all last names on the MASTER-FILE in a right-justified format.

3. Set up tests for the student's college on the MASTER-FILE using the level 88 conditionals.

4. Set up a test for a student's class on the MASTER-FILE using level 88 conditionals. Classes are defined this way:

CREDITS	CLASS
0–29	Freshman
30–59	Sophomore
60–89	Junior
90 and above	Senior

5. Redo the grade summary example of Chapter 10 using indexes and index-handling statements where possible.

6. Rewrite the definition for the MASTER-RECORD to allow the table of courses to be of variable length. Use indexes to access this table.

7. Set up a program that will rewrite the MASTER-FILE to implement your definitions in exercise 6. Also set up your definitions so that the courses are in course number order.

8. Set up a program that will count the number of students from each city in the college's area. Since you do not know what these cities are in advance,

you will have to build the table as you search. Use the OCCURS–DEPENDING ON option to set the table size. If an incoming student's city is not found in the list, add it to the bottom of the list and increase the table size.

9. Write a program that will produce a set of mailing labels for the students on the MASTER-FILE. The labels should look like this:

```
MR. CHARLES R. JACKSON
2179 CHARLESTON CT.
NEWPORT BEACH, CA 92663
```

Use the STRING statement to squeeze out the unneccessary blanks in the label. Also make sure that the correct title for the individual (either MR. or MS.) is included with the label.

10. Write a program that will produce a form letter. The text of the letter and the date of the letter should be read into variable-sized tables for the text using ACCEPT statements. The general format of the letter should be:

```
                                          JANUARY 3, 1980


MR. CHARLES R. JACKSON
2179 CHARLESTON CT.
NEWPORT BEACH, CA 92663

DEAR MR. JACKSON:
                        (text of letter)



                 SINCERELY,

            (your name)
```

If a lower-case alphabet is available at your installation, you might find out how to print this letter in lower-case letters. If you choose to do this, be sure that you translate the name and address into lower-case letters as well to make the letter look correct.

11. Write a COBOL text-edit program that will read in cards with text on them and process them this way:

   1. It will print out the text lines in double-spaced pages with page numbers at the top of the page.

   2. Set the length of the line at n spaces per line. The value for n is initially read in using an ACCEPT statement.

   3. Skip to a new line and indent five spaces any time the character # is encountered in the text.

12 1
2 12
12
12 1
2 12
12
12 1
2 12
12
12 1
2 12
12

THE REPORT WRITER

12.0 INTRODUCTION

The most common use of the COBOL language is to generate reports. We have already generated many kinds of management reports using the MASTER-FILE we defined. An example was the report giving a list of the graduating seniors that we produced in Chapter 5. This report is typical of the kind for which COBOL might be used. In business, there are many similar types of reports—for example, sales reports, payroll registers, account activity reports, and so on. With the COBOL statements we have discussed up to this point, you should be able to generate any of these reports without too much difficulty given the initial data files. As you begin to write COBOL programs to produce different types of reports, you will notice that the computer code you are generating is somewhat stereotyped, and you will find yourself doing the same things over and over. Because of the repetitive nature of report programs the COBOL designers built in a report-generating feature so that programmers working in the language are spared some of the tedious detail of setting up the same type of code over and over to generate reports.

The report writer facility in COBOL can be very useful, and you should learn to use it. You may find a few problems with it, however. First, the report writer may not be available on smaller computers. It takes up a lot of computer memory (but so does a COBOL program capable of producing an elaborate report without the use of the report writer). Check the manual for your computer to see whether the report writer is available. In addition, some installations discourage the use of the report writer because of the large amount of core it requires, and you will no doubt encounter professional COBOL programmers who have nothing good to say about the report feature because of its supposed "inefficiency." The reason for this may be that many COBOL programmers got their training on old, second-generation machines with small computer memories on which space was at a premium. As a result, they tend to use a variety of tricks to make their programs as small as possible because they think smallness means efficiency. This may be a false measure of economy. The real question is how much money can be saved by the use of the report feature because today the cost of programmer time is the most important consideration. The programmer time you can save using the report feature will probably make it well worth the additional memory required.

Learning to use the report writer from a reference manual can be quite difficult. This is not because the report statements are difficult in themselves but because the terminology used can be very confusing. The easiest way to learn how to use the report feature is to do it backwards. First, we start with an example of a report and identify the components that make up the report. Then we introduce the report statements and show how to use them to generate the report itself.

As an example of a report, we have generated a tuition and fees report from our MASTER-FILE. In this report we print out the amount of money that each student pays in tuition and fees. These are summed to give a total payment. The students are listed in order by college, and within each college the students are listed alphabetically. We also generate a total for tuition and fees for each college, and then at the end of the report, we generate a total for the entire university.

Figure 12.1 shows the report as it is produced from the students listed on the MASTER-FILE. The report in Figure 12.1 is self-explanatory because it is very similar to the grade report that you did in Chapter 5. We have numbered the parts of the report to make their function clear. These parts are:

1. REPORT HEADER—The report header appears only once for the entire report. It is at the beginning and is a kind of overall title for the report.

2. PAGE HEADER—The page header is a title that appears at the top of each report page. It may be used to identify the page as belonging to a particular report. This can be useful in case the printout is broken up. Ideally, it should contain the report name and date and perhaps page numbers as well.

3. CONTROL HEADER—The control header is a heading that is printed each time some particular control break occurs. In the example in Figure 12.1, we are using the field COLLEGE as our control field. This means that the input data that we use to generate the report is sorted in order by college, and that each time the value in the COLLEGE field changes, a control header is printed. In the report feature, a control break can also be specified for initial (the first record reported) and final (the last record reported).

FIGURE 12.1
Sample Tuition and Fees
Report.

COLLEGE TUITION AND FEES REPORT

TUITION AND FEES BY COLLEGE   JANUARY, 1980.

COLLEGE: AGRICULTURE

STUDENT	TUITION	FEES	OTHER	TOTAL
AVANT, LUPE W.	1,400.00	275.00	90.28	1,765.28
AVANT, TOBY V.	1,400.00	275.00	106.00	2,531.00
BACH, JULIA V.	1,400.00	275.00	40.01	1,715.01
BATES, ANGELA M.	1,400.00	275.00	39.52	1,714.52
BETZEN, KNOX J.	1,400.00	275.00	285 91	1,960.91
DOUGLAS, GAIL T.	1,400.00	275.00	105.49	2,680.49
FLOYD, GARY V.	1,400.00	275.00	36.29	2,611.29
GARLAND, ANTHONY S.	1,400.00	275.00	80.24	2,505.24
JAMES, IRENE G.	1,400.00	275.00	52.75	2,477.75
JOHNSON, KAY Y.	1,400.00	275.00	13.85	1,688.85
KING, JAMES B.	1,400.00	275.00	35.80	2,610.80
NEWCOMER, KATHRYN R.	1,400.00	275.00	93.51	2,668.51
PATRICK, DORIS Y.	1,400.00	275.00	49.00	2,624.00
SALVINO, MARTHA S.	1,400.00	275.00	110.76	1,785.76
SPENCER, CASEY A.	1,400.00	275.00	205.33	2,780.33
SPENCER, MARILYN A.	1,400.00	275.00	247.04	1,922.04
TROTTER, GRANT K.	1,400.00	275.00	116.68	1,791.68
VARGAS, GEOFFREY M.	1,400.00	275.00	170.83	2,745.83

COLLEGE TOTALS   25,200.00 4,950.00 1,879.29   81,158.58

COLLEGE: ARTS AND SCIENCES

STUDENT	TUITION	FEES	OTHER	TOTAL
ADDISON, WILSON S.	1,400.00	275.00	110.70	2,685.70
AIRINGTON, KENT I.	1,400.00	275.00	70.02	1,745.02
ALDRICH, LOREN U.	1,400.00	275.00	13.02	2,588.02
ALEXANDER, ANN W.	1,400.00	275.00	29.81	2,454.81
ALEXANDER, JEWELL Q.	1,400.00	275.00	46.11	1,721.11
ALLDAY, DEBORAH C.	1,400.00	275.00	36.29	1,711.29
ASHTON, BARBARA K.	1,400.00	275.00	5.92	2,580.92
AYLOR, KEVIN T.	1,400.00	275.00	118.73	2,693.73
AYLOR, PATRICIA P.	1,400.00	275.00	174.99	1,849.99
AYLOR, RODNEY I.	1,400.00	275.00	45.49	2,470.49
BABSON, TRAVIS U.	1,400.00	275.00	7.52	1,682.52
BARNETT, GARY A.	1,400.00	275.00	14.98	1,689.98
BARTLETT, DEAN V.	1,400.00	275.00	48.54	1,723.54
BATES, LAWRENCE T.	1,400.00	275.00	74.95	1,749.95
BETTZ, CASEY J.	1,400.00	275.00	83.68	2,658.68

TUITION AND FEES REPORT   PAGE- 0001

FIGURE 12.1
(Continued)

TUITION AND FEES BY COLLEGE   JANUARY, 1980.

BETTZ, RANDALL Z.	1,400.00	275.00	46.42	2,621.42
BIGGS, PAMELA D.	1,400.00	275.00	180.57	1,855.57
BOWLING, PAT Y.	1,400.00	275.00	22.53	1,697.53
BROWN, CINDY A.	1,400.00	275.00	72.14	1,747.14
CAINS, RICHARD Q.	1,400.00	275.00	24.70	1,699.70
CAMERON, ELLEN O.	1,400.00	275.00	186.16	1,861.16
CAMERON, SARA W.	1,400.00	275.00	59.94	1,734.94
CAMP, MARIE H.	1,400.00	275.00	39.08	1,714.08
CARRERA, JOANN L.	1,400.00	275.00	190.15	2,615.15
CARRERA, JOHN M.	1,400.00	275.00	17.99	1,692.99
CHAMBERS, DEBRA Y.	1,400.00	275.00	111.02	2,686.02
CHAMBERS, SANDRA D.	1,400.00	275.00	132.43	2,707.43
CHANDLER, CONNIE X.	1,400.00	275,00	35.69	1,710.69
CHAPMAN, SHELLY N.	1,400.00	275.00	42.44	2,617.44
CHRISTIAN, GORDON D.	1,400.00	275.00	214.08	2,789.08
COKER, DANIEL B.	1,400.00	275.00	59.80	2,484.80
COKER, TONY K.	1,400.00	275.00	58.36	2,633.36
DAVIDSON, JULIANNE R.	1,400.00	275.00	52.76	2,627.76
ELLIS, GEORGE F.	1,400.00	275.00	129.48	2.554.48
ESTES, ALICIA T.	1,400.00	275.00	54.78	2,629.78
EUBANKS, DEBORAH F.	1,400.00	275.00	38.80	2,613.80
EVANS, MARSHALL I.	1,400.00	275.00	109.72	1,784.72
FINNEY, WAGNER I.	1,400.00	275.00	71.69	2,646.69
GARLAND, ALAN C.	1,400.00	275.00	20.85	1,695.85
GLEASON, JACKIE D.	1,400.00	275.00	1.21	1,676.21
HERRERA, BARRY Z.	1,400.00	275.00	57.48	2,632.48
HERRERA, JOEL R.	1,400.00	275.00	81.44	1,756.44
HERRERA, MARK A.	1,400.00	275.00	13.58	2,588.58
HOLLOWAY, JANE Z.	1,400.00	275.00	61.02	2,636.02
JACKSON, VANESSA I.	1,400.00	275.00	6.41	1,681.41
JARVIS, MARTHA C.	1,400.00	275.00	277.26	1,952.26
LAING, BERT V.	1,400.00	275.00	18.12	2,593.12
LAND, BENJAMIN M.	1,400.00	275.00	183.76	2,758.76
LAND, WILLIAM M.	1,400.00	275.00	42.87	1,717.87
MARTINI, CHARLES T.	1,400.00	275.00	110.92	2,685.92
MULLEN, DONNA V.	1,400.00	275.00	95.44	1,770.44
NOEL, MELONIE D.	1,400.00	275.00	47.55	2,622.55
NOEL, STEWART Q.	1,400.00	275.00	186.62	2,761.62
PHILLIPS, DORIS C.	1,400.00	275.00	19.12	2,594.12
PORTER, MARION I.	1,400.00	275.00	2.24	1,677.24
PRUETT, JOHN X.	1,400.00	275,00	86.78	1.761.78
PURCELL, ELBERT K.	1,400.00	275.00	36.64	2,611.64
RAMIEREZ, LINDA E.	1,400.00	275.00	53.20	2,628.20
REDFORD, RENALDO I.	1,400.00	275.00	63.13	2,488.13
ROWELL, JANE O.	1,400.00	275.00	147.65	2,722.65
SALVINO, HOLLY O.	1,400.00	275.00	114.62	1,789.62
SETTLE, BRENDA D.	1,400.00	275.00	184.82	2,609.82

FIGURE 12.1
(Continued)

TUITION AND FEES BY COLLEGE   JANUARY, 1980.

SHAFER, JULIAN T.	1,400.00	275.00	20.38	1,695.38
SHAFER, KNOX K.	1,400.00	275.00	112.99	2,687.99
SHERIDAN, MARSHALL Y.	1,400.00	275.00	64.62	2,639.62
SLIDER, BILLY S.	1,400.00	275.00	88.33	1,763.33
SPEIGHT, BRAD X.	1,400.00	275.00	176.18	1,851.18
SPEIGHT, PEARL G.	1,400.00	275.00	71.61	2,496.61
STROUD, TRAVIS Q.	1,400.00	275.00	68.38	1,743.38
TERRY, VICKI H.	1,400.00	275.00	10.22	1,685.22
THOMPSON, GERALD H.	1,400.00	275.00	2.33	1,677.33
THOMPSON, JOLYON O.	1,400.00	275.00	26.78	1,701.78
THOMPSON, JON J.	1,400.00	275,00	73.63	1,748.63
TURNER, PHYLLIS Q.	1,400.00	275.00	78.82	2,653.82
VARGAS, RICKY A.	1,400.00	275.00	120.81	1,795.81
WALKER, STEWART V.	1,400.00	275.00	110.12	2,685.12
WILCOX, EUGENIA E.	1,400.00	275.00	86.64	1,761.64
WILCOX, JEROLD A.	1,400.00	275.00	102.57	2,677.57
WILLIAMS, JILL E.	1,400.00	275.00	66.76	1,741.76
ZACHARY, TERRI I.	1,400.00	275.00	60.27	1,735.27

COLLEGE TOTALS	112,000.00	22,000.00	6,085.65	349,771.30

COLLEGE: BUSINESS

STUDENT	TUITION	FEES	OTHER	TOTAL
AIRINGTON, JOANN B.	1,400.00	275.00	71.35	2,496.35
ALEXANDER, LUCY U.	1,400.00	275.00	12.12	1,687.12
ALEXANDER, WALTER M.	1,400.00	275.00	44.53	1,719.53
BARNETT, DEAN N.	1,400.00	275.00	3.86	2,428.86
BETTZ, RUBY C.	1,400.00	275.00	90.44	2,515.44
BOWLING, MARK X.	1,400.00	275.00	188.78	1,863.78
BRYANT, ALICE M.	1,400.00	275.00	142.57	2,717.57
CARRERA, KENNETH O.	1,400.00	275.00	3.41	2,428.41
CHRISTIAN, PAMELA P.	1,400.00	275.00	34.93	2,609.93
COLE, ELIZABETH J.	1,400.00	275.00	15.99	2,590.99
COLE, KELLY V.	1,400.00	275.00	34.76	1,709.76
COOK, PHILLIP H.	1,400.00	275.00	10.59	1,685.59
CRAWFORD, LUPE O.	1,400.00	275.00	14.64	2,589.64
DICKERSON, BARTON S.	1,400.00	275.00	62.33	1,737.33
DOUGLAS, NANCY V.	1,400.00	275.00	60.21	1,735.21
EUBANKS, BRUCE D.	1,400.00	275.00	5.05	1,680.05
FELLERS, PATRICK Z.	1,400.00	275.00	17.08	2,592.08
FOSTER, ROBIN F.	1,400.00	275.00	26.55	2,601.55
FREITAG, PAT V.	1,400.00	275.00	57.17	2,632.17

TUITION AND FEES REPORT   PAGE- 0003

FIGURE 12.1
(Continued)

```
TUITION AND FEES BY COLLEGE                    JANUARY, 1980.

GARLOCK, SHERRI K.        1,400.00    275.00     101.42    1,776.42
HILL, ETHEL S.            1,400.00    275.00     278.59    2,853.59
HOLLOWAY, FREDRICK V.     1,400.00    275,00      35.82    2,460.82
JACOBS, KEITH N.          1,400.00    275.00     132.14    1,807.14
JAMES, DONALD J.          1,400.00    275.00      10.55    2,585.55
JAMES, LILLY F.           1,400.00    275.00     253.47    2,828.47
KING, WILLIAM F.          1,400.00    275.00      22.85    1,697.85
LIND, SOAMES W.           1,400.00    275.00     243.06    2,818.06
MCALLISTER, PENNY I.      1,400.00    275.00     102.96    2,677.96
NEWCOMER, HAROLD R.       1,400.00    275.00      68.72    1,743.72
RAYMER, WINIFRED K.       1,400.00    275.00       4.07    2,579.07
REED, HERMAN Z.           1,400.00    275.00      61.99    2,636.99
SLIDER, CAROL Z.          1,400.00    275.00       5.16    2,430.16
SLIDER, ELAINE T.         1,400.00    275.00      35.86    2,610.86
SPENCER, ALAN H.          1,400.00    275.00      16.58    2,591.58
TAYLOR, KAREN D.          1,400.00    275.00      93.47    2,668.47
TRACY, JAMES D.           1,400.00    275.00     197.16    1,872.16
TROTTER, JANNA F.         1,400.00    275.00      11.77    2,586.77
TURNER, ANTONIO L.        1,400.00    275.00      85.50    1,760.50
WILCOX, HERBERT W.        1,400.00    275.00      53.06    2,628.06
WILLIAMS, NORMAN L.       1,400.00    275.00      80.09    1,755.09
YOUNG, VIOLET A.          1,400.00    275.00      32.80    2,607.80
                       ------------------------------------------
COLLEGE TOTALS          57,400.00 11,275.00   2,823.45  187,996.90

             COLLEGE:  EDUCATION

     STUDENT              TUITION     FEES      OTHER      TOTAL

AIRINGTON, DANIEL C.      1,400.00    275.00      51.61    1,726.61
ARNOLD, ELMER V.          1,400.00    275.00      33.55    2,458.55
AVANT, LORI D.            1,400.00    275.00      44.97    1,719.97
BOWLING, SHERRI S.        1,400.00    275.00      39.41    2,614.41
BROWN, ANTHONY R.         1,400.00    275.00     189.22    1,864.22
DUKE, TERRENCE Q.         1,400.00    275.00      16.10    2,441.10
EVANS, MARY J.            1,400.00    275.00     165.19    2,740.19
FELLERS, NANCY B.         1,400.00    275.00      44.67    1,719.67
FULLER, VICTORIA I.       1,400.00    275.00       4.60    1,679.60
GARLOCK, JOSEPH D.        1,400.00    275.00      50.32    2,625.32
GARLOCK, NICHOLAS G.      1,400.00    275.00     136.16    2,711.16
GARY, ALICIA X.           1,400.00    275.00      55.29    1,730.29
HOWELL, DIANNE U.         1,400.00    275.00      26.54    1,701.54
LANE, JUDITH C.           1,400.00    275.00       7.18    2,582.18
MAHAN, SCOTT V.           1,400.00    275.00      39.34    1,714.34


TUITION AND FEES REPORT                        PAGE- 0004
```

FIGURE 12.1
(Continued)

```
TUITION AND FEES BY COLLEGE                        JANUARY, 1980.

NEWCOMER, JOHN P.         1,400.00    275.00     13.08    1,688.08
PATRICK, POLLY Q.         1,400.00    275.00     21.31    1,696.31
RAYMER, GEORGE N.         1,400.00    275.00     72.47    2,647.47
SAVAGE, ELMER L.          1,400.00    275.00     21.01    1,696.01
SHERIDAN, RENALDO S.      1,400.00    275.00     10.15    2,585.15
SPARKS, KATHRYN O.        1,400.00    275.00      5.23    1,680.23
SPARKS, MARY C.           1,400.00    275.00     10.08    2,585.08
SPROULS, MARGARET C.      1,400.00    275.00      8.54    2,433.54
WALL, PETER B.            1,400.00    275.00     16.14    1,691.14
WHATLEY, TIMOTHY E.       1,400.00    275.00     33.16    1,708.16
WILCOX, STEPHEN L.        1,400.00    275.00     55.40    2,630.40
                         ----------------------------------------
COLLEGE TOTALS           36,400.00  7,150.00  1,170.72  110,141.44

                 COLLEGE:  ENGINEERING

    STUDENT               TUITION    FEES     OTHER     TOTAL

ABBE, CAMILLE O.          1,400.00    275.00     31.39    1,706.39
ADDISON, MICHAEL M.       1,400.00    275.00     98.73    1,773.73
ALEXANDER, LORI F.        1,400.00    275.00    122.45    1,797.45
AYLOR, RENE M.            1,400.00    275.00    230.27    2,805.27
BACH, VERNON T.           1,400.00    275.00    146.00    1,821.00
BARCLAY, KAREN L.         1,400.00    275.00    126.41    2,701.41
BARCLAY, KELLY E.         1,400.00    275.00    111.99    2,536.99
BARCLAY, NELL T.          1,400.00    275.00     60.25    1,735.25
BARNETT, ALICIA P.        1,400.00    275.00     31.90    1,706.90
BRYANT, HESTER T.         1,400.00    275.00     95.93    2,670.93
CHAMBERLAIN, KENNETH P.   1,400.00    275.00    179.29    1,854.29
CRAIG, RICHARD O.         1,400.00    275.00    408.27    2,083.27
DAVIS, CONNIE K.          1,400.00    275.00     12.19    2,587.19
DAVIS, STEPHEN X.         1,400.00    275.00      6.74    2,581.74
DOWELL, ALLEN J.          1,400.00    275.00     56.68    2,631.58
DRAKE, SUSAN F.           1,400.00    275.00      3.84    1,678.84
ELLIS, CANDACE C.         1,400.00    275.00     28.82    2,603.82
ELLIS, KELLY V.           1,400.00    275.00     89.52    2,514.52
FLOYD, MARLA Z.           1,400.00    275.00     33.18    2,608.18
FREITAG, ANN N.           1,400.00    275.00    139.34    2,714.34
GALLAWAY, KENT J.         1,400.00    275.00     10.46    2,585.46
JACKSON, LOUIS Y.         1,400.00    275.00    123.25    1,798.25
JONES, CHERYL F.          1,400.00    275.00     47.63    1,722.63
JONES, LISA H.            1,400.00    275.00     93.66    2,668.66
KING, MARGARET U.         1,400.00    275.00     11.34    2,586.34
LACY, ELIZABETH T.        1,400.00    275.00     71.84    2,646.84
```

TUITION AND FEES REPORT   PAGE- 0005

FIGURE 12.1
(Continued)

TUITION AND FEES BY COLLEGE

```
MCALLISTER, MICHAEL Z.      1,400.00   275.00    133.38    2,558.38
PORTER, RUSSELL H.          1,400.00   275.00      1.38    1,676.38
ROGERS, PHYLLIS O.          1,400.00   275.00     97.85    2,672.85
SHAFER, ELAINE S.           1,400 00   275.00     51.53    2,626.53
SKIPPER, ANITA L.           1,400.00   275.00     40.25    1,715.25
SPEIGHT, CHARLES Z.         1,400.00   275.00    126.42    1,801.42
TRACY, MARIA T.             1,400.00   275.00    105.73    1,780.73
TURNER, BRENDA K.           1,400.00   275.00     45.14    1,720.14
TURNER, STEVE K.            1,400.00   275.00     86.37    1,761.37
WEIR, EUGENE O.             1,400.00   275.00    245.22    1,920.22
                           -------------------------------------------

COLLEGE TOTALS             50,400.00  9,900.00  3,304.54  158,709.08

UNIVERSITY TOTALS         281,400.00 55,275.00 15,263.65  887,777.30
```

⑦

TUITION AND FEES REPORT   PAGE- 0006
END OF TUITION AND FEES REPORT   JANUARY, 1980.

⑧

4. DETAIL LINE—The detail line is the basic line of the report. There may be several different types of detail lines in a report, although in this example, we have only one type, which gives the student name and the fees.

5. CONTROL FOOTING—The control footing is printed at the end of a series of detail lines when a control break occurs.

6. PAGE FOOTING—The page footing appears at the bottom of each page of a report. Like the page heading, it can be used for identification purposes or for page numbers. In our example, we have a title and the page number in the page footing.

7. CONTROL FOOTING—This is an example of a final control footing. It is used to print out cleanup information (in this case the sum of the university totals for tuition and fees) after all the work in the report has been done.

8. REPORT FOOTING—This line is printed out after the entire report is completed and is used to identify the end of the report.

As you can see from the figure, any of the material in it could be generated using statements you have already learned. However, the program to do this would not be an easy proposition. For instance, you would have to set up counters in your program to make sure that the various types of header and footing lines appeared in the proper place. You would have to check for control breaks using IF statements, and you would have to maintain count of the pages generated in your report so that you could print out the page numbers. To get yourself in the proper frame of mind for reading the rest of the material in this chapter, you might try writing a COBOL program that would produce Figure 12.1 without using the report feature. After you have done that, you should be very interested in learning how to use the material that follows.

12.1 DATA DIVISION ENTRIES FOR REPORTS

A report is simply a special type of file, and as such, it needs a set of ENVIRONMENT and DATA DIVISION entries similar to those you have already used in setting up other COBOL files. The only ENVIRONMENT entry needed is a SELECT entry in the FILE SECTION. This SELECT entry gives the name of the file that the report will be produced on and associates that name with some external I/O device. Some examples of the SELECT entries that might be used with report files are:

```
SELECT PRINT-FILE ASSIGN TO UT-S-PRINTER.
SELECT LABEL-FILE ASSIGN TO UT-S-MAILER.
```

These are conventional SELECT statements that could be used with the DATA DIVISION entries given later. Note that we have used two different external file names. This would cause COBOL to separate the output from the two reports and print them on different sections of the printed output generated by our program.

In the DATA DIVISION, we must give two entries for a report. First of all, there must be an entry in the FILE SECTION that gives the name of the file on which the report will be produced. This can be a very simple file declaration that only specifies the maximum record size for the report, usually the length of the print line on which the report will be printed. You do not need to give detailed entries on the format of the report line because these will be handled in the report definition itself. Some examples of file definitions for reports might be:

```
FD PRINT-FILE REPORTS ARE SALES-REPORT, EXPENSE-
   REPORT, LABEL RECORDS ARE STANDARD.
01 PRINT-RECORD PICTURE X(120).
FD LABEL-FILE REPORT IS MAILING-LABELS,
   LABEL RECORDS ARE OMITTED.
01 LABEL-DATA PICTURE X(50).
```

These look like ordinary file definitions except that we have an additional clause specifying the names of the reports that are to be printed on this file. It is possible to print multiple reports on a single file as we have done in our first example, or we can link only one report with the file as we have done in our second example. As with any file definition, we must give a LABEL RECORDS clause, and we could give the other clauses discussed for use with the FD statement in Chapter 8 if we wished. The general format for the REPORT **clause** is:

REPORT clause

$$\left\{ \begin{array}{l} \underline{\text{REPORT}} \ \underline{\text{IS}} \\ \underline{\text{REPORTS}} \ \text{ARE} \end{array} \right\} \quad \text{report-name-1} \quad [\ \text{report-name-2} \ ] \ \ldots$$

Finally, in the DATA DIVISION itself, we have to add a new section, the REPORT SECTION. It comes after the FILE SECTION and the WORKING-STORAGE SECTION, making it the third section in our DATA DIVISION. In the REPORT SECTION, we give a series of report definitions similar in concept to the file definitions in the FILE SECTION. To help you see what is going on in the discussion in this section, refer back to Figure 12.1 for specific examples of some of the concepts discussed in this section.

We start our report definition with a header much like that used for files. The general format of this header is:

```
RD report-name

    [ CODE clause ]

    [ CONTROL clause ]

    [ PAGE LIMIT clause ]
```

We will first discuss each of the clauses separately and then give examples of a completed-report definition.

The first clause is the CODE **clause**. It is used to produce a single character code at the beginning of each report line. This is useful if more than one report is to be given on a file at one time. The general format is:

CODE clause

```
CODE mnemonic-name
```

The mnemonic name must be a single character defined in the SPECIAL-NAMES paragraph of the ENVIRONMENT DIVISION.

The CONTROL clause is used to identify the control breaks used in our report. We discussed the concept of a control break in Chapter 5. A control field is a field the value of which we are monitoring when printing out reports. In the report in Figure 12.1, we were using the field COLLEGE as a control field. This means that we will sort the input file that contains the college names in order by the field COLLEGE. When we are reading in data to generate the reports, a change in the value in the COLLEGE field will generate a control break. This triggers the printing of a special set of lines called a control footing and then a new control heading for the next part of the report. The CONTROL clause tells the report writer which variables are being used as controls in the generation of this particular report. Some examples of the CONTROL clause might be:

```
CONTROL IS FINAL
CONTROLS ARE FINAL, SALES-DISTRICT, SALES-REGION
CONTROL IS MAJOR OF MASTER-RECORD,
        COLLEGE OF MASTER-RECORD
```

The fields given in the list after the CONTROL clause tell which fields will be treated as control breaks. The word FINAL means that when the program runs out of data, this also is to be treated as a control break, and a control line is to be printed. Recall that the file should be sorted in order by the control field. If this were not the case, we would get all sorts of "control breaks" as we encountered the different values in the field for the different records. The general format for the CONTROL **clause** is: CONTROL clause

$$
\left\{ \begin{array}{l} \underline{\text{CONTROL}} \text{ IS} \\ \underline{\text{CONTROLS}} \text{ ARE} \end{array} \right\} \left\{ \begin{array}{l} \underline{\text{FINAL}} \\ \text{identifier-1 [identifier-2] ...} \\ \underline{\text{FINAL}} \text{ identifier-1 [identifier-2] ...} \end{array} \right\}
$$

The PAGE LIMIT clause defines the placement of the report on the physical page. The use of this clause can be somewhat confusing, so read the material carefully. The best way to approach the problem is to take a specific PAGE LIMIT clause as an example and break it down. Suppose we have:

```
PAGE LIMIT IS 59 LINES,
        HEADING 2,
        FIRST DETAIL 6,
        LAST DETAIL 52,
        FOOTING 55.
```

The PAGE LIMIT clause tells us how large the page is and where on the page various segments of the report may begin. In the example above, the

page contains a maximum of 59 lines. The number following the HEAD-
ING phrase tells us where report headings and page headings may begin.
In the example above, no report heading or page heading line will begin
before line 2 of the report page.

The FIRST DETAIL phrase tells us where the detail lines and the
control headings may begin. In our example no detail lines or control
headings may begin above line 6. The last detail line tells where the last
detail line may be printed. No detail lines or control headings will begin
after line 53 in our example. Finally, the FOOTING phrase tells us where
the control footings must end in a report. No control footing will extend
beyond line 55 in our example. The restrictions imposed on control footings do not apply to the report footing or the page footing. The report
heading in our example may begin anywhere from line 2 to line 59. The
page footing may begin only on line 56 since it must start on the line after
the one given on the FOOTING phrase, and it may extend to the end of the
page.

The general format of the PAGE LIMIT **clause** is:

PAGE LIMIT clause

$$
\underline{\text{PAGE}} \quad
\begin{bmatrix} \text{LIMIT IS} \\ \text{LIMITS ARE} \end{bmatrix}
\quad \text{integer-1} \quad
\begin{Bmatrix} \underline{\text{LINE}} \\ \underline{\text{LINES}} \end{Bmatrix}
$$

[$\underline{\text{HEADING}}$ integer-2]

[$\underline{\text{FIRST}}$ $\underline{\text{DETAIL}}$ integer-3]

[$\underline{\text{LAST}}$ $\underline{\text{DETAIL}}$ integer-4]

[$\underline{\text{FOOTING}}$ integer-5]

Figure 12.2 shows the relationship between the values given in the PAGE
LIMITS clause and the placement of data on the report page. It shows the
different types of lines in a report and the positions at which they may
start on a page.

As you can see from the figure, a report heading or report footing
may begin at line integer-2 or any line through integer-1. A page heading
must not begin before integer-2, and it must stop before integer-3. A
detail line or a control heading line must not begin before integer-3, and
it must not extend beyond integer-4. A control footing must not begin
before integer-3, and it must not extend beyond integer-5. A page footing
must begin after integer-5, and it must not extend beyond integer-1. The
diagram in Figure 12.2 may prove helpful to you later on when you begin
writing report definitions in COBOL. Review the specifications at that
time to make sure you have set up your page in the way you intended.

At this point, we are ready to begin our discussion of the report groups that make up the report definition itself. The report groups are similar to the record descriptions that make up the file definition except that there will normally be several types of report groups associated with a report (report heading, page heading, page footing, etc.), and the elements in a report group are concerned with the line and column placement of the data so that we can specify the exact format of the report much more readily than we could by using a simple file definition. Each of the report groups in the report description will begin at level 01 and be similar in concept to an ordinary data item description in a file definition. For example, let us take a sample report group definition that shows a detail line in a report. The group is:

```
01  EMPLOYEE-LINE TYPE IS DETAIL.
    02  LINE NUMBER IS 10.
        03  COLUMN 10 PICTURE X(11) VALUE IS
                'EMPLOYEE:'.
        03  COLUMN 22 PICTURE X(30) SOURCE IS
                FULL-NAME.
        03  COLUMN 60 PICTURE $$$$,$$9.99 SOURCE
                IS SALARY.
    02  LINE NUMBER IS 11.
        03  COLUMN 22 PICTURE X(30) SOURCE IS
                DEPARTMENT.
    02  LINE NUMBER IS 12.
        03  COLUMN 22 PICTURE X(6) SOURCE IS
                PHONE.
```

FIGURE 12.2
Placement Diagram for Report Lines

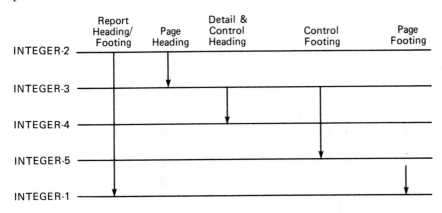

The detail line here is referred to by the name EMPLOYEE-LINE, and, in fact, it defines three lines of the report. The first line begins on line 10 of our report, and it has three entries on that line, one giving a literal, one giving the full name of the employee, and one giving the salary. At line 11, we have a department name, and at line 12, we have a phone number. The data generated by this detail line might look something like this

```
EMPLOYEE:     SMITH, JOHN              $25,375.00
              ACCOUNTING
              2-7562
```

In examining the clauses in the detail line, you will see some that look familiar to you (like PICTURE) and some that do not (like SOURCE and COLUMN). In fact, we can use a number of the same clauses that we used in the file definitions in report definitions as well. The clauses that can be used in both are:

```
USAGE clause
JUSTIFIED clause
PICTURE clause
BLANK WHEN ZERO clause
```

Of those listed above, only the PICTURE clause is really necessary. The others are optional and may be used as needed. They all have the same interpretation they did in the earlier material on file definitions, and they will not be discussed further here.

The new clauses that can be used with reports are:

```
TYPE clause
LINE clause
COLUMN clause
SOURCE clause
VALUE clause
SUM clause
RESET clause
GROUP clause
NEXT GROUP clause
```

These clauses and the ones given earlier are used to qualify the description of the data given in the report. Some of them can only be used at the highest level, level 01, to describe a report group entry. Others can be used at any level. In a report, as in any other data description, each elementary data item must have a level number associated with it.

The first clause we will discuss is the TYPE clause. The TYPE clause must be used with the level 01 description defining the report group itself. It cannot be omitted in the report group definition because it defines the type of report group and tells when it is to be printed. In our earlier example, you have seen a TYPE clause that was used to define the EMPLOYEE-LINE as a detail line with the clause TYPE IS DETAIL. In fact, we can use the TYPE clause for defining all the different types of report groups that will be used in our report.

The general format of a TYPE **clause** is: TYPE clause

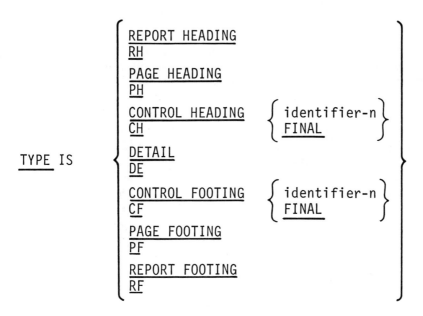

TYPE IS

REPORT HEADING
RH

PAGE HEADING
PH

CONTROL HEADING   { identifier-n
CH   FINAL }

DETAIL
DE

CONTROL FOOTING   { identifier-n
CF   FINAL }

PAGE FOOTING
PF

REPORT FOOTING
RF

In the set of definitions that make up a report, there will be only one REPORT HEADING, PAGE HEADING, PAGE FOOTING, and REPORT FOOTING. The REPORT HEADING and the REPORT FOOTING items will be printed only once, at the beginning and end of the report, respectively. The items defined by the PAGE HEADING and PAGE FOOTING will be printed at the beginning and end of every page. The CONTROL HEADING and CONTROL footing items are used to specify the report groups that are to be printed at the control breaks. With these, you must also name the identifier that is to be used as the control variable. It must be one of the ones named in the report definition header as well. You will have some sort of report group for every control variable specified. All of these types of report groups are printed automatically by the report writer when it senses the condition requiring one of them has occurred. The only thing you will have to specifically require to be printed are the report groups defining detail lines. How to cause report printing will be covered in the next section.

The next type of clause is the LINE clause, which gives the absolute or relative line number of a line printed in a report group. Some examples of LINE clauses are:

```
LINE NUMBER IS 10
LINE 5
LINE NUMBER IS PLUS 2
LINE NUMBER IS PLUS 1
LINE NUMBER IS NEXT PAGE
LINE PLUS 5
```

In the first example the data item will be printed on line 10. In the second example it is printed on line 5. The words NUMBER IS are simply filler words and can be omitted. The third example takes care of a problem that may have already occurred to you in defining a report. Suppose we have a report like the one defined in Figure 12.1, which prints out an un-specified number of detail lines. In that report we generated one detail line for each student on the MASTER-FILE. In general, we would not know exactly how many students would be on the file, so it would not be possible to specify exactly the line on which each student's name would be printed. Even if we could, it would make the report impossibly long. This problem is handled by using a relative line number. Thus, the third example says that the data item is to be printed two lines past the current line (in this case). The use of relative line numbers makes it possible to let the report writer control the printing of detail lines and control headers and footings.

The general format for the LINE **clause** is:

LINE clause

$$
\underline{\text{LINE}} \text{ NUMBER IS} \quad
\left\{
\begin{array}{l}
\text{integer-1} \\
\underline{\text{PLUS}} \text{ integer-2} \\
\underline{\text{NEXT}} \ \underline{\text{PAGE}}
\end{array}
\right\}
$$

The next type of clause in the definition of an elementary data item in a report group is the COLUMN clause. Some examples are:

```
COLUMN NUMBER IS 3
COLUMN 45
COLUMN NUMBER IS 55
```

The general format for the COLUMN **clause** is:

COLUMN clause

```
COLUMN NUMBER IS integer-1
```

The COLUMN clause indicates that the left-most character of the elementary data item should be placed in the column specified by the integer. In our first example the data would begin in column 3 of the print line. We must give a COLUMN clause with every elementary data item in a report group. When you define your report you should make sure that the COLUMN clause does not try to place the data so that it falls outside the report record boundary. When several COLUMN clauses are given without an intervening LINE clause, the report writer assumes that all the data will go on the same line.

The next clause is the SOURCE clause. It tells the report writer which variable contains the data that will be printed in that particular location. Some examples of the use of the SOURCE clause (and some of the other clauses as well) are:

```
02  LINE 30 COLUMN 10 PICTURE X(30) SOURCE IS
            LAST-NAME.
   03 COLUMN 40 PICTURE X(20) SOURCE IS
            FIRST-NAME.
   03 COLUMN 60 PICTURE X SOURCE IS INIT.
```

In this example the variables LAST-NAME, FIRST-NAME, and INIT are being used as the source for the data printed at different column locations on line 30. Notice in the definition of the print line that we must give a new level number for each elementary data item just as we did earlier in record definitions. The LINE, COLUMN, and SOURCE phrases are treated as additional qualifiers for the data on these lines. The general format of the SOURCE **clause** is:

SOURCE clause

```
SOURCE IS identifier-1
```

Suppose, however, that the data that we want to print in a specific column is a literal value. Then we can use the VALUE clause to set the value of the data to be printed in a particular location. An example is:

```
02 LINE 30 COLUMN 10 PICTURE X(15) VALUE IS
            'STUDENT NUMBER:'.
   03 COLUMN 27 PICTURE X(40) SOURCE IS
            STUDENT-NO OF STUDENT.
```

In this example we want to have a title printed out beside the data. The words STUDENT NUMBER: will be printed on line 30 beginning in column 10. The general format of the VALUE **clause** is:

VALUE clause

```
VALUE IS literal
```

The same rules apply for the VALUE clause in the report definitions as applied in the record definitions.

In writing reports, we will sometimes want to be able to sum up certain variable values. For instance, we might like to have a field in the report represent the sum of two variables in the program. This can be done by ADD statements in the PROCEDURE DIVISION, or in certain cases, it can be done using declaratives at the beginning of the PROCE-DURE DIVISION (to be discussed in the next section). However, it is also possible to perform sums using the SUM clause in the report definition itself. Some examples of the SUM clause are:

```
SUM VAR-COST, FIXED-COST
SUM FEE1, FEE2 UPON TOT-FEE
SUM X
```

The SUM clause is used to indicate the source of the data in the same way that a SOURCE clause is used, but it also causes transformation of the data. The general form of the SUM clause is: SUM clause

$$\underline{\text{SUM}} \text{ identifier-1 [identifier-2] ... [} \underline{\text{UPON}} \text{ data-name]}$$

The SUM clause may appear only in elementary items in a control footing in a report. It causes automatic summation of the variable or variables given in the list that follows. Generally, you use the SUM to refer back to previous fields in the report and cause them to be summed for the control footing line in the report.

Along with the SUM clause, we also have the RESET clause, which causes the summation counters to be set back to zero. An example of the RESET clause is:

```
RESET ON COLLEGE OF MASTER-RECORD.
RESET ON CLASS OF STUDENT.
RESET ON FINAL.
```

When a control break occurs on the identifier named after the RESET, the counter for the SUM will be set to zero. The RESET statement would be used in conjunction with the SUM to allow subtotaling of variables in the report group. The general format of the RESET statement is: RESET statement

$$\underline{\text{RESET}} \text{ ON } \begin{Bmatrix} \text{identifier-1} \\ \text{FINAL} \end{Bmatrix}$$

The next clause we can use is one called the GROUP clause. It must be used at the elementary data item level, and it is used to suppress the printing of the field under certain conditions. To see how it might work, suppose we had the definition for a report detail line that looked like this:

```
01 STUDENT-LINE TYPE IS DETAIL LINE NUMBER IS
          PLUS 1.
   02 COLUMN 10 PICTURE X(25) SOURCE IS COLLEGE
          OF MASTER-RECORD.
   02 COLUMN 35 PICTURE X(30) SOURCE IS FULL-NAME.
```

Suppose we had the file sorted in order by college, and within each college, we had the names in alphabetical order. If we generated print-out using the detail line above, the printout would look something like this:

```
AGRICULTURE          ADAMS, PETER
AGRICULTURE          ALLEN, CHARLES
AGRICULTURE          ALTMANN, PHILLIP
AGRICULTURE          ATWATER, KENNETH
        .                .
        .                .
        .                .
```

In the printout, the college name would be printed out with each student line. The result would be difficult to read. The only time we are really interested in seeing the college name is when the college changes—that is, at the occurrence of a control break. The GROUP clause will suppress the printing of the item except immediately after a control or page break. If we had written our detail line like this:

```
01 STUDENT-LINE TYPE IS DETAIL LINE NUMBER IS
          PLUS 1.
   02 COLUMN 10 PICTURE X(25) GROUP INDICATE SOURCE
          IS COLLEGE OF MASTER-RECORD.
   02 COLUMN 35 PICTURE X(30) SOURCE IS FULL-NAME.
```

The report lines we would have generated would have looked like this:

```
AGRICULTURE          ADAMS, PETER
                     ALLEN, CHARLES
                     ALTMANN, PHILLIP
                     ATWATER, KENNETH
                         .
                         .
                         .
```

The college name would be printed only at the control break for the new college.

The general format of the GROUP **clause** is:

```
GROUP INDICATE
```

As a final type of control phrase, we have the NEXT GROUP phrase. It is used only in a report group entry, and it sets the spacing condition following the last line of the report group in which it appears. Some examples of the NEXT GROUP clause are:

```
NEXT GROUP IS 3
NEXT GROUP IS PLUS 10
NEXT GROUP PLUS 6
NEXT GROUP IS NEXT PAGE
NEXT GROUP NEXT PAGE
```

The first example indicates that the next group is to appear on line 3. The second example shows that the next group is to be printed 10 lines down from the current group. The final examples show that there should be a page eject before printing the next group. The general format of the NEXT GROUP **phrase** is:

$$
\underline{\text{NEXT GROUP}} \text{ IS } \left\{ \begin{array}{l} \text{integer-1} \\ \underline{\text{PLUS}} \text{ integer-2} \\ \underline{\text{NEXT PAGE}} \end{array} \right\}
$$

In this section, we have given the report definition clauses used to control the printing of the data in a report. It may seem difficult to understand how to use them all. The best approach is to refer to the program at the end of the chapter and study the way in which specific clauses were used to produce the report in Figure 12.1.

12.2 PROCEDURE DIVISION ENTRIES FOR REPORTS

Up to this point, the material we have had on reports has been the DATA DIVISION entries, which give the information on how to format the reports. In addition to this material, we also have to know when to print out the reports, and the statements for this action will be found in the PROCEDURE DIVISION. We frequently have to manipulate the data before we can generate a report, and this must also be done in the PROCE-

DURE DIVISION, using statements that we have already had. One example of this could be found in the report in Figure 12.1 where we had to pack the first name, middle initial, and last name of each student in the report into a full-name field before we could print a detail line.

The statements in the PROCEDURE DIVISION for generating reports are few and simple, but there are some points that we should be aware of before we begin to use them. The generation of reports basically involves the use of some special printing statements that are not too different from the ones we have had earlier.

The first new feature we will introduce is called the DECLARATIVES section. This is a special section in the PROCEDURE DIVISION that is called in asynchronously. This means that it is not executed when it is encountered like the other PROCEDURE DIVISION sections and paragraphs, but, rather, it is executed when some special condition is encountered. The DECLARATIVES section is used for two things. It is used for special user-written label-checking routines for magnetic tapes and other files. We have not covered this material in this book because most computer installations do not write their own label-checking routines but, instead, use those supplied by the manufacturer. The second thing that the DECLARATIVES section is used for is manipulation of the data items to be printed in reports. Before we print a control footing or heading, we frequently like to manipulate the data values to be printed. One example of this might be the modification of a total in a control footing for a bill to reflect a quantity discount. We would use some code in the DECLARATIVES section to perform this function.

The general format of the DECLARATIVES **section** is:

**DECLARATIVES
section**

```
PROCEDURE DIVISION.

DECLARATIVES.

section-name    SECTION.   USE sentence.

paragraph-name.     sentence    ...    ...    ...

END DECLARATIVES.
```

As you can see from this definition, the DECLARATIVES section must be given first in the PROCEDURE DIVISION. It is broken up into different sections, and each section outlines a condition under which the section is to be invoked and an action to be taken when it is invoked. To set the condition under which the section is to be invoked, we use the USE sentence. The general format of the USE **sentence** is:

USE sentence

```
USE BEFORE REPORTING data-name.
```

The data name in this definition is a report group name from some report definition. It cannot be a detail line, but any other report group is all right. The actions outlined in the paragraphs that follow the USE sentence tell what is to be done before this particular report group is printed.

As an example of a USE sentence, let us suppose that a company had the policy that all orders over $100 would get a 5 percent discount. The DECLARATIVES section could contain the code to calculate this discount before the control footing for the total bill was printed. The following code could handle this calculation (assuming that the appropriate fields were defined elsewhere in the program):

```
PROCEDURE DIVISION.
DECLARATIVES.
CALC-TOTAL SECTION. USE BEFORE REPORTING TOTAL-
        BILL-LINE.
FIGURE-TOTAL.
    IF TOTAL-SALES IS GREATER THAN 100
        COMPUTE TOTAL-BILL = .95 * TOTAL-SALES
    ELSE
        MOVE TOTAL-SALES TO TOTAL-BILL.
END DECLARATIVES.
```

In this example, the CALC-TOTAL section would be invoked before the report group TOTAL-BILL-LINE was printed. This line would be some sort of control footing that would print out the total bill. Before we print this line, the section would check to see if the total were greater than 100. If it were, then the 5 percent discount would be taken, which would give the amount of the total bill. Otherwise, the total sales would simply give the total bill, and this value would be printed out in our report. You can also use the DECLARATIVES section for a variety of types of summing and initialization that would be very useful in reports.

Another useful feature in the report writer that we have not covered so far is the existence of certain special variables used by the report writer. There are two of these, and their names are:

```
PAGE-COUNTER
LINE-COUNTER
```

The PAGE-COUNTER gives the number of the current page that the report is printing; the LINE-COUNTER gives the current line. They are updated automatically by the report writer as you are generating detail lines. The PAGE-COUNTER is the more useful of this pair of values. It can be used to print out the page numbers on the report (as we did in Figure 12.1) by putting a line in the report like:

`SOURCE IS PAGE-COUNTER`

at the appropriate location in the page heading or page footing.

At this point, we are ready for the statements to generate the report. Since a report is much like any other input–output statement, we have to have statements for initializing the report as well as one for printing out a detail line from the report. The first of these, the INITIATE statement, initializes the report. Its general form is:

INITIATE statement

`INITIATE report-name-1 [ report-name-2 ] ...`

This statement sets up the initial values for the counters. It does not open the file on which the report is to be printed. This must be done using an ordinary OPEN statement. The INITIATE statement must be given once and only once for a given report without an intervening TERMINATE.

The next statement corresponds to the CLOSE in our other input–output statements. Its general format is:

`TERMINATE report-name-1 [ report-name-2 ] ...`

The TERMINATE **statement** causes cleanup processing for the report and triggers printing of the ending material on the report. We can continue to use the report in our program after we have terminated it only if we issue another INITIATE statement for that report.

TERMINATE statement

Finally, to generate the report itself, we have the GENERATE **statement.** Its general format is:

GENERATE statement

`GENERATE identifier`

The identifier in this definition may be either a report name or a detail line. If it is a detail line, it causes that particular detail line to be printed (remember that a report could have many different detail lines). If it is a report name, then the entire report (except for the detail lines) will be printed as a sort of summary report. This last feature can be very useful, because it allows us to use a report either as highly detailed report or as a summary, depending on the form of the GENERATE statement that we use.

The best way to understand these statements is to go to the next section where the program example that generated the report in Figure 12.1 is explained.

12.3   PROGRAM EXAMPLE USING REPORT

In Section 12.0, we had a report that gave a breakdown of tuition and fees on a college-by-college basis. For each college, we printed out the students' full names in alphabetical order, last name first. Then we printed out the tuition, fees, miscellaneous fees, and total balance owed by each student. At the end of the report for each college, we printed out the totals for the college and then finally, we printed out the grand totals for the university. The report had both page headings and page footings to identify the date, report title, and page number of each page. Refer to Figure 12.1 for the printout generated in this report.

The program to generate this report is fairly simple. Most of the work is done in the REPORT SECTION of the DATA DIVISION, where the report format is laid out. The work done in the PROCEDURE DIVISION to actually generate the report is minimal. The HIPO diagram for the PROCEDURE DIVISION is shown in Figure 12.3. In the program we have only four paragraphs, a CONTROL-SECTION to handle the calling of the subordinate routines, an INITIALIZE routine, a GENERATE-REPORT routine, and finally, a CLEANUP routine. In addition, we have a DECLARATIVES section that will be explained when we look more closely at the report definition. Figure 12.4 gives a listing of the program that produces the report.

The INITIALIZE routine is the first routine of any consequence (the CONTROL-SECTION that precedes it is conventional). First, we read in a value for the REPORT-DATE using an ACCEPT. You might wonder why we did not use the form ACCEPT REPORT-DATE FROM DATE to initialize the REPORT-DATE. The answer would be that in a typical computer shop, we might have to run this program several days in advance of the date that we would like to have our listing appear. To compensate for this, we simply read in the date that we would like to have appear on our report as another piece of data, and that way, we can set it to any convenient date. In the next lines of the INITIALIZE routine, we sort the data on the

FIGURE 12.3
Hierarchy Diagram for Tuition and Fees Report

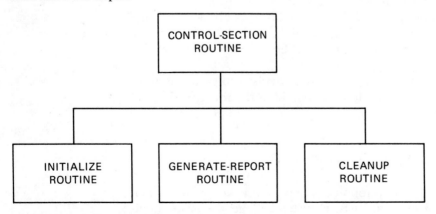

FIGURE 12.4
Program Listing for Tuition
and Fees Report.

```
000010 IDENTIFICATION DIVISION.
000020 PROGRAM-ID. COLLTOT.
000030 AUTHOR.  NORMAN LYONS.
000040 DATE-WRITTEN.  JANUARY, 1980.
000050 DATE-COMPILED.  JANUARY, 1980.
000060 SECURITY.  NONE.
000070********************VERSION 1.0 - LAST MODIFIED, JANUARY, 1980*****
000080*    THE COLLTOT PROGRAM USES THE REPORT FEATURE TO PROVIDE A    *
000090*    REPORT ON THE TUITION AND FEES PAID IN BY EACH STUDENT      *
000100*    IN ALL COLLEGES.  IN ADDITION, THE TOTAL TUITION AND FEES FOR*
000110*    EACH COLLEGE AND FOR THE UNIVERSITY AS A WHOLE ARE GIVEN.   *
000120**************************************************************
000130 ENVIRONMENT DIVISION.
000140 CONFIGURATION SECTION.
000150 SOURCE-COMPUTER.  IBM-370-145.
000160 OBJECT-COMPUTER.  IBM-370-145.
000170 INPUT-OUTPUT SECTION.
000180 FILE-CONTROL.
000190     SELECT MASTER-FILE ASSIGN TO UT-S-OLDMAST.
000200     SELECT REPORT-FILE ASSIGN TO UT-S-SORTOUT.
000210     SELECT SORT-FILE ASSIGN TO UT-S-SORTIN.
000220     SELECT TUITION-FILE ASSIGN TO UT-S-TUITION.
000230 DATA DIVISION.
000240 FILE SECTION.
000250 FD  MASTER-FILE LABEL RECORDS ARE STANDARD.
000260 01  MASTER-RECORD          PICTURE X(387).
000270 FD  REPORT-FILE LABEL RECORDS ARE STANDARD.
000280 01  REPORT-RECORD.
000290     02  STUDENT-NO          PICTURE X(10).
000300     02  LAST-NAME           PICTURE X(20).
000310     02  FIRST-NAME          PICTURE X(20).
000320     02  INIT                PICTURE X.
000330     02  FILLER              PICTURE X(63).
000340     02  COLLEGE             PICTURE X(20).
000350     02  FILLER              PICTURE X(225).
000360     02  TUITION-BAL         PICTURE 99999V99.
000370     02  FEE-BAL             PICTURE 99999V99.
000380     02  OTHER-BAL           PICTURE 99999V99.
000390     02  TOTAL-BAL           PICTURE 99999V99.
000400 SD  SORT-FILE DATA RECORDS ARE SORT-RECORDS.
000410 01  SORT-RECORDS.
000420     02  FILLER.             PICTURE X(10).
000430     02  LAST-NAME           PICTURE X(20).
000440     02  FIRST-NAME          PICTURE X(20).
000450     02  INIT                PICTURE X.
000460     02  FILLER              PICTURE X(63).
000470     02  COLLEGE             PICTURE X(20).
000480     02  FILLER              PICTURE X(253).
000490 FD  TUITION-FILE REPORT IS TUITION-REPORT,
000500     LABEL RECORDS ARE STANDARD.
000510 WORKING-STORAGE SECTION.
000520 77  FULL-NAME               PICTURE X(40).
000530 77  MORE-DATA               PICTURE X(3) VALUE IS 'YES'.
000540 77  REPORT-DATE             PICTURE X(15).
```

FIGURE 12.4
(Continued)

```
000550 77  TOTAL-MONEY           PICTURE 999999V99 VALUE IS ZERO.
000560 77  UNIV-FEES             PICTURE 999999V99 VALUE IS ZERO.
000570 77  UNIV-MISC             PICTURE 999999V99 VALUE IS ZERO.
000580 77  UNIV-TOTAL            PICTURE 999999V99 VALUE IS ZERO.
000590 77  UNIV-TUITION          PICTURE 999999V99 VALUE IS ZERO.
000600 REPORT SECTION.
000610 RD  TUITION-REPORT
000620     CONTROLS ARE FINAL,  COLLEGE OF REPORT-RECORD,
000630     PAGE LIMIT IS 59 LINES,
000640     HEADING 2, FIRST DETAIL 6, LAST DETAIL 52, FOOTING 55.
000650 01  TYPE IS REPORT HEADING.
000660     02  LINE NUMBER IS 2.
000670         03  COLUMN 30 PICTURE X(31) VALUE IS
000680         'COLLEGE TUITION AND FEES REPORT'.
000690 01  PAGE-HEAD TYPE IS PAGE HEADING.
000700     04  LINE NUMBER IS 4.
000710         03  COLUMN 10 PICTURE X(27) VALUE IS
000720         'TUITION AND FEES BY COLLEGE'.
000730         03  COLUMN 65 PICTURE X(15) SOURCE IS REPORT-DATE.
000740 01  COLLEGE-HEADER TYPE IS CONTROL HEADING
000750     COLLEGE OF REPORT-RECORD NEXT GROUP IS PLUS 1.
000760     02  LINE NUMBER IS PLUS 4.
000770         03  COLUMN 30 PICTURE X(10) VALUE IS 'COLLEGE:'.
000780         03  COLUMN 40 PICTURE X(20) SOURCE IS
000790             COLLEGE OF REPORT-RECORD.
000800     02  LINE NUMBER IS PLUS 2.
000810         03  COLUMN 15 PICTURE X(7) VALUE IS 'STUDENT'.
000820         03  COLUMN 42 PICTURE X(7) VALUE IS 'TUITION'.
000830         03  COLUMN 54 PICTURE X(4) VALUE IS 'FEES'.
000840         03  COLUMN 64 PICTURE X(5) VALUE IS 'OTHER'.
000850         03  COLUMN 72 PICTURE X(5) VALUE IS 'TOTAL'.
000860 01  STUDENT-FEES TYPE IS DETAIL.
000870     02  LINE NUMBER IS PLUS 1.
000880         03  COLUMN 10 PICTURE X(29) SOURCE IS FULL-NAME.
000890         03  COLUMN 39 PICTURE ZZZ,ZZZ.99 BLANK WHEN ZERO
000900             SOURCE IS TUITION-BAL OF REPORT-RECORD.
000910         03  COLUMN 50 PICTURE ZZ,ZZZ.99 BLANK WHEN ZERO
000920             SOURCE IS FEE-BAL OF REPORT-RECORD.
000930         03  COLUMN 60 PICTURE ZZ,ZZZ.99 BLANK WHEN ZERO
000940             SOURCE IS OTHER-BAL OF REPORT-RECORD.
000950         03  TOT-FEE COLUMN 70 PICTURE ZZZ,ZZZ.99
000960             BLANK WHEN ZERO SOURCE IS TOTAL-BAL.
000970 01  COLLEGE-FOOTING TYPE IS CONTROL FOOTING.
000980     COLLEGE OF REPORT-RECORD.
000990     02  LINE NUMBER IS PLUS 1.
001000         03  COLUMN 39 PICTURE X(40) VALUE IS ALL '-'.
001010     02  LINE NUMBER IS PLUS 2.
001020         03  COLUMN 10 PICTURE X(14) VALUE IS 'COLLEGE TOTALS'.
001030         03  COLLEGE-TUITION COLUMN 39 PICTURE ZZZ,ZZZ.99
001040             SUM TUITION-BAL RESET ON COLLEGE OF REPORT-RECORD.
001050         03  COLLEGE-FEES COLUMN 50 PICTURE ZZ,ZZZ.99
001060             SUM FEE-BAL RESET ON COLLEGE OF REPORT-RECORD.
001070         03  COLLEGE-MISC COLUMN 60 PICTURE ZZ,ZZZ.99
001080             SUM OTHER-BAL RESET ON COLLEGE OF REPORT-RECORD.
001090         03  COLLEGE-TOTAL COLUMN 70 PICTURE ZZZ,ZZZ.99
```

FIGURE 12.4
(Continued)

```
001100           SUM TOTAL-BAL RESET ON COLLEGE OF REPORT-RECORD.
001110 01  TYPE IS CONTROL FOOTING FINAL.
001120     02  LINE NUMBER PLUS 2.
001130         03  COLUMN 10 PICTURE X(17)
001140             VALUE IS 'UNIVERSITY TOTALS'.
001150         03  COLUMN 39 PICTURE ZZZ,ZZZ.99 SOURCE IS UNIV-TUITION.
001160         03  COLUMN 50 PICTURE ZZ,ZZZ.99 SOURCE IS UNIV-FEES.
001170         03  COLUMN 60 PICTURE ZZ,ZZZ.99 SOURCE IS UNIV-MISC.
001180         03  COLUMN 70 PICTURE ZZZ,ZZZ.99 SOURCE IS UNIV-TOTAL.
001190 01  TYPE IS PAGE FOOTING.
001200     02  LINE NUMBER PLUS 2.
001210         03  COLUMN 10 PICTURE X(23) VALUE IS
001220             'TUITION AND FEES REPORT'.
001230         03  COLUMN 70 PICTURE X(5) VALUE IS 'PAGE-'.
001240         03  COLUMN 76 PICTURE 9999 SOURCE IS PAGE-COUNTER.
001250 01  TYPE REPORT FOOTING.
001260     02  LINE NUMBER PLUS 1.
001270         03  COLUMN 10 PICTURE X(30) VALUE IS
001280             'END OF TUITION AND FEES REPORT'.
001290         03  COLUMN 65 PICTURE X(15) SOURCE IS REPORT-DATE.
001300 PROCEDURE DIVISION.
001310 DECLARATIVES.
001320 UNIVERSITY-TOTALS SECTION.
001330     USE BEFORE REPORTING COLLEGE-FOOTING.
001340 ADD-COLLEGES.
001350     ADD COLLEGE-TUITION TO UNIV-TUITION.
001360     ADD COLLEGE-FEES TO UNIV-FEES.
001370     ADD COLLEGE-MISC TO UNIV-MISC.
001380     ADD COLLEGE-TOTAL TO UNIV-TOTAL.
001390 END UNIVERSITY-TOTALS.  EXIT.
001400 END DECLARATIVES.
001410 CONTROL-SECTION.
001420     PERFORM INITIALIZE.
001430     PERFORM GENERATE-REPORT UNTIL MORE-DATA IS EQUAL TO 'NO'.
001440     PERFORM CLEANUP.
001450     STOP RUN.
001460 INITIALIZE.
001470     ACCEPT REPORT-DATE.
001480     SORT SORT-FILE ON ASCENDING KEY COLLEGE OF SORT-RECORDS,
001490         ASCENDING LAST-NAME OF SORT-RECORDS,
001500         ASCENDING FIRST-NAME OF SORT-RECORDS,
001510         ASCENDING INIT OF SORT-RECORDS,
001520         USING MASTER-FILE,
001530         GIVING REPORT-FILE.
001540     OPEN INPUT REPORT-FILE, OUTPUT TUITION-FILE.
001550     READ REPORT-FILE AT END MOVE 'NO' TO MORE-DATA.
001560     INITIATE TUITION-REPORT.
001570 GENERATE-REPORT.
001580     STRING LAST-NAME OF REPORT-RECORD DELIMITED BY ' '.
001590         ', ' DELIMITED BY SIZE,
001600         FIRST-NAME OF REPORT-RECORD DELIMITED BY ' ',
001610         INIT OF REPORT-RECORD, '.', DELIMITED BY SIZE
001620         INTO FULL-NAME.
001630     GENERATE STUDENT-FEES.
001640     ADD TUITION-BAL OF REPORT-RECORD TO COLLEGE-TUITION.
```

FIGURE 12.4

(Continued)

```
001650      ADD FEE-BAL OF REPORT-RECORD TO COLLEGE-FEES.
001660      ADD OTHER-BAL TO COLLEGE-MISC.
001670      ADD TOTAL-BAL TO COLLEGE-TOTAL.
001680      READ REPORT-FILE AT END MOVE 'NO' TO MORE-DATA.
001690 CLEANUP.
001700      TERMINATE TUITION-REPORT.
001710      CLOSE REPORT-FILE, TUITION-FILE.
001720      DISPLAY 'SUCCESSFUL END OF REPORT PROGRAM'.
```

MASTER-FILE by college and by full name. This way, all the students in a college will be grouped together in alphabetical order. It is necessary to do this because we will be using the field COLLEGE as a control break when we generate our report. The sorted data is written on the REPORT-FILE and will be read in as needed to generate the reports. We then open the REPORT-FILE for input and the TUITION-FILE (which is the printer file for the reports we generate) to output. Finally, we initiate the TUITION-REPORT and leave the INITIALIZE routine.

The GENERATE-REPORT routine does the actual work of generating the report itself. It begins by packing the LAST-NAME, FIRST-NAME, and INIT into the single field FULL-NAME so that these may be printed out in the detail line, STUDENT-FEES. After the values have been packed, we issue the report statement, GENERATE STUDENT-FEES. This will print out the detail line, STUDENT-FEES. The checking to see whether or not it is time to print the other report groups (report headers, page headers, control headers, control footings, etc.) will be handled automatically by the report writer when the GENERATE statement for a detail group is given. After the GENERATE, we have a series of ADD statements that produce the totals for the college in each of the tuition and fee categories. We could also have done this with SUM and RESET statements in the report definition if we had chosen. Finally, we finish the GENERATE-REPORT routine by reading in the next record from the REPORT-FILE.

The CLEANUP routine is also fairly conventional. We issue the TERMINATE statement to complete the generation of the reports, close both our open files, and terminate with a success message.

Look at the REPORT SECTION beginning at line 600 in the program in Figure 12.4. It might be helpful to refer back to Figure 12.1 to see what report groups in the section generated the specific lines of the report. In line 610 we give the report definition, which lists the controls as FINAL and as COLLEGE OF REPORT-RECORD. The definition also sets up the page limits as was explained earlier.

The first report group is the report heading that begins on line 650 of the program. It gives the overall title of the report, and its contents are printed only once, at the beginning of the report. If we had wished, we could have caused the report heading to be printed on a separate page and used it as a title page for the report to follow. In this example, we have chosen to have it simply be another line of the report.

The next report group is the page heading beginning on line 690. It gives the header that is printed at the top of each page of the report. After that, we have the control header called COLLEGE-HEADER. This report group has two lines, which give the college name and the column headings for the tuition and fees for the students in that college. Notice that in this report group, we are using the relative line numbers because we do not know the exact lines on which these items will have to appear.

The next report group is the detail line that lists the name and amounts for each individual student. Note that the student's name is taken from the FULL-NAME field in WORKING-STORAGE. The value in this field is set by the STRING statement we execute before we generate the detail line. The columns of the detail line have been adjusted so that they come out under the proper column headings on the COLLEGE-HEADER.

In line 970 we have the footing line, COLLEGE-FOOTING. This line prints out a line of minus signs to separate the individual student totals from the college totals, and then it prints out the college totals. These totals were previously computed in the GENERATE-REPORT paragraph. Note that in the DECLARATIVES section, we execute another piece of code before reporting the COLLEGE-FOOTING. In this code we add the college totals into the university totals, which are reported as the final control footing. Note that in the footing and header report detail lines, we must tell which control variable the line is associated with.

In line 1110, we have the FINAL control footing, which prints out the university totals for tuition and fees. This footing line is printed only after all report records have been read in. It is initiated by the TERMINATE statement as is the final report footing line beginning on line 1250.

The only other report group we have in this definition is the page footing, which begins on line 1190. The page footing gives the format of the data to be printed at the bottom of every page of the report. In this example we use the PAGE-COUNTER to print out the page number of the report page at the bottom of each page. In a large report it is a good idea to number the pages to provide a way of telling whether any pages are missing when you use the report later on.

The report writer is one of the most useful features in COBOL. It allows us a great deal of flexibility in printing out standard information systems reports and can result in great savings in programmer time and effort. We pay for this in terms of increased execution time and core storage, but the convenience of using the feature makes it well worth it.

STUDY EXERCISES

1. Redo the grade summary program of Chapter 10 using the report writer feature.

2. Write a COBOL program using the report writer that will produce a printed copy of a student record from the MASTER-FILE similar in format to the one in Figure 2.1.

3. Prepare a COBOL program using the report writer that will produce a report of the names of students in academic difficulty as in the example in Figure 5.4.

4. Prepare a COBOL program using the report writer that will produce a report of the names of probable graduating seniors as in the example in Figure 5.7.

5. Prepare a COBOL program using the report writer that will produce a count of the number of men and women majoring in different subjects. The report should be formatted like this:

```
              MAJOR REPORT BY SEX

     MAJOR         MALE        FEMALE        TOTAL
     XXXXX         XXXX         XXXX         XXXX

                     .            .            .
                     .            .            .
                     .            .            .

  UNIV. TOTAL       XXXX         XXXX         XXXX
```

6. Prepare a COBOL program using the report writer that will produce a count of the number of students in each college on a class-by-class basis. The classes are defined as:

CLASS	CREDITS
Freshman	0–29
Sophomore	30–59
Junior	60–89
Senior	90 and above

The general format of the report should look like this:

STUDENT COUNT BY CLASS

COLLEGE	FRESHMEN	SOPHOMORES	JUNIORS	SENIORS	TOTAL
XXXX	XXXX	XXXX	XXXX	XXXX	XXXX
.	.	.	.	.	.
.	.	.	.	.	.
.	.	.	.	.	.
UNIV. TOTAL	XXXX	XXXX	XXXX	XXXX	XXXX

7. Write a COBOL program using the report writer to prepare a student grade report for the semester. Assume that the GPA given in the field AVERAGE is the average for last semester without the present grades added. Compute a new AVERAGE for the student using the grades in the COURSE table and print out the grade report. The format of the report should be:

GRADE REPORT FOR   xxxx SEMESTER, yyyy

STUDENT: student name   OVERALL GPA: x.xxx
COLLEGE: college name
MAJOR: major name

COURSES

COURSE NUMBER	COURSE NAME	HOURS	PASS/FAIL	GRADE
XXXXX	XXXXX	XXXX	XXXX	X
.	.	.	.	.
.	.	.	.	.
.	.	.	.	.

SEMESTER GRADE AVERAGE: x.xxx

Courses taken pass/fail (P–F is equal to 1) are not counted in computing the average. For printing out the report, transform all numeric grades to their letter equivalents (A = 4, B = 3, etc.).

8. Prepare a COBOL program using the report writer that will give the students' bills for the semester. The report should look like this:

```
        TOTAL BILL FOR xxx SEMESTER, yyyy

STUDENT:  full name
          street address
          city, state zip

          TUITION:        xxxxx
          ROOM AND BOARD:xxxxx
          FEES:           xxxxx
          MISCELLANEOUS: xxxxx

          TOTAL           xxxxx
```

Print the bills in order by zip code and pack all the data in the name and address.

COBOL RESERVED WORDS

This appendix gives a list of the COBOL reserved words. If the word has an asterisk in front of it, it is not a standard 1974 ANSI COBOL word but is an IBM 370 OS/VS COBOL extension. COBOL compilers vary from machine to machine. The full ANSI COBOL instruction set is not implemented on all compilers, and almost all compilers have some extensions to 1974 ANSI COBOL. Consult the manual for your particular machine in case of a problem.

ACCEPT	ACCESS	*ACTUAL
ADD	*ADDRESS	ADVANCING
AFTER	ALL	ALPHABETIC
ALSO	ALTERNATE	AND
*APPLY	ARE	AREA
AREAS	ASCENDING	ASSIGN
AT	AUTHOR	*BASIS
*BEGINNING	BLANK	BLOCK
BOTTOM	BY	CALL
CANCEL	*CBL	CD
CF	CH	*CHANGED
CHARACTER	CHARACTERS	CLOCK-UNITS
CLOSE	COBOL	CODE
CODE-SET	COLLATING	COLUMN
COMMA	COMMUNICATION	COMP
*COMP-1	*COMP-2	*COMP-3
*COMP-4	*COMPUTATIONAL-1	*COMPUTATIONAL-2
*COMPUTATIONAL-3	*COMPUTATIONAL-4	COMPUTE
CONFIGURATION	*CONSOLE	CONTAINS
CONTROL	CONTROLS	COPY
*CORE-INDEX	CORR	CORRESPONDING
COUNT	*CSP	CURRENCY
*CURRENT-DATE	*CO1	*CO2
*CO3	*CO4	*CO5
*CO6	*CO7	*CO8
*CO9	*C10	*C11
*C12	DATA	DATE
DATE-COMPILED	DATE-WRITTEN	DAY
DE	*DEBUG	DEBUG-CONTENTS
DEBUG-ITEM	DEBUG-LINE	DEBUG-NAME
DEBUG-SUB-1	DEBUG-SUB-2	DEBUG-SUB-3
DEBUGGING	DECIMAL-POINT	DECLARATIVES
DELETE	DELIMITED	DELIMITER
DEPENDING	DELIMITED	DESCENDING
DESTINATION	DETAIL	DISABLE
*DISP	DISPLAY	*DISPLAY-ST

299

DIVIDE	DIVISION	DOWN
DUPLICATES	DYNAMIC	EGI
EJECT	ELSE	EMI
ENABLE	END	END-OF-PAGE
*ENDING	ENTER	*ENTRY
ENVIRONMENT	EOP	EQUAL
ERROR	ESI	EVERY
*EXAMINE	*EXCEPTION	*EXHIBIT
EXIT	EXTEND	*EXTENDED-SEARCH
FD	FILE	FILE-CONTROL
*FILE-LIMIT	*FILE-LIMITS	FILLER
FINAL	FIRST	FOOTING
FOR	FROM	GENERATE
GIVING	GO	*GOBACK
GREATER	GROUP	HEADING
HIGH-VALUE	HIGH-VALUES	I-O
I-O-CONTROL	*ID	IDENTIFICATION
IF	IN	INDEX
INDEXED	INDICATE	INITIAL
INITIATE	INPUT	INPUT-OUTPUT
INSPECT	*INSERT	INSTALLATION
INTO	INVALID	IS
JUST	JUSTIFIED	KEY
LABEL	*LABEL-RETURN	LAST
LEADING	*LEAVE	LESS
LIMIT	LIMITS	LINAGE
LINAGE-COUNTER	LINE	LINE-COUNTER
LINES	*LINKAGE	LOCK
LOW-VALUE	LOW-VALUES	MEMORY
MERGE	MESSAGE	MODE
MODULES	*MORE-LABELS	MOVE
MULTIPLE	MULTIPLY	*NAMED
NATIVE	NEGATIVE	NEXT
NO	*NOMINAL	NOT
*NOTE	NUMBER	NUMERIC
OBJECT-COMPUTER	OCCURS	OF
OFF	OMITTED	ON
OPEN	OPTIONAL	OR
ORGANIZATION	*OTHERWISE	OUTPUT
OVERFLOW	PAGE	PAGE-COUNTER
*PASSWORD	PERFORM	PF
PH	PIC	PICTURE
PLUS	POINTER	POSITION
*POSITIONING	POSITIVE	*PRINT-SWITCH
PRINTING	PROCEDURE	PROCEDURES
PROCEED	*PROCESSING	PROGRAM
PROGRAM-ID	QUEUE	QUOTE
QUOTES	RANDOM	RD
READ	*READY	RECEIVE
RECORD	*RECORD-OVERFLOW	*RECORDING
RECORDS	REDEFINES	REEL
REFERENCES	RELATIVE	RELEASE
*RELOAD	REMAINDER	*REMARKS
RENAMES	*REORG-CRITERIA	REPLACING
REPORT	REPORTING	REPORTS
*REREAD	RERUN	RESERVE
RESET	RETURN	*RETURN-CODE
REVERSED	REWIND	REWRITE

RF
ROUNDED
SD
SECURITY
SEGMENT-LIMIT
SENTENCE
*SERVICE
SIZE
*SKIP3
*SORT-FILE-SIZE
*SORT-MODE-SIZE
SOURCE-COMPUTER
SPECIAL-NAMES
START
SUB-QUEUE-3
SUPPRESS
SYNCHRONIZED
*SYSPUNCH
TABLE
TAPE
*TEXT
THROUGH
*TIME-OF-DAY
*TOTALED
*TRACK
*TRACKS
TYPE
UNTIL
USAGE
VALUE
WHEN
WORDS
*WRITE-ONLY
ZEROS

RH
RUN
SEARCH
*SEEK
SELECT
SEPARATE
SET
*SKIP1
SORT
SORT-MERGE
*SORT-RETURN
SPACE
STANDARD
STRING
SUB-QUEUE-1
SUBTRACT
*SYMBOLIC
*SYSIN
*SO1
TALLY
TERMINAL
THAN
THRU
TIMES
*TOTALING
*TRACK-AREA
TRAILING
UNIT
UP
USE
VALUES
*WHEN-COMPILED
WORKING-STORAGE
ZERO

RIGHT
SAME
SECTION
SEGMENT
SEND
SEQUENTIAL
SIGN
*SKIP2
*SORT-CORE-SIZE
*SORT-MESSAGE
SOURCE
SPACES
STANDARD-1
SUB-QUEUE-2
SUM
SYNC
*SYSOUT
*SO2
TALLYING
TERMINATE
*THEN
TIME
TO
*TRACE
*TRACK-LIMIT
*TRANSFORM
UNSTRING
UPON
USING
VARYING
WITH
WRITE
ZEROES

APPENDIX B
STRUCTURE OF COBOL STATEMENTS

Appendix B gives a summary of the statement definitions for all major COBOL statements. These definitions are from 1974 ANSI COBOL. As such, they may look slightly different from some of the definitions given earlier in this book. Some of the earlier definitions were abbreviated for pedagogical purposes; others were modified slightly (examples are the SELECT and COPY statements) to conform to the more common IBM usages. In general, the definitions will be the same.

You can obtain a complete copy of the ANSI COBOL standard by writing to:

American National Standards Institute, Inc.
1430 Broadway
New York, NY 10018

The ANSI standard version of COBOL is not completely implemented on any machine. There are always minor (and sometimes major) differences between a particular version of COBOL and the ANSI COBOL. Having a copy of the standard for COBOL could be useful if you are ever asked to evaluate a particular version of COBOL in an equipment selection process. The definitions in this appendix are a reasonable substitute for the entire standard. The following acknowledgment must accompany all reproductions of the COBOL material.

ACKNOWLEDGMENT

COBOL is an industry language and is not the property of any company or group of companies, or of any organization or group of organizations. No warranty, expressed or implied, is made by any contributor or by the CODASYL Programming Language Committee as to the accuracy and functioning of the programming system and language. Moreover, no responsibility is assumed by any contributor, or by the committee in connection therewith. The authors and copyright holders of the copyright material used herein,

FLOW-MATIC (trademark of Sperry Rand Coporation), Programming for the UNIVAC I and II, Data Automation Systems copyrighted 1958 and 1959, by Sperry Rand Corporation

GENERAL FORMAT FOR IDENTIFICATION DIVISION

```
IDENTIFICATION DIVISION.

PROGRAM-ID.  program-name.

[AUTHOR.  [comment-entry] ...]

[INSTALLATION.  [comment-entry] ...]

[DATE-WRITTEN.  [comment-entry] ...]

[DATE-COMPILED.  [comment-entry] ...]

[SECURITY.  [comment-entry]  ...]
```

GENERAL FORMAT FOR ENVIRONMENT DIVISION

```
ENVIRONMENT DIVISION.

CONFIGURATION SECTION.

SOURCE-COMPUTER.  computer-name  [WITH DEBUGGING MODE]  .

OBJECT-COMPUTER.  computer-name

    ⎡                          ⎧ WORDS      ⎫ ⎤
    ⎢ , MEMORY SIZE integer    ⎨ CHARACTERS ⎬ ⎥
    ⎣                          ⎩ MODULES    ⎭ ⎦

    [, PROGRAM COLLATING SEQUENCE IS alphabet-name]

    [, SEGMENT-LIMIT IS segment-number]  .

[ SPECIAL-NAMES.  [, implementor-name

    ⎧ IS mnemonic-name [, ON STATUS IS condition-name-1 [, OFF STATUS IS condition-name-2 ]] ⎫ ⎤
    ⎪ IS mnemonic-name [, OFF STATUS IS condition-name-2 [, ON STATUS IS condition-name-1 ]] ⎪ ⎪   ...
    ⎨ ON STATUS IS condition-name-1 [, OFF STATUS IS condition-name-2]                        ⎬ ⎥
    ⎩ OFF STATUS IS condition-name-2 [, ON STATUS IS condition-name-1]                        ⎭ ⎦
```

GENERAL FORMAT FOR ENVIRONMENT DIVISION (cont.)

```
    ┌                    ┌ STANDARD-1                                              ┐ ┐
    │ , alphabet-name IS │ NATIVE                                                  │ │ ...
    │                    │ implementor-name                                        │ │
    │                    │          ┌ ┌ THROUGH ┐                            ┐     │ │
    │                    │ literal-1│ │ THRU    │ literal-2                   │     │ │
    │                    │          │ └ ALSO literal-3 [, ALSO literal-4]...  │     │ │  ...
    │                    │          │   ┌ ┌ THROUGH ┐                      ┐  │     │ │
    │                    │          │   │ │ THRU    │ literal-6             │  │     │ │
    │                    └          └   │ └ ALSO literal-7 [, ALSO literal-8]...│  │     │ │
    └                                                                               ┘ ┘
```

[, CURRENCY SIGN IS literal-9]

[, DECIMAL-POINT IS COMMA] .]

[INPUT-OUTPUT SECTION.

FILE-CONTROL.

    {file-control-entry} ...

[I-O-CONTROL.

```
    ┌                  ┌    ┌ file-name-1        ┐ ┐
    │ ; RERUN          │ ON │ implementor-name   │ │
    │                  └    └                    ┘ │
    │          ┌ ┌ [END OF] ┌ REEL ┐            ┐ ┐
    │          │ │          │ UNIT │ OF file-name-2│
    │  EVERY   │ │ integer-1 RECORDS             │ │ ...
    │          │ │ integer-2 CLOCK-UNITS         │ │
    │          └ │ condition-name                ┘ ┘
```

```
    ┌         ┌ RECORD    ┐                                      ┐
    │ ; SAME  │ SORT      │ AREA FOR file-name-3 {, file-name-4} ... │ ...
    │         └ SORT-MERGE ┘                                      ┘
```

```
    ┌ ; MULTIPLE FILE TAPE CONTAINS file-name-5 [POSITION integer-3]        ┐
    │    [, file-name-6  [POSITION integer-4]]...  ]...   .]]
```

GENERAL FORMAT FOR FILE CONTROL ENTRY

FORMAT 1:

SELECT [OPTIONAL] file-name

    ASSIGN TO implementor-name-1 [, implementor-name-2] ...

    [; RESERVE integer-1 [AREA / AREAS]]

    [; ORGANIZATION IS SEQUENTIAL]

GENERAL FORMAT FOR FILE CONTROL ENTRY (cont.)

    [; ACCESS MODE IS SEQUENTIAL]

    [; FILE STATUS IS data-name-1].

FORMAT 2:

SELECT file-name

    ASSIGN TO implementor-name-1 [, implementor-name-2] ...

$$\left[\; ; \text{RESERVE integer-1} \begin{bmatrix} \text{AREA} \\ \text{AREAS} \end{bmatrix} \right]$$

    ; ORGANIZATION IS RELATIVE

$$\left[\; ; \text{ACCESS MODE IS} \left\{ \begin{array}{l} \text{SEQUENTIAL} \quad [, \text{RELATIVE KEY IS data-name-1}] \\ \left\{ \begin{array}{l} \text{RANDOM} \\ \text{DYNAMIC} \end{array} \right\} , \text{RELATIVE KEY IS data-name-1} \end{array} \right\} \right]$$

    [; FILE STATUS IS data-name-2] .

FORMAT 3:

SELECT file-name

    ASSIGN TO implementor-name-1 [, implementor-name-2] ...

$$\left[\; ; \text{RESERVE integer-1} \begin{bmatrix} \text{AREA} \\ \text{AREAS} \end{bmatrix} \right]$$

    ; ORGANIZATION IS INDEXED

$$\left[\; ; \text{ACCESS MODE IS} \left\{ \begin{array}{l} \text{SEQUENTIAL} \\ \text{RANDOM} \\ \text{DYNAMIC} \end{array} \right\} \right]$$

    ; RECORD KEY IS data-name-1

$$\left[\; ; \underline{\text{ALTERNATE}} \; \underline{\text{RECORD}} \text{ KEY IS data-name-2 } [\text{WITH } \underline{\text{DUPLICATES}}] \right] \; ...$$

    [; FILE STATUS IS data-name-3] .

FORMAT 4:

SELECT file-name ASSIGN TO implementor-name-1 [, implementor-name-2] ...

GENERAL FORMAT FOR DATA DIVISION

    DATA DIVISION.

    [FILE SECTION.

    [FD file-name

GENERAL FORMAT FOR DATA DIVISION (cont.)

$$\left[\; ; \; \underline{\text{BLOCK}} \text{ CONTAINS } [\text{integer-1} \; \underline{\text{TO}}] \text{ integer-2} \left\{\begin{array}{l}\underline{\text{RECORDS}}\\ \underline{\text{CHARACTERS}}\end{array}\right\}\right]$$

$$\left[\; ; \; \underline{\text{RECORD}} \text{ CONTAINS } [\text{integer-3} \; \underline{\text{TO}}] \quad \text{integer-4 CHARACTERS}\right]$$

$$; \; \underline{\text{LABEL}} \left\{\begin{array}{l}\underline{\text{RECORD}} \text{ IS}\\ \underline{\text{RECORDS}} \text{ ARE}\end{array}\right\} \left\{\begin{array}{l}\underline{\text{STANDARD}}\\ \underline{\text{OMITTED}}\end{array}\right\}$$

$$\left[\; ; \; \underline{\text{VALUE}} \; \underline{\text{OF}} \text{ implementor-name-1 IS} \left\{\begin{array}{l}\text{data-name-1}\\ \text{literal-1}\end{array}\right\}\right.$$

$$\left.\left[, \text{ implementor-name-2 IS } \left\{\begin{array}{l}\text{data-name-2}\\ \text{literal-2}\end{array}\right\}\right]\ldots\right]$$

$$\left[\; ; \; \underline{\text{DATA}} \left\{\begin{array}{l}\text{RECORD IS}\\ \text{RECORDS ARE}\end{array}\right\} \text{ data-name-3 } [, \text{ data-name-4}] \ldots\right]$$

$$\left[\; ; \; \underline{\text{LINAGE}} \text{ IS } \left\{\begin{array}{l}\text{data-name-5}\\ \text{integer-5}\end{array}\right\} \text{ LINES } \left[, \text{ WITH } \underline{\text{FOOTING}} \text{ AT } \left\{\begin{array}{l}\text{data-name-6}\\ \text{integer-6}\end{array}\right\}\right]\right.$$

$$\left.\left[, \text{ LINES AT } \underline{\text{TOP}} \left\{\begin{array}{l}\text{data-name-7}\\ \text{integer-7}\end{array}\right\}\right]\left[, \text{ LINES AT } \underline{\text{BOTTOM}}\left\{\begin{array}{l}\text{data-name-8}\\ \text{integer-8}\end{array}\right\}\right]\right]$$

$$\left[\; ; \; \underline{\text{CODE-SET}} \text{ IS alphabet-name}\right]$$

$$\left[\; ; \left\{\begin{array}{l}\underline{\text{REPORT}} \text{ IS}\\ \underline{\text{REPORTS}} \text{ ARE}\end{array}\right\} \text{ report-name-1 } [, \text{ report-name-2}] \ldots\right].$$

[record-description-entry] ...] ...

[SD file-name

$$\left[\; ; \; \underline{\text{RECORD}} \text{ CONTAINS } [\text{integer-1} \; \underline{\text{TO}}] \quad \text{integer-2 CHARACTERS}\right]$$

$$\left[\; ; \; \underline{\text{DATA}} \left\{\begin{array}{l}\underline{\text{RECORD}} \text{ IS}\\ \underline{\text{RECORDS}} \text{ ARE}\end{array}\right\} \text{ data-name-1 } [, \text{ data-name-2}] \ldots\right].$$

{record-description-entry} ...] ...]

$$\left[\underline{\text{WORKING-STORAGE}} \; \underline{\text{SECTION}}.\right.$$

$$\left[\begin{array}{l}\text{77-level-description-entry}\\ \text{record-description-entry}\end{array}\right] \quad \ldots\right]$$

$$\left[\underline{\text{LINKAGE}} \; \underline{\text{SECTION}}.\right.$$

$$\left[\begin{array}{l}\text{77-level-description-entry}\\ \text{record-description-entry}\end{array}\right] \quad \ldots\right]$$

$$\left[\underline{\text{COMMUNICATION}} \; \underline{\text{SECTION}}.\right.$$

[communication-description-entry

[record-description-entry] ...] ...]

GENERAL FORMAT FOR DATA DIVISION (cont.)

[REPORT SECTION.

[RD report-name

    [; CODE literal-1]

$$\left[; \begin{Bmatrix} \text{CONTROL IS} \\ \text{CONTROLS ARE} \end{Bmatrix} \begin{Bmatrix} \text{data-name-1} \ [, \text{data-name-2}] \ \dots \\ \text{FINAL} \ [, \text{data-name-1} \ [, \text{data-name-2}] \ \dots] \end{Bmatrix} \right]$$

$$\left[; \underline{\text{PAGE}} \begin{bmatrix} \text{LIMIT IS} \\ \text{LIMITS ARE} \end{bmatrix} \text{integer-1} \begin{bmatrix} \text{LINE} \\ \text{LINES} \end{bmatrix} \quad [, \underline{\text{HEADING}} \ \text{integer-2}] \right.$$

      [, FIRST DETAIL integer-3]   [, LAST DETAIL integer-4]

      $$\left. [, \underline{\text{FOOTING}} \ \text{integer-5}] \ \right] .$$

{report-group-description-entry} ...] ...]

GENERAL FORMAT FOR DATA DESCRIPTION ENTRY

FORMAT 1:

$$\text{level-number} \begin{Bmatrix} \text{data-name-1} \\ \underline{\text{FILLER}} \end{Bmatrix}$$

    [; REDEFINES data-name-2]

$$\left[; \begin{Bmatrix} \underline{\text{PICTURE}} \\ \underline{\text{PIC}} \end{Bmatrix} \text{IS character-string} \right]$$

$$\left[; \ [\underline{\text{USAGE}} \ \text{IS}] \begin{Bmatrix} \underline{\text{COMPUTATIONAL}} \\ \underline{\text{COMP}} \\ \underline{\text{DISPLAY}} \\ \underline{\text{INDEX}} \end{Bmatrix} \right]$$

$$\left[; \ [\underline{\text{SIGN}} \ \text{IS}] \begin{Bmatrix} \underline{\text{LEADING}} \\ \underline{\text{TRAILING}} \end{Bmatrix} [\underline{\text{SEPARATE}} \ \text{CHARACTER}] \right]$$

$$\left[; \ \underline{\text{OCCURS}} \begin{Bmatrix} \text{integer-1} \ \underline{\text{TO}} \ \text{integer-2 TIMES} \ \underline{\text{DEPENDING}} \ \text{ON data-name-3} \\ \text{integer-2} \ \overline{\text{TIMES}} \end{Bmatrix} \right.$$

      $$\left[\begin{Bmatrix} \underline{\text{ASCENDING}} \\ \underline{\text{DESCENDING}} \end{Bmatrix} \text{KEY IS data-name-4} \ [, \text{data-name-5}] \ \dots \ \right] \ \dots$$

        $$\left. [\text{INDEXED BY index-name-1} \ [, \text{index-name-2}] \ \dots] \right]$$

$$\left[; \begin{Bmatrix} \underline{\text{SYNCHRONIZED}} \\ \underline{\text{SYNC}} \end{Bmatrix} \begin{bmatrix} \underline{\text{LEFT}} \\ \underline{\text{RIGHT}} \end{bmatrix} \right]$$

$$\left[; \begin{Bmatrix} \underline{\text{JUSTIFIED}} \\ \underline{\text{JUST}} \end{Bmatrix} \text{RIGHT} \right]$$

GENERAL FORMAT FOR DATA DESCRIPTION ENTRY (cont.)

[; <u>BLANK</u> WHEN ZERO]

[; <u>VALUE</u> IS literal].

<u>FORMAT 2</u>:

66 data-name-1; <u>RENAMES</u> data-name-2 $\left[\left\{ \begin{array}{l} \underline{THROUGH} \\ \underline{THRU} \end{array} \right\} \text{data-name-3} \right]$.

<u>FORMAT 3</u>:

88 condition-name; $\left\{ \begin{array}{l} \underline{VALUE} \text{ IS} \\ \underline{VALUES} \text{ ARE} \end{array} \right\}$ literal-1 $\left[\left\{ \begin{array}{l} \underline{THROUGH} \\ \underline{THRU} \end{array} \right\} \text{literal-2} \right]$

$\left[\text{, literal-3} \left[\left\{ \begin{array}{l} \underline{THROUGH} \\ \underline{THRU} \end{array} \right\} \text{literal-4} \right] \right]$ ... .

GENERAL FORMAT FOR COMMUNICATION DESCRIPTION ENTRY

<u>FORMAT 1</u>:

CD cd-name;

$$\text{FOR} \left[\underline{INITIAL} \right] \text{INPUT} \left[\begin{array}{l} \left[\text{; SYMBOLIC } \underline{QUEUE} \text{ IS data-name-1} \right] \\ \left[\text{; SYMBOLIC } \underline{SUB\text{-}QUEUE\text{-}1} \text{ IS data-name-2} \right] \\ \left[\text{; SYMBOLIC } \underline{SUB\text{-}QUEUE\text{-}2} \text{ IS data-name-3} \right] \\ \left[\text{; SYMBOLIC } \underline{SUB\text{-}QUEUE\text{-}3} \text{ IS data-name-4} \right] \\ \left[\text{; } \underline{MESSAGE} \ \underline{DATE} \text{ IS data-name-5} \right] \\ \left[\text{; } \underline{MESSAGE} \ \underline{TIME} \text{ IS data-name-6} \right] \\ \left[\text{; SYMBOLIC } \underline{SOURCE} \text{ IS data-name-7} \right] \\ \left[\text{; } \underline{TEXT} \ \underline{LENGTH} \text{ IS data-name-8} \right] \\ \left[\text{; } \underline{END} \ \underline{KEY} \text{ IS data-name-9} \right] \\ \left[\text{; } \underline{STATUS} \ \underline{KEY} \text{ IS data-name-10} \right] \\ \left[\text{; } \underline{MESSAGE} \ \underline{COUNT} \text{ IS data-name-11} \right] \\ \left[\text{data-name-1, data-name-2, ..., data-name-11} \right] \end{array} \right]$$

<u>FORMAT 2</u>:

<u>CD</u> cd-name; FOR <u>OUTPUT</u>

[; <u>DESTINATION</u> <u>COUNT</u> IS data-name-1]

[; <u>TEXT</u> <u>LENGTH</u> IS data-name-2]

GENERAL FORMAT FOR COMMUNICATION DESCRIPTION ENTRY (cont.)

[; STATUS KEY IS data-name-3]

[; DESTINATION TABLE OCCURS integer-2 TIMES

      [; INDEXED BY index-name-1 [, index-name-2]...]]

[; ERROR KEY IS data-name-4]

[; SYMBOLIC DESTINATION IS data-name-5] .

GENERAL FORMAT FOR REPORT GROUP DESCRIPTION ENTRY

FORMAT 1:

01 [data-name-1]

$$\left[\text{; } \underline{\text{LINE}} \text{ NUMBER IS } \left\{ \begin{array}{l} \text{integer-1 [ON } \underline{\text{NEXT}} \text{ } \underline{\text{PAGE}}] \\ \underline{\text{PLUS}} \text{ integer-2} \end{array} \right\} \right]$$

$$\left[\text{; } \underline{\text{NEXT}} \text{ } \underline{\text{GROUP}} \text{ IS } \left\{ \begin{array}{l} \text{integer-3} \\ \underline{\text{PLUS}} \text{ integer-4} \\ \underline{\text{NEXT}} \text{ } \underline{\text{PAGE}} \end{array} \right\} \right]$$

$$\text{; } \underline{\text{TYPE}} \text{ IS } \left[\begin{array}{l} \left\{ \begin{array}{l} \underline{\text{REPORT}} \text{ } \underline{\text{HEADING}} \\ \underline{\text{RH}} \end{array} \right\} \\ \left\{ \begin{array}{l} \underline{\text{PAGE}} \text{ } \underline{\text{HEADING}} \\ \underline{\text{PH}} \end{array} \right\} \\ \left\{ \begin{array}{l} \underline{\text{CONTROL}} \text{ } \underline{\text{HEADING}} \\ \underline{\text{CH}} \end{array} \right\} \left\{ \begin{array}{l} \text{data-name-2} \\ \underline{\text{FINAL}} \end{array} \right\} \\ \left\{ \begin{array}{l} \underline{\text{DETAIL}} \\ \underline{\text{DE}} \end{array} \right\} \\ \left\{ \begin{array}{l} \underline{\text{CONTROL}} \text{ } \underline{\text{FOOTING}} \\ \underline{\text{CF}} \end{array} \right\} \left\{ \begin{array}{l} \text{data-name-3} \\ \underline{\text{FINAL}} \end{array} \right\} \\ \left\{ \begin{array}{l} \underline{\text{PAGE}} \text{ } \underline{\text{FOOTING}} \\ \underline{\text{PF}} \end{array} \right\} \\ \left\{ \begin{array}{l} \underline{\text{REPORT}} \text{ } \underline{\text{FOOTING}} \\ \underline{\text{RF}} \end{array} \right\} \end{array} \right]$$

$$\left[\text{; [}\underline{\text{USAGE}} \text{ IS] } \underline{\text{DISPLAY}} \right] \text{ .}$$

FORMAT 2:

level-number [data-name-1]

$$\left[\text{; } \underline{\text{LINE}} \text{ NUMBER IS } \left\{ \begin{array}{l} \text{integer-1 [ON } \underline{\text{NEXT}} \text{ } \underline{\text{PAGE}}] \\ \underline{\text{PLUS}} \text{ integer-2} \end{array} \right\} \right]$$

$$\left[\text{; [}\underline{\text{USAGE}} \text{ IS] } \underline{\text{DISPLAY}} \right] \text{ .}$$

GENERAL FORMAT FOR REPORT GROUP DESCRIPTION ENTRY (cont.)

```
FORMAT 3:

level-number  [data-name-1]

    [; BLANK WHEN ZERO ]

    [; GROUP INDICATE ]
    [ ; { JUSTIFIED
          JUST      } RIGHT ]
    [ ; LINE NUMBER IS { integer-1  [ON NEXT PAGE]
                         PLUS integer-2            } ]


    [; COLUMN NUMBER IS integer-3]

      ; { PICTURE
          PIC     } IS character-string


    {  ; SOURCE IS identifier-1

       ; VALUE IS literal

      {; SUM identifier-2  [, identifier-3]  ...

            [UPON data-name-2  [, data-name-3]  ... ]} ...

         [RESET ON { data-name-4
                     FINAL      } ]                       }

    [; [USAGE IS] DISPLAY ] .
```

GENERAL FORMAT FOR PROCEDURE DIVISION

```
FORMAT 1:

PROCEDURE DIVISION [ USING data-name-1  [, data-name-2]  ... ] .
[DECLARATIVES.

{section-name SECTION [segment-number] .    declarative-sentence
[paragraph-name. [sentence] ... ] ...} ...
END DECLARATIVES. ]
{section-name SECTION [segment-number] .
[paragraph-name. [sentence ] ... ] ...} ...
FORMAT 2:

PROCEDURE DIVISION [USING data-name-1  [, data-name-2 ] ... ] .
{paragraph-name. [sentence]  ... }  ...
```

GENERAL FORMAT FOR VERBS

```
ACCEPT identifier [FROM mnemonic-name]
                         ┌ DATE ┐
ACCEPT identifier FROM  { DAY  }
                         └ TIME ┘

ACCEPT cd-name MESSAGE COUNT

ADD { identifier-1 } [, identifier-2 ] ... TO identifier-m [ROUNDED]
    { literal-1    } [, literal-2    ]

    [, identifier-n [ROUNDED]] ... [; ON SIZE ERROR imperative-statement]

ADD { identifier-1 } , { identifier-2 } [ , identifier-3 ] ...
    { literal-1    }   { literal-2    } [ , literal-3    ]

    GIVING identifier-m [ROUNDED] [, identifier-n [ROUNDED]] ...

    [; ON SIZE ERROR imperative-statement]

ADD { CORRESPONDING } identifier-1 TO identifier-2 [ROUNDED]
    { CORR          }

    [; ON SIZE ERROR imperative-statement]

ALTER procedure-name-1 TO [PROCEED TO] procedure-name-2

    [; procedure-name-3 TO [PROCEED TO] procedure-name-4] ...

CALL { identifier-1 } [USING data-name-1 [, data-name-2] ...]
     { literal-1    }

    [; ON OVERFLOW imperative-statement]

CANCEL { identifier-1 } [, identifier-2 ] ...
       { literal-1    } [, literal-2    ]

                      ┌ ┌ REEL ┐ ┌ WITH NO REWIND ┐ ┐
                      │ { UNIT }  │ FOR REMOVAL     │ │
CLOSE file-name-1     │           └                 ┘ │
                      │                  ┌ NO REWIND ┐ │
                      │       WITH       { LOCK      } │
                      └                               ┘

  ┌                 ┌ ┌ REEL ┐ ┌ WITH NO REWIND ┐ ┐ ┐
  │                 │ { UNIT }  │ FOR REMOVAL     │ │ │
  │ , file-name-2   │           └                 ┘ │ │ ...
  │                 │                  ┌ NO REWIND ┐ │ │
  │                 │       WITH       { LOCK      } │ │
  └                 └                               ┘ ┘

CLOSE file-name-1 [WITH LOCK] [, file-name-2 [WITH LOCK]] ...

COMPUTE identifier-1 [ROUNDED] [ , identifier-2 [ROUNDED]] ...

    = arithmetic-expression [; ON SIZE ERROR imperative-statement ]
```

GENERAL FORMAT FOR VERBS (cont.)

<u>DELETE</u> file-name RECORD [; <u>INVALID</u> KEY imperative-statement]

<u>DISABLE</u> $\left\{ \begin{array}{l} \underline{\text{INPUT}} \quad [\underline{\text{TERMINAL}}] \\ \underline{\text{OUTPUT}} \end{array} \right\}$ cd-name WITH <u>KEY</u> $\left\{ \begin{array}{l} \text{identifier-1} \\ \text{literal-1} \end{array} \right\}$

<u>DISPLAY</u> $\left\{ \begin{array}{l} \text{identifier-1} \\ \text{literal-1} \end{array} \right\} \left[\begin{array}{l} , \text{ identifier-2} \\ , \text{ literal-2} \end{array} \right]$ ... [<u>UPON</u> mnemonic-name]

<u>DIVIDE</u> $\left\{ \begin{array}{l} \text{identifier-1} \\ \text{literal-1} \end{array} \right\}$ <u>INTO</u> identifier-2 [<u>ROUNDED</u>]

$\left[, \text{ identifier-3} \quad [\underline{\text{ROUNDED}}] \right]$ ... [; ON <u>SIZE</u> <u>ERROR</u> imperative-statement]

<u>DIVIDE</u> $\left\{ \begin{array}{l} \text{identifier-1} \\ \text{literal-1} \end{array} \right\}$ <u>INTO</u> $\left\{ \begin{array}{l} \text{identifier-2} \\ \text{literal-2} \end{array} \right\}$ <u>GIVING</u> identifier-3 [<u>ROUNDED</u>]

$\left[, \text{ identifier-4} \quad [\underline{\text{ROUNDED}}] \right]$ ... [; ON <u>SIZE</u> <u>ERROR</u> imperative-statement]

<u>DIVIDE</u> $\left\{ \begin{array}{l} \text{identifier-1} \\ \text{literal-1} \end{array} \right\}$ <u>BY</u> $\left\{ \begin{array}{l} \text{identifier-2} \\ \text{literal-2} \end{array} \right\}$ <u>GIVING</u> identifier-3 [<u>ROUNDED</u>]

$\left[, \text{ identifier-4} \quad [\underline{\text{ROUNDED}}] \right]$ ... [; ON <u>SIZE</u> <u>ERROR</u> imperative-statement]

<u>DIVIDE</u> $\left\{ \begin{array}{l} \text{identifier-1} \\ \text{literal-1} \end{array} \right\}$ <u>INTO</u> $\left\{ \begin{array}{l} \text{identifier-2} \\ \text{literal-2} \end{array} \right\}$ <u>GIVING</u> identifier-3 [<u>ROUNDED</u>]

<u>REMAINDER</u> identifier-4 [; ON <u>SIZE</u> <u>ERROR</u> imperative-statement]

<u>DIVIDE</u> $\left\{ \begin{array}{l} \text{identifier-1} \\ \text{literal-1} \end{array} \right\}$ <u>BY</u> $\left\{ \begin{array}{l} \text{identifier-2} \\ \text{literal-2} \end{array} \right\}$ <u>GIVING</u> identifier-3 [<u>ROUNDED</u>]

<u>REMAINDER</u> identifier-4 [; ON <u>SIZE</u> <u>ERROR</u> imperative-statement]

<u>ENABLE</u> $\left\{ \begin{array}{l} \underline{\text{INPUT}} \quad [\underline{\text{TERMINAL}}] \\ \underline{\text{OUTPUT}} \end{array} \right\}$ cd-name WITH <u>KEY</u> $\left\{ \begin{array}{l} \text{identifier-1} \\ \text{literal-1} \end{array} \right\}$

<u>ENTER</u> language-name [routine-name] .

<u>EXIT</u> [<u>PROGRAM</u>]

<u>GENERATE</u> $\left\{ \begin{array}{l} \text{data-name} \\ \text{report-name} \end{array} \right\}$

<u>GO</u> TO [procedure-name-1]

<u>GO</u> TO procedure-name-1 [, procedure-name-2] ...   , procedure-name-n

<u>DEPENDING</u> ON identifier

GENERAL FORMAT FOR VERBS (cont.)

```
IF condition;  ⎰ statement-1    ⎱ ⎰ ; ELSE statement-2      ⎱
               ⎱ NEXT SENTENCE  ⎰ ⎱ ; ELSE NEXT SENTENCE    ⎰


INITIATE report-name-1 [, report-name-2] ...


INSPECT identifier-1 TALLYING

   ⎰              ⎰  ⎰  ⎰ ALL      ⎱ ⎰ identifier-3 ⎱ ⎰ BEFORE ⎱          ⎰ identifier-4 ⎱ ⎱  ⎱    ⎱
   ⎱ ,identifier-2 FOR ⎱  ⎱ , ⎱ LEADING  ⎰ ⎱ literal-1    ⎰ ⎱ AFTER  ⎰ INITIAL ⎱ literal-2    ⎰ ⎰ ... ⎰ ...
                        ⎱ CHARACTERS ⎰


INSPECT identifier-1 REPLACING

  ⎡ CHARACTERS BY ⎰ identifier-6 ⎱ ⎡ ⎰ BEFORE ⎱ INITIAL ⎰ identifier-7 ⎱ ⎤ ⎤
  ⎢               ⎱ literal-4    ⎰ ⎣ ⎱ AFTER  ⎰         ⎱ literal-5    ⎰ ⎦ ⎥
  ⎨                                                                        ⎬
  ⎢ ⎰   ⎰ ALL     ⎱ ⎰  ⎰ identifier-5 ⎱    ⎰ identifier-6 ⎱ ⎡ ⎰ BEFORE ⎱ INITIAL ⎰ identifier-7 ⎱ ⎤ ⎱    ⎱ ⎥
  ⎣ ⎱ , ⎱ LEADING ⎰ ⎱ , ⎱ literal-3    ⎰ BY ⎱ literal-4    ⎰ ⎣ ⎱ AFTER  ⎰         ⎱ literal-5    ⎰ ⎦ ⎰ ... ⎰ ... ⎦
        ⎱ FIRST   ⎰


INSPECT identifier-1 TALLYING

   ⎰              ⎰  ⎰  ⎰ ALL      ⎱ ⎰ identifier-3 ⎱ ⎡ ⎰ BEFORE ⎱          ⎰ identifier-4 ⎱ ⎱    ⎱
   ⎱ ,identifier-2 FOR ⎱  ⎱ , ⎱ LEADING  ⎰ ⎱ literal-1    ⎰ ⎣ ⎱ AFTER  ⎰ INITIAL ⎱ literal-2    ⎰ ⎰ ... ⎰ ...
                        ⎱ CHARACTERS ⎰


REPLACING

  ⎡ CHARACTERS BY ⎰ identifier-6 ⎱ ⎡ ⎰ BEFORE ⎱ INITIAL ⎰ identifier-7 ⎱ ⎤ ⎤
  ⎢               ⎱ literal-4    ⎰ ⎣ ⎱ AFTER  ⎰         ⎱ literal-5    ⎰ ⎦ ⎥
  ⎨                                                                        ⎬
  ⎢ ⎰   ⎰ ALL     ⎱ ⎰  ⎰ identifier-5 ⎱    ⎰ identifier-6 ⎱ ⎡ ⎰ BEFORE ⎱ INITIAL ⎰ identifier-7 ⎱ ⎤ ⎱    ⎱ ⎥
  ⎣ ⎱ , ⎱ LEADING ⎰ ⎱ , ⎱ literal-3    ⎰ BY ⎱ literal-4    ⎰ ⎣ ⎱ AFTER  ⎰         ⎱ literal-5    ⎰ ⎦ ⎰ ... ⎰ ... ⎦
        ⎱ FIRST   ⎰


MERGE file-name-1 ON ⎰ ASCENDING  ⎱ KEY data-name-1 [, data-name-2] ...
                     ⎱ DESCENDING ⎰
                    ⎡ ON ⎰ ASCENDING  ⎱ KEY data-name-3 [, data-name-4] ... ⎤ ...
                    ⎣    ⎱ DESCENDING ⎰                                      ⎦


   [COLLATING SEQUENCE IS alphabet-name]

   USING file-name-2, file-name-3 [, file-name-4] ...

   ⎰ OUTPUT PROCEDURE IS section-name-1 ⎡ ⎰ THROUGH ⎱ section-name-2 ⎤ ⎱
   ⎨                                    ⎣ ⎱ THRU    ⎰                ⎦ ⎬
   ⎱ GIVING file-name-5                                               ⎰
```

GENERAL FORMAT FOR VERBS (cont.)

$\underline{MOVE} \begin{Bmatrix} identifier\text{-}1 \\ literal \end{Bmatrix} \underline{TO}$ identifier-2 [, identifier-3] ...

$\underline{MOVE} \begin{Bmatrix} \underline{CORRESPONDING} \\ \underline{CORR} \end{Bmatrix}$ identifier-1 $\underline{TO}$ identifier-2

$\underline{MULTIPLY} \begin{Bmatrix} identifier\text{-}1 \\ literal\text{-}1 \end{Bmatrix} \underline{BY}$ identifier-2 [$\underline{ROUNDED}$]

  [, identifier-3 [$\underline{ROUNDED}$]] ... [; ON $\underline{SIZE}$ $\underline{ERROR}$ imperative-statement]

$\underline{MULTIPLY} \begin{Bmatrix} identifier\text{-}1 \\ literal\text{-}1 \end{Bmatrix} \underline{BY} \begin{Bmatrix} identifier\text{-}2 \\ literal\text{-}2 \end{Bmatrix} \underline{GIVING}$ identifier-3 [$\underline{ROUNDED}$]

  [, identifier-4 [$\underline{ROUNDED}$]] ... [; ON $\underline{SIZE}$ $\underline{ERROR}$ imperative-statement]

$\underline{OPEN} \begin{Bmatrix} \underline{INPUT} \text{ file-name-1} \begin{bmatrix} \underline{REVERSED} \\ \underline{WITH} \underline{NO} \underline{REWIND} \end{bmatrix} \left[, \text{ file-name-2} \begin{bmatrix} \underline{REVERSED} \\ \underline{WITH} \underline{NO} \underline{REWIND} \end{bmatrix}\right] ... \\ \underline{OUTPUT} \text{ file-name-3}[\text{WITH } \underline{NO} \text{ } \underline{REWIND}], \left[\text{file-name-4 } [\text{WITH } \underline{NO} \text{ } \underline{REWIND}]\right] ... \\ \underline{I\text{-}O} \text{ file-name-5 } [, \text{ file-name-6}] ... \\ \underline{EXTEND} \text{ file-name-7 } [, \text{ file-name-8}] ... \end{Bmatrix} ...$

$\underline{OPEN} \begin{Bmatrix} \underline{INPUT} \text{ file-name-1 } [, \text{ file-name-2}] ... \\ \underline{OUTPUT} \text{ file-name-3 } [, \text{ file-name-4}] ... \\ \underline{I\text{-}O} \text{ file-name-5 } [, \text{ file-name-6}] ... \end{Bmatrix} ...$

$\underline{PERFORM}$ procedure-name-1 $\left[\begin{Bmatrix} \underline{THROUGH} \\ \underline{THRU} \end{Bmatrix} \text{procedure-name-2} \right]$

$\underline{PERFORM}$ procedure-name-1 $\left[\begin{Bmatrix} \underline{THROUGH} \\ \underline{THRU} \end{Bmatrix} \text{procedure-name-2} \right] \begin{Bmatrix} identifier\text{-}1 \\ integer\text{-}1 \end{Bmatrix} \underline{TIMES}$

$\underline{PERFORM}$ procedure-name-1 $\left[\begin{Bmatrix} \underline{THROUGH} \\ \underline{THRU} \end{Bmatrix} \text{procedure-name-2} \right] \underline{UNTIL}$ condition-1

$\underline{PERFORM}$ procedure-name-1 $\left[\begin{Bmatrix} \underline{THROUGH} \\ \underline{THRU} \end{Bmatrix} \text{procedure-name-2} \right]$

  $\underline{VARYING} \begin{Bmatrix} identifier\text{-}2 \\ index\text{-}name\text{-}1 \end{Bmatrix} \underline{FROM} \begin{Bmatrix} identifier\text{-}3 \\ index\text{-}name\text{-}2 \\ literal\text{-}1 \end{Bmatrix}$

  $\underline{BY} \begin{Bmatrix} identifier\text{-}4 \\ literal\text{-}3 \end{Bmatrix} \underline{UNTIL}$ condition-1

  $\left[\underline{AFTER} \begin{Bmatrix} identifier\text{-}5 \\ index\text{-}name\text{-}3 \end{Bmatrix} \underline{FROM} \begin{Bmatrix} identifier\text{-}6 \\ index\text{-}name\text{-}4 \\ literal\text{-}3 \end{Bmatrix} \right.$

GENERAL FORMAT FOR VERBS (cont.)

$$\underline{BY} \left\{ \begin{array}{l} \text{identifier-7} \\ \text{literal-4} \end{array} \right\} \underline{UNTIL} \text{ condition-2}$$

$$\left[\underline{AFTER} \left\{ \begin{array}{l} \text{identifier-8} \\ \text{index-name-4} \end{array} \right\} \underline{FROM} \left\{ \begin{array}{l} \text{identifier-9} \\ \text{index-name-6} \\ \text{literal-5} \end{array} \right\} \right.$$

$$\left. \underline{BY} \left\{ \begin{array}{l} \text{identifier-10} \\ \text{literal-6} \end{array} \right\} \underline{UNTIL} \text{ condition-3} \right]\Bigg]$$

<u>READ</u> file-name RECORD [<u>INTO</u> identifier] [; AT <u>END</u> imperative-statement]

<u>READ</u> file-name [<u>NEXT</u>] RECORD [<u>INTO</u> identifier]

  [; AT <u>END</u> imperative-statement]

<u>READ</u> file-name RECORD [<u>INTO</u> identifier] [; <u>INVALID</u> KEY imperative-statement]

<u>READ</u> file-name RECORD [<u>INTO</u> identifier]

  [; <u>KEY</u> IS data-name]

  [; <u>INVALID</u> KEY imperative-statement]

$$\underline{RECEIVE} \text{ cd-name} \left\{ \begin{array}{l} \underline{MESSAGE} \\ \underline{SEGMENT} \end{array} \right\} \underline{INTO} \text{ identifier-1} \quad [; \underline{NO}\ \underline{DATA} \text{ imperative-statement}]$$

<u>RELEASE</u> record-name [<u>FROM</u> identifier]

<u>RETURN</u> file-name RECORD [<u>INTO</u> identifier] ; AT <u>END</u> imperative-statement

<u>REWRITE</u> record-name [<u>FROM</u> identifier]

<u>REWRITE</u> record-name [<u>FROM</u> identifier] [; <u>INVALID</u> KEY imperative-statement]

$$\underline{SEARCH} \text{ identifier-1} \left[\underline{VARYING} \left\{ \begin{array}{l} \text{identifier-2} \\ \text{index-name-1} \end{array} \right\} \right] [; \text{ AT } \underline{END} \text{ imperative-statement-1}]$$

$$; \underline{WHEN} \text{ condition-1} \left\{ \begin{array}{l} \text{imperative-statement-2} \\ \underline{NEXT}\ \underline{SENTENCE} \end{array} \right\}$$

$$\left[; \underline{WHEN} \text{ condition-2} \left\{ \begin{array}{l} \text{imperative-statement-3} \\ \underline{NEXT}\ \underline{SENTENCE} \end{array} \right\} \right] \ldots$$

<u>SEARCH</u> <u>ALL</u> identifier-1 [; AT <u>END</u> imperative-statement-1]

$$; \underline{WHEN} \left\{ \begin{array}{l} \text{data-name-1} \left\{ \begin{array}{l} \text{IS } \underline{EQUAL} \text{ TO} \\ \text{IS } \underline{=} \end{array} \right\} \left\{ \begin{array}{l} \text{identifier-3} \\ \text{literal-1} \\ \text{arithmetic-expression-1} \end{array} \right\} \\ \text{condition-name-1} \end{array} \right\}$$

$$\left[\underline{AND} \left\{ \begin{array}{l} \text{data-name-2} \left\{ \begin{array}{l} \text{IS } \underline{EQUAL} \text{ TO} \\ \text{IS } = \end{array} \right\} \left\{ \begin{array}{l} \text{identifier-4} \\ \text{literal-2} \\ \text{arithmetic-expression-2} \end{array} \right\} \\ \text{condition-name-2} \end{array} \right\} \right] \ldots$$

GENERAL FORMAT FOR VERBS (cont.)

$$\left\{ \begin{array}{l} \text{imperative-statement-2} \\ \underline{\text{NEXT}}\ \underline{\text{SENTENCE}} \end{array} \right\}$$

$\underline{\text{SEND}}$ cd-name $\underline{\text{FROM}}$ identifier-1

$\underline{\text{SEND}}$ cd-name [$\underline{\text{FROM}}$ identifier-1] $\left\{ \begin{array}{l} \text{WITH identifier-2} \\ \text{WITH } \underline{\text{ESI}} \\ \text{WITH } \underline{\text{EMI}} \\ \text{WITH } \underline{\text{EGI}} \end{array} \right\}$

$$\left[\underline{\underset{\text{AFTER}}{\text{BEFORE}}}\ \ \text{ADVANCING} \left\{ \begin{array}{l} \left\{ \begin{array}{l} \text{identifier-3} \\ \text{integer} \end{array} \right\} \left[\begin{array}{l} \text{LINE} \\ \text{LINES} \end{array} \right] \\ \left\{ \begin{array}{l} \text{mnemonic-name} \\ \underline{\text{PAGE}} \end{array} \right\} \end{array} \right\} \right]$$

$\underline{\text{SET}} \left\{ \begin{array}{ll} \text{identifier-1} & \text{[, identifier-2]} \ \dots \\ \text{index-name-1} & \text{[, index-name-2]} \ \dots \end{array} \right\} \underline{\text{TO}} \left\{ \begin{array}{l} \text{identifier-3} \\ \text{index-name-3} \\ \text{integer-1} \end{array} \right\}$

$\underline{\text{SET}}$ index-name-4 [, index-name-5] $\dots \left\{ \begin{array}{l} \underline{\text{UP}}\ \underline{\text{BY}} \\ \underline{\text{DOWN}}\ \underline{\text{BY}} \end{array} \right\} \left\{ \begin{array}{l} \text{identifier-4} \\ \text{integer-2} \end{array} \right\}$

$\underline{\text{SORT}}$ file-name-1 ON $\left\{ \begin{array}{l} \underline{\text{ASCENDING}} \\ \underline{\text{DESCENDING}} \end{array} \right\}$ KEY data-name-1 [, data-name-2] $\dots$

$\left[\text{ON} \left\{ \begin{array}{l} \underline{\text{ASCENDING}} \\ \underline{\text{DESCENDING}} \end{array} \right\} \text{KEY data-name-3 [, data-name-4] } \dots \right] \dots$

[COLLATING $\underline{\text{SEQUENCE}}$ IS alphabet-name]

$\left\{ \begin{array}{l} \underline{\text{INPUT}}\ \underline{\text{PROCEDURE}} \text{ IS section-name-1} \left[\left\{ \begin{array}{l} \underline{\text{THROUGH}} \\ \text{THRU} \end{array} \right\} \text{section-name-2} \right] \\ \underline{\text{USING}} \text{ file-name-2 [, file-name-3] } \dots \end{array} \right\}$

$\left\{ \begin{array}{l} \underline{\text{OUTPUT}}\ \underline{\text{PROCEDURE}} \text{ IS section-name-3} \left[\left\{ \begin{array}{l} \underline{\text{THROUGH}} \\ \text{THRU} \end{array} \right\} \text{section-name-4} \right] \\ \underline{\text{GIVING}} \text{ file-name-4} \end{array} \right\}$

$\underline{\text{START}}$ file-name $\left[\underline{\text{KEY}} \left\{ \begin{array}{l} \text{IS } \underline{\text{EQUAL}} \text{ TO} \\ \text{IS =} \\ \text{IS } \underline{\text{GREATER}} \text{ THAN} \\ \text{IS >} \\ \text{IS } \underline{\text{NOT}}\ \underline{\text{LESS}} \text{ THAN} \\ \text{IS } \underline{\text{NOT}} \text{ <} \end{array} \right\} \text{data-name} \right]$

[; $\underline{\text{INVALID}}$ KEY imperative-statement]

$\underline{\text{STOP}} \left\{ \begin{array}{l} \underline{\text{RUN}} \\ \text{literal} \end{array} \right\}$